ENTERTAINING WITH
GOOD
HOUSEKEEPING

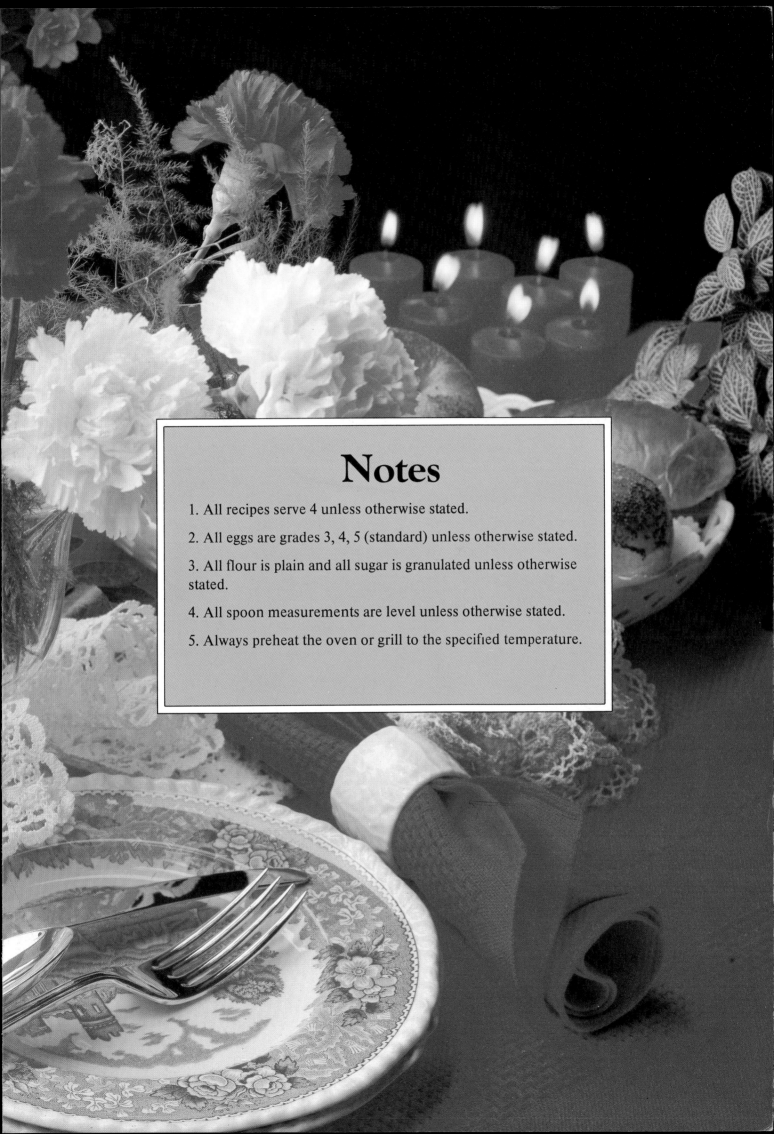

Notes

1. All recipes serve 4 unless otherwise stated.

2. All eggs are grades 3, 4, 5 (standard) unless otherwise stated.

3. All flour is plain and all sugar is granulated unless otherwise stated.

4. All spoon measurements are level unless otherwise stated.

5. Always preheat the oven or grill to the specified temperature.

ENTERTAINING WITH
GOOD HOUSEKEEPING

CONTENTS

ISBN 0 86273 055 4

Entertaining with Good Housekeeping was
first published in 1979 in hard cover
by Sundial Publications Limited
59 Grosvenor Street, London W.1.

Paperback edition first published 1982

Produced by Mandarin Publishers Limited
22a Westlands Road, Quarry Bay, Hong Kong
Printed in Hong Kong

INTRODUCTION

Parties of all sorts can be great fun and enormously rewarding but no hostess gets by on inspiration alone. It needs careful arrangements for looking after your guests and a bit of hard work in the kitchen beforehand if you're to avoid driving yourself and the family into a frenzy. Work things out ahead, follow a few basic rules and everything on the day will be fine.

Menu Planning

Always plan a menu that has plenty of variety and keep within the limitations of your skill and circumstances. If timing worries you choose a casserole dish as a main course, accompanied by oven baked potatoes and a salad. It sounds obvious to say don't try anything new on the night – but don't. An old favourite perfectly served is far, far better than an experiment which flops. You wouldn't of course serve a quiche followed by steak and kidney pudding and then a fruit pie – three pastry dishes – but beware also of serving three rather sloppy courses. A general principle is 'wet' followed by 'dry', so soup with a crisp tasting main course followed by a soufflé is a good choice. Be careful with flavours too and don't paralyse the palate with curried soup before serving a delicately flavoured fish or chicken dish.

Serve foods in season when you can; for example, if melons or strawberries are plentiful choose these instead of making an elaborate dessert. Don't dismiss the possibility of serving convenience foods, especially at a buffet party. There are some excellent quiches, pâtés and cold meats available but buy them only from a tried and tested source. Try not to leave shopping until the last minute; always make a list. Remember, too, if you need to have a joint or chicken boned give the butcher as much notice as you can.

Laying the Table

This is one of the pleasanter pre-tasks of entertaining. Don't overdo it though. China, glasses and cutlery provide a lot of detail and too much decoration can look fussy. What is important is to have everything sparklingly clean. Tablecloths for buffet and informal meals need to be freshly ironed and paper table napkins chosen in subtle colours to match the cloth or mats. The cutlery should be placed neatly, knife blades pointing inwards and always on the right in the order in which they will be used, with forks to match on the left. The dessert spoon and fork may be laid nearest the plate or across the top in neat alignment with the spoon handle to the right and fork handle to the left.

Flower arrangements should be low and not overpoweringly scented. The photographs in the following chapters give ideas of how flowers can complement food. On a buffet table use taller arrangements in candlestick holders to keep the flowers above the food. Candlelight is more flattering than electric light but if you must have the latter have it casting light on the food and not faces.

Choosing Wine

There are no rules about wines to be served with food. It is very much a personal choice. It is generally accepted, however, that dry wines should come before sweet ones and light before the full bodied ones, for the good reason that the reverse order turns the dry wine bitter and the light wine insipid. It is also commonsense to serve dry white wine with fish and white meats rather than to obliterate their delicate flavour with heavier reds. Red meats and game, however, need the stronger company of a full red wine. Sweet desserts need sweet wine for a partner. Two wines are usually considered enough for entertaining at home though many a dinner party gets by very happily with one – chosen to go with the main course. For buffet parties and informal suppers a sparkling wine is often a good choice, with a light red table wine as an alternative. Seek the advice of your local wine merchant if you are not sure what to buy but at the same time don't despise wine from the better chain stores and supermarkets which is often explicitly labelled to help your choice. Play safe and buy a bottle to try before the party. Always serve wine correctly. All white wines should be served chilled but not iced. One to two hours in the refrigerator should be enough. Most red wines should be served at room temperature so let them stand in a room at about 15°-18°C (60°-65°F) for a few hours and uncork them at least an hour before serving. Wine glasses should be clear, colourless and thin, preferably with a bowl curving in towards the rim so as to hold the wine's bouquet. The glass should be stemmed – long or short. A 162-175 ml (5½-6 fl oz) glass is a good all purpose size. Never fill the glass more than half to two-thirds full.

Streamlining the Work

Having the right equipment does wonders for one's kitchen morale. Most of us can't change the cooker just because we've decided to entertain but if you happen to be buying one choose a model with two ovens, a large grill, good plate warming facilities and a reliable simmering hot plate or burner. If you have to make do with a small cooker, consider buying a plug-in electric frypan, casserole or grill to give extra cooking facilities.

For food preparation sharp knives, a pair of kitchen scissors and cooking tongs for lifting food from a frying pan, are all indispensable. An electric blender can halve the time it takes to make soups, pâtés and puréed desserts, while a mixer for whipping and beating and an attachment for shredding and slicing are invaluable when cooking for numbers. A pop-up toaster solves the problem of last minute hot toast to serve with pâtés and an electric coffee maker – the filter or percolator type – can be left to make coffee on its own. Use a vacuum flask to keep the milk hot.

A plug-in hot plate on the sideboard will ensure that food is kept hot and the plates warm. A trolley is also an asset for bringing the food into the dining room and for whisking the unattractive remains quickly away.

How A Freezer Can Help

A freezer can help as much as anything in the preparation of a party. Many cooked dishes can be made in advance, put in the freezer and brought out to thaw the day before the party. Casseroles and quiches can be put straight into the oven for reheating. The tables on pages 184-5 give an idea of what freezes well, how to wrap food for the freezer and how long foods take to thaw. Unless you have a microwave oven, there is nothing much that can be safely done to speed the process of thawing, so get food out of the freezer in good time. As a general rule it's best to allow most foods to thaw overnight in the refrigerator. Don't wrap and freeze food in very large portions. For instance, it's much better to make two pâtés for six to eight people than one huge one for twelve or more.

If you want to serve pâté in slices, cut it when it is nearly frozen and wrap the slices, interleaved with cling film or waxed paper. Write the number of slices on the label and place back in the freezer, fully wrapped, to finish freezing. The same can be done with cream filled cakes. It helps on the day and the slices look neat and even.

Don't forget to label everything. It's so easy to forget which package is which and it's not funny to find you've taken a loaf of bread out of the freezer instead of a pie when it is too late to do anything about it.

INFORMAL SUPPER PARTIES

Even informal meals need careful thought. These menus have been planned so that most of the preparation can be done beforehand and all but the finishing touches completed before the guests arrive. Cold dishes complement hot ones and this means departures to the kitchen for progress checks can be kept to a minimum once the party has started.

The meals cover a wide variety of informal occasions and are for a varying number of guests. The dishes are easy to prepare and include such things as soups, quiches and pies which do not need elaborate last minute dishing up. Table settings can be just as informal as the food. Use a plug-in electric hot plate, if you have one, to keep food and plates warm on the serving table. To drink, choose litre bottles of table wine or dry cider and have soft drinks available.

SOUPS AND SALADS FOR TEN

Lentil broth, Toasted flapovers/Smoked sausage and cheese salad, Beef salad niçoise/Apricot orange flan, Almond cream

BEFOREHAND

Make the soup. Shape the flapovers. Complete the sausage and beef salads. Refrigerate, covered.

Apricot orange flan

The custard-filled bases can be completed the day before and kept, loosely covered, in a cool place – not the refrigerator.

Almond cream

Whip up the ingredients, except the almonds, up to 2 hours ahead and refrigerate.

LENTIL BROTH

Metric	Imperial
50 g butter	2 oz butter
100 g smoked bacon rashers, rinds removed, diced	4 oz smoked bacon rashers, rinds removed, diced
225 g onions, peeled and chopped	8 oz onions, peeled and chopped
225 g carrots, peeled and chopped	8 oz carrots, peeled and chopped
225 g celery, trimmed and chopped	8 oz celery, trimmed and chopped
350 g lentils	12 oz lentils
3.5 litres light stock	$6\frac{1}{4}$ pints light stock
4 cloves	4 cloves
1 bay leaf	1 bay leaf
1 x 5 ml spoon dried oregano	1 teaspoon dried oregano
1 x 5 ml spoon dried thyme	1 teaspoon dried thyme
Salt	Salt
Freshly ground black pepper	Freshly ground black pepper

Melt the butter in a large saucepan. Add the bacon, onions, carrots and celery and fry for 5 minutes. Add the remaining ingredients with salt and pepper to taste and bring to the boil. Reduce the heat, cover and simmer for $1\frac{1}{2}$ hours.

Remove the cloves and bay leaf. Purée the soup in an electric blender. Reheat, and adjust the seasoning.

TOASTED FLAPOVERS

Cut the crusts from a small, thinly sliced white loaf. Spread each slice liberally with softened butter. Fold over the two opposite corners to the centre and thread the flapover on a skewer. Repeat, using all the slices. Lightly dust the flapovers with mild curry powder. Cover with kitchen foil or cling film, or keep in a plastic bag until needed. Grill until crisp and golden on both sides.

Right: Lentil broth. Far right: Smoked sausage and cheese salad; Toasted flapovers.

SMOKED SAUSAGE AND CHEESE SALAD

Metric	Imperial
100 g onion, peeled and chopped	4 oz onion, peeled and chopped
4 x 15 ml spoons chopped fresh parsley	4 tablespoons chopped fresh parsley
4 x 15 ml spoons salad oil	4 tablespoons salad oil
2 x 15 ml spoons wine vinegar	2 tablespoons wine vinegar
4 x 5 ml spoons French mustard	4 teaspoons French mustard
Salt	Salt
Freshly ground black pepper	Freshly ground black pepper
500 g smoked pork sausage, cut into 3 mm thick slices	1 lb smoked pork sausage, cut into $\frac{1}{8}$ inch thick slices
350 g Gouda cheese, cut into 1 cm cubes	12 oz Gouda cheese, cut into $\frac{1}{2}$ inch cubes

Combine the onion, parsley, oil, vinegar, mustard and salt and pepper to taste in a screwtop jar. Shake them well together.

Put the sausage and cheese in a serving bowl and pour over the dressing. Toss well to mix. Cover and leave to infuse the flavours for about 1 hour. Serve lightly chilled.

Beef salad niçoise.

BEEF SALAD NIÇOISE

Metric	Imperial
275 g pasta bows	10 oz pasta bows
Salt	Salt
20 black olives	20 black olives
225 g cooked brisket, thinly sliced and cut into strips	8 oz cooked brisket, thinly sliced and cut into strips
5 anchovy fillets, chopped	5 anchovy fillets, chopped
5 tomatoes, skinned, seeded and cut into strips	5 tomatoes, skinned, seeded and cut into strips
7.5 cm piece cucumber	3 inch piece cucumber
For the dressing:	**For the dressing:**
150 ml thick mayonnaise	¼ pint thick mayonnaise
4 x 15 ml spoons salad oil	4 tablespoons salad oil
2 x 15 ml spoons garlic vinegar	2 tablespoons garlic vinegar
1 x 2.5 ml spoon salt	½ teaspoon salt
Freshly ground black pepper	Freshly ground black pepper

Cook the pasta in boiling salted water until tender – about 10 minutes. Drain and refresh in cold water. Drain thoroughly. Leave to cool.

Combine the olives, beef, anchovies, tomatoes and pasta in a bowl.

Place the dressing ingredients with pepper to taste in a screwtop jar. Shake well, then add to the bowl and toss lightly.

Run the prongs of a fork down the skin of the cucumber. Cut into thin slices and arrange, overlapping, around the edge of a dish to give a scalloped effect. Spoon in the salad. Cover and chill for about 1 hour before serving.

APRICOT ORANGE FLAN

Metric	Imperial
275 g plain flour	10 oz plain flour
2 oranges	2 oranges
150 g butter	5 oz butter
300 ml soured cream	½ pint soured cream
2 eggs, separated	2 eggs, separated
2 x 15 ml spoons sugar	2 tablespoons sugar
2 x 822 g cans apricot halves	2 x 1 lb 13 oz cans apricot halves
1 x 15 ml spoon arrowroot	1 tablespoon arrowroot
2 x 15 ml spoons water	2 tablespoons water
Pistachio nuts, blanched and halved	Pistachio nuts, blanched and halved

Sift the flour into a bowl. Grate the rind from one orange into the flour. Thinly pare the rind from the other orange and cut it into julienne strips. Set aside. Squeeze the juice from both oranges and set aside. Rub the butter into the flour until the mixture resembles fine breadcrumbs. Add enough of the orange juice to knit the dough together – about 3 x 15 ml spoons (3 tablespoons). Chill for 1 hour.

Divide the dough into two and roll out each piece to line a 23.5 cm (9¼ inch) French fluted flan tin. Bake blind in a preheated moderately hot oven (200°C/400°F, Gas Mark 6) for 20 minutes. Remove the paper lining and bake for 10 minutes more. Remove from the oven and allow to cool.

Mix the soured cream with the egg yolks and sugar. Beat the whites until stiff and fold through the soured cream mixture. Divide equally between the pastry cases and spread evenly. Return to the oven and bake for 10 minutes. Leave to cool.

Drain the apricots. Arrange, hollow sides up, over the filling. Put the apricot can syrup, the rest of the orange juice and the orange rind strips in a saucepan and bring to the boil. Boil until reduced by half. Dissolve the arrowroot in the water. Pour into the pan and cook, stirring, until clear. Cool. Use to glaze the fruit. Decorate with halved pistachio nuts.

ALMOND CREAM

Metric	Imperial
150 ml soured cream	¼ pint soured cream
150 ml single cream	¼ pint single cream
150 ml double cream	¼ pint double cream
2 x 5 ml spoons caster sugar	2 teaspoons caster sugar
1 egg white	1 egg white
50 g flaked almonds, toasted	2 oz flaked almonds, toasted

Whisk the creams and sugar together until frothy and lightly thickened. Beat the egg white until stiff and fold into the cream mixture. Chill. Fold in the almonds just before serving.

Apricot orange flan; Almond cream.

HARVEST HOME FOR EIGHT

Cole slaw appetiser/Crackers and pretzels/Harvest pie, Tomatoes with lemon/Almond-stuffed apples, Butterscotch sauce

BEFOREHAND

Cole slaw appetiser
Shred the cabbage, chop the celery and onion and mix together in a lidded bowl. Combine the walnuts and raisins, but store separately. All the slaw ingredients can be combined several hours ahead of the meal and then spooned into dishes 1 hour ahead; cover with cling film.

Harvest pie
Make the pie filling and refrigerate. Keep the reserved onion in cling film. Rub margarine into self-raising flour for the topping mixture. (Add milk just before cooking.)

Tomatoes with lemon
Skin the tomatoes and refrigerate, covered.

Almond-stuffed apples with Butterscotch sauce
Up to 1 hour ahead, arrange the apples ready for cooking and brush with butter. (Time the cooking so that they're nearly ready when supper begins, then reduce the heat and keep them warm.) Make the sauce. (Reheat later in a double saucepan or in a heatproof bowl over a pan of simmering water.)

Tomatoes with lemon.

TOMATOES WITH LEMON

Metric	Imperial
75 g butter	3 oz butter
1 garlic clove, crushed	1 garlic clove, crushed
Finely grated rind of ½ lemon	Finely grated rind of ½ lemon
1 x 15 ml spoon lemon juice	1 tablespoon lemon juice
1 x 2.5 ml spoon salt	½ teaspoon salt
Freshly ground black pepper	Freshly ground black pepper
2 x 15 ml spoons chopped parsley	2 tablespoons chopped parsley
1 x 5 ml spoon caster sugar	1 teaspoon caster sugar
8 large tomatoes, skinned	8 large tomatoes, skinned

Melt the butter in a frying pan. Add the garlic, lemon rind, lemon juice, salt, pepper to taste, parsley and sugar and stir well. Heat very gently for about 3 minutes, for the flavours to blend. Add the tomatoes and cook for 5 minutes, turning frequently to baste.

COLE SLAW APPETISER

Metric	Imperial
225 g white cabbage, cored and finely shredded	8 oz white cabbage, cored and finely shredded
75 g celery, trimmed and finely chopped	3 oz celery, trimmed and finely chopped
75 g onion, peeled and finely chopped	3 oz onion, peeled and finely chopped
75 g walnuts, roughly chopped	3 oz walnuts, roughly chopped
75 g seedless raisins, cleaned	3 oz seedless raisins, cleaned
Grated rind and juice of 1 small lemon	Grated rind and juice of 1 small lemon
150 ml thick mayonnaise	¼ pint thick mayonnaise
2 x 15 ml spoons oil	2 tablespoons oil
1 x 15 ml spoon vinegar	1 tablespoon vinegar
1 x 5 ml spoon dry mustard	1 teaspoon dry mustard
Salt	Salt
Freshly ground black pepper	Freshly ground black pepper
Paprika for garnish	Paprika for garnish

Put the cabbage, celery, onion, walnuts and raisins in a bowl. Combine the lemon rind and juice with the mayonnaise, oil, vinegar and mustard. Adjust the seasoning to taste. Fold the mayonnaise dressing through the vegetables. Serve on individual dishes, garnished with a dusting of paprika. Accompany with crackers and pretzels.

Cole slaw appetiser.

HARVEST PIE

Metric	Imperial
1 x 1.5 kg lean collar joint of bacon	1 x 3 lb lean collar joint of bacon
500 g carrots, peeled and diced	1 lb carrots, peeled and diced
Salt	Salt
50 g butter	2 oz butter
500 g onions, peeled and thinly sliced	1 lb onions, peeled and thinly sliced
50 g plain flour	2 oz plain flour
1 x 326 g can sweetcorn kernels	1 x 11½ oz can sweetcorn kernels
Milk	Milk
Freshly ground black pepper	Freshly ground black pepper
Oil	Oil
For the topping:	**For the topping:**
350 g self-raising flour	12 oz self-raising flour
1 x 2.5 ml spoon salt	½ teaspoon salt
75 g margarine	3 oz margarine
Milk	Milk

Put the bacon in a saucepan and cover with cold water. Bring slowly to the boil. Simmer for about 1 hour 35 minutes. Drain and cool. Cut into cubes. Meanwhile, cook the carrots in boiling salted water until tender. Drain.

Melt the butter in a saucepan. Reserve 16 slices of onion and add the rest to the butter. Cook gently until soft. Stir in the flour and cook, stirring, for 1 to 2 minutes.

Drain the sweetcorn and make the can liquid up to 900 ml (1½ pints) with milk. Add the liquid to the pan, and bring to the boil, stirring. Simmer until thickened, then remove from the heat. Fold in the carrots, corn and bacon. Season to taste. Divide between two shallow 1.7 litre (3 pint) ovenproof dishes.

To make the topping, sift the flour and salt into a bowl. Rub the margarine into the flour, then add enough milk to give a light scone dough. Roll out to 1 cm (½ inch) thick. Cut out sixteen 5 cm (2 inch) rounds with a plain cutter. Lay an onion slice on each, and arrange, overlapping, over the bacon and vegetables in the dishes. Brush with oil. Bake in a preheated very hot oven (240°C/450°F, Gas Mark 8) for about 25 minutes, or until the topping is risen and golden brown.

Harvest pie.

Almond-stuffed apples; Butterscotch sauce.

ALMOND-STUFFED APPLES

Metric	Imperial
8 large cooking apples	8 large cooking apples
100 g marzipan	4 oz marzipan
8 walnut halves	8 walnut halves
50 g butter, melted	2 oz butter, melted

Wipe the apples and core with an apple corer. With a pointed knife, make a slit around the middle circumference of each apple. On the top half make 5 to 6 slits down to the middle. Place the apples in a roasting tin.

Cut the marzipan into eight long sticks and insert one into each core cavity. Top with a walnut half. Brush all over with melted butter and cover with foil. Bake in the bottom of a preheated very hot oven (240°C/450°F, Gas Mark 8) for 25 minutes. Lower the oven temperature to moderate (180°C/350°F, Gas Mark 4), remove the foil and bake in the centre of the oven for a further 30 to 40 minutes or until soft but not floppy. Serve with Butterscotch sauce and pouring cream.

BUTTERSCOTCH SAUCE

Metric	Imperial
100 g butter	4 oz butter
50 g cane or golden syrup	2 oz cane or golden syrup
225 g soft brown sugar	8 oz soft brown sugar
300 ml single cream	½ pint single cream
2 x 15 ml spoons lemon juice	2 tablespoons lemon juice

Melt the butter in a saucepan. Add the syrup and sugar and heat slowly, stirring until dissolved. Stir in the remaining ingredients. Bring to the boil. Keep at a 'rolling boil' for 5 minutes, stirring occasionally. Allow to cool. Serve warm.

Pasta Party for Twelve

Cannelloni with chicken and ham or Macaroni and smoked cod with soured cream sauce/Wholewheat and ale loaves/Orange bavarois

Beforehand

Cannelloni with chicken and ham
Complete preparation, but do not bake; cover with foil and refrigerate.
Macaroni and smoked cod with soured cream sauce
Poach the fish and use to make the sauce; store, covered, in the refrigerator. Hard-boil the eggs.
Wholewheat and ale loaves
Bake the day before, cool and foil-wrap, ready to refresh when required.
Orange bavarois
Make the day before and keep in the refrigerator.

Cannelloni with Chicken and Ham

Metric	Imperial
750 g onions, peeled and sliced	1½ lb onions, peeled and sliced
150 g butter	6 oz butter
225 g lean cooked ham, minced	8 oz lean cooked ham, minced
500 g cold cooked chicken meat, chopped	1 lb cold cooked chicken meat, chopped
225 g mushrooms, finely chopped	8 oz mushrooms, finely chopped
250 g fresh white breadcrumbs	9 oz fresh white breadcrumbs
6 x 15 ml spoons chopped fresh parsley	6 tablespoons chopped fresh parsley
1 x 5 ml spoon dried sage	1 teaspoon dried sage
Salt	Salt
Freshly ground black pepper	Freshly ground black pepper
2 eggs, beaten	2 eggs, beaten
24 cannelloni tubes	24 cannelloni tubes
75 g plain flour	3 oz plain flour
1.4 litres milk	2½ pints milk
500 g tomatoes, skinned, seeded and sliced	1 lb tomatoes, skinned, seeded and sliced

Finely chop 225 g (8 oz) of the onions. Melt 50 g (2 oz) of the butter in a frying pan and fry the chopped onions until soft. Stir in the ham and chicken and fry for 5 minutes. Add the mushrooms and stir well. Remove from the heat.

In a large bowl, combine 225 g (8 oz) of the breadcrumbs, the parsley, sage, chicken mixture and plenty of seasoning. Bind with the eggs. Use to stuff the cannelloni.

Melt 75 g (3 oz) of the remaining butter in a saucepan. Add the rest of the onions, sliced, and soften without colouring – about 10 minutes. Stir in the flour and cook for 1 minute. Off the heat, stir in the milk, then bring to the boil, stirring, and simmer for 5 minutes. Season well. Spoon some of the onion sauce onto the bottom of two shallow ovenproof serving dishes, each large enough to take half the cannelloni in a single layer.

Divide the cannelloni between the two dishes. Pour over the rest of the sauce. Sprinkle with the rest of the breadcrumbs and bake in a preheated moderate oven (180°C/350°F, Gas Mark 4) for 40 to 45 minutes or until the top is browned.

Meanwhile, melt the remaining butter in the cleaned-out frying pan. Add the tomatoes and fry for 2 to 3 minutes, turning to coat with the butter. Garnish the dishes of cannelloni with the tomato slices and sprinkle with plenty of black pepper.

Wholewheat and Ale Loaves

Metric	Imperial
1 x 15 ml spoon dried yeast	1 tablespoon dried yeast
450 ml brown ale	¾ pint brown ale
25 g butter	1 oz butter
450 g plain wholewheat flour	1 lb plain wholewheat flour
225 g strong plain flour, sifted	8 oz strong plain flour, sifted
2 x 5 ml spoons salt	2 teaspoons salt
50 g Cheddar cheese, grated	2 oz Cheddar cheese, grated

Dissolve the dried yeast in 6 x 15 ml spoons (6 tablespoons) of the brown ale and leave in a warm place until frothy. Put the remaining ale and the butter in a saucepan and bring to the boil. Cool until lukewarm.

Mix the flours and salt together in a large bowl. Add the warm ale mixture and the yeast liquid and work to a dough. Turn onto a floured surface and knead for about 10 minutes, until smooth and elastic. Shape into a ball and place in a lightly oiled polythene bag. Leave to rise in a warm place until doubled in size.

Turn the dough onto a floured surface and knead for 2 to 3 minutes. Shape into 12 even-sized balls and place in a 25 by 20 cm (10 by 8 inch) oblong roasting tin. Cover lightly and leave to rise for 30 to 35 minutes, until doubled in size.

Sprinkle the cheese over the tops and bake in a preheated moderately hot oven (200°C/400°F, Gas Mark 6) for about 30 minutes. Cool on a wire rack. Break apart into small loaves for eating. Makes 12

Cannelloni with chicken and ham.

MACARONI AND SMOKED COD WITH SOURED CREAM SAUCE

Metric	Imperial
500 g wholewheat short-style macaroni	1¼ lb wholewheat short-style macaroni
Salt	Salt
1.25 kg smoked cod fillets	2½ lb smoked cod fillets
1.2 litres milk	2 pints milk
1 slice of onion	1 slice of onion
1 slice of carrot	1 slice of carrot
6 peppercorns	6 peppercorns
1 bay leaf	1 bay leaf
50 g butter	2 oz butter
4 x 15 ml spoons plain flour	4 tablespoons plain flour
300 ml soured cream	½ pint soured cream
2 eggs, hard-boiled and chopped	2 eggs, hard-boiled and chopped
Freshly ground black pepper	Freshly ground black pepper
Snipped fresh chives to garnish	Snipped fresh chives to garnish

Cook the macaroni in plenty of boiling salted water as directed on the packet. Drain and cool under cold running water.

Place the fish in a roasting tin with the milk, onion, carrot, peppercorns and bay leaf. Cover and cook in a preheated moderate oven (180°C/350°F, Gas Mark 4) for about 20 minutes or until the fish flakes when forked. Strain off the milk and reserve. Flake the fish, removing any skin and bones. Increase the oven temperature to moderately hot (200°C/400°F, Gas Mark 6).

Melt the butter in a large saucepan. Stir in the flour and cook, stirring, for 1 minute. Off the heat, stir in the reserved milk from the fish. Bring to the boil, stirring, and simmer for 2 minutes. Stir in the soured cream, flaked fish and the hard-boiled eggs. Season well.

Fold the cooked macaroni into the fish mixture, combining well to coat the pasta. Adjust the seasoning. Divide between two lightly buttered casserole dishes. Cover and cook in the oven for about 25 minutes until piping hot. Stir well to loosen the pasta and garnish with snipped chives.

Wholewheat and ale loaves.

Above: Orange bavarois. Right: Macaroni and smoked cod with soured cream sauce; Green salad.

ORANGE BAVAROIS

Make three

Metric	Imperial
3 oranges	3 oranges
300 ml milk	½ pint milk
1 x 142 g lemon jelly tablet	1 x 5 oz lemon jelly tablet
1 x 15 ml spoon lemon juice	1 tablespoon lemon juice
1 x 15 ml spoon custard powder	1 tablespoon custard powder
2 x 5 ml spoons castor sugar	2 teaspoons castor sugar
150 ml double cream	¼ pint double cream
To decorate:	**To decorate:**
Whipped cream	Whipped cream
Orange slices	Orange slices

Finely grate the rind from one orange into the milk. Using a serrated knife, pare all the oranges, removing all traces of white pith. Remove the fleshy segments free of white pith over a measure – to catch any juice. Squeeze out any juice from the remaining membrane. Divide the jelly tablet in half. Place one half in the measure with the lemon juice and make up to 300 ml (½ pint) with boiling water. Stand the measure in hot water and stir to dissolve the jelly. When dissolved leave in a cold place until set to the consistency of unbeaten egg white. Fold the orange segments into the half-set jelly and spoon into a 900 ml (1½ pint) jelly mould. Leave to set.

Make a thin custard with the milk, custard powder and sugar. While the custard is still hot, add the rest of the jelly tablet, broken up, and stir until it is dissolved. Cool, stirring occasionally to prevent a skin forming. Whip the cream to the consistency of the custard and fold it into the custard mixture. Spoon over the jelly base. Leave overnight to set. Unmould onto a serving dish and decorate with cream and orange slices.

CUT AND COME AGAIN QUICHE PARTY FOR SIX

Mushroom cream flan or Bacon, celery and cream cheese quiche, Tossed green salad, Tomato cole slaw/ Frozen cranberry meringue ring

BEFOREHAND

Make the flans (heat just before serving). Make the slaw, omitting the apple; add this just before serving. Make the sweet. Prepare the salad ingredients; toss shortly before serving.

MUSHROOM CREAM FLAN

Metric	Imperial
For the pastry:	**For the pastry:**
125 g wholemeal flour	4 oz wholemeal flour
125 g plain flour, sifted	4 oz plain flour, sifted
1 x 2.5 ml spoon salt	½ teaspoon salt
125 g block margarine	4 oz block margarine
For the filling:	**For the filling:**
25 g butter or margarine	1 oz butter or margarine
225 g button mushrooms, quartered	8 oz button mushrooms, quartered
2 eggs	2 eggs
1 egg yolk	1 egg yolk
150 ml unsweetened natural yogurt	¼ pint unsweetened natural yogurt
6 x 15 ml spoons single cream	6 tablespoons single cream
Salt	Salt
Freshly ground black pepper	Freshly ground black pepper
2 x 15 ml spoons snipped fresh chives	2 tablespoons snipped fresh chives

Put the flours and salt into a mixing bowl and rub in the margarine until the mixture resembles breadcrumbs. Mix in enough water to bind to a dough. Roll out and use to line a 23 cm (9 inch) loose-bottomed flan tin. Bake blind in a preheated moderately hot oven (190°C/375°F, Gas Mark 5) for 15 minutes or until dry and just beginning to colour.

Meanwhile, melt the butter or margarine for the filling in a frying pan. Add the mushrooms and fry for 2 minutes. Drain. Whisk the whole eggs, egg yolk, yogurt, cream, seasoning and chives together. Scatter the mushrooms over the bottom of the flan case and pour over the yogurt mixture. Return to the moderately hot oven and bake for about 30 minutes, or until just set and golden brown. Serve hot or cold.

BACON, CELERY AND CREAM CHEESE QUICHE

Metric	Imperial
For the pastry:	**For the pastry:**
150 g butter or margarine	5 oz butter or margarine
300 g plain flour, sifted	10 oz plain flour, sifted
175 g Cheddar cheese, grated	6 oz Cheddar cheese, grated
2 egg yolks	2 egg yolks
For the filling:	**For the filling:**
350 g streaky bacon rashers, rinds removed, diced	12 oz streaky bacon rashers, rinds removed, diced
175 g celery, trimmed and thinly sliced	6 oz celery, trimmed and thinly sliced
4 eggs, beaten	4 eggs, beaten
175 g cream cheese	6 oz cream cheese
300 ml milk	½ pint milk
Freshly ground black pepper	Freshly ground black pepper

Rub the butter or margarine into the flour until it resembles fine breadcrumbs. Stir in the Cheddar cheese, egg yolks and just enough cold water to bind together. Knead lightly. Roll out the dough and use to line two 20 cm (8 inch) fluted flan rings, placed on a baking sheet. Bake blind in a preheated hot oven (220°C/425°F, Gas Mark 7) for 10 minutes.

Fry the bacon in its own fat until crisp and golden. Add the celery and cook gently for 2 to 3 minutes. Drain. Beat the eggs into the cream cheese and stir in the milk. Season with black pepper.

Fill the flan cases with the bacon and celery and pour over the egg mixture. Return the flans to the oven to bake for a further 10 minutes, then reduce the heat to moderately hot (190°C/375°F, Gas Mark 5). Bake for a further 15 to 20 minutes. Serve hot or cold.

TOMATO COLE SLAW

Metric	Imperial
500 g crisp green eating apples, cored and diced	1 lb crisp green eating apples, cored and diced
Juice of 1 lemon	Juice of 1 lemon
500 g white cabbage, cored and finely shredded	1 lb white cabbage, cored and finely shredded
75 g seedless raisins, cleaned	3 oz seedless raisins, cleaned
300 ml thick mayonnaise	½ pint thick mayonnaise
Salt	Salt
Freshly ground black pepper	Freshly ground black pepper
500 g tomatoes, sliced	1 lb tomatoes, sliced

Put the apples in a bowl with the lemon juice and toss lightly to coat the pieces with the juice.

In a large bowl, combine the cabbage with the raisins, mayonnaise and drained apple. Season well. Place two-thirds of the cabbage mixture in a deep serving dish, levelling the surface. Season the tomato slices and place most in a layer over the slaw. Cover with the remaining cabbage mixture, piling up in the centre. Arrange the remaining tomato slices around the top edge. Keep in a cool place.

Left: Mushroom cream flan.

FROZEN CRANBERRY MERINGUE RING

Metric	Imperial
350 g whole cranberries	12 oz whole cranberries
60 g granulated sugar	2½ oz granulated sugar
200 ml water	⅓ pint water
3 x 15 ml spoons cornflour	3 tablespoons cornflour
300 ml skimmed milk	½ pint skimmed milk
60 g soft margarine	2½ oz soft margarine
60 g icing sugar	2½ oz icing sugar
75 g meringue shells, roughly broken up	3 oz meringue shells, roughly broken up
A few meringue pieces for decoration	A few meringue pieces for decoration

Place the cranberries, granulated sugar and water in a pan and cook gently until the fruit pops and softens. Cool.

Mix the cornflour with a little of the milk to a smooth paste. Bring the remaining milk to the boil and pour onto the cornflour, stirring. Return this mixture to the pan and bring to the boil, still stirring. Cover and leave to cool.

Blend the margarine, cornflour mixture, sifted icing sugar and half the cranberry mixture in an electric blender until smooth. Fold together the meringue pieces, puréed mixture, and nearly all the remaining whole cranberry mixture (reserve a few cranberries for decoration). Turn into a lightly oiled 900 ml (1½ pint) non-stick ring mould. Cover and freeze until firm. To serve, unmould and decorate with extra broken meringue and the reserved whole cranberries.

Below: Bacon, celery and cream cheese quiche; Green salad; Tomato cole slaw; Frozen cranberry meringue ring.

ONE-POT SUPPER FOR SIX

Avocado-stuffed tomatoes/Lamb bourguignon, Fluffy boiled rice, Glazed carrots (oven-cooked)/Chocolate and orange ice cream

BEFOREHAND

Avocado-stuffed tomatoes
Stuff the tomatoes. Store, covered with cling film, in the refrigerator for not more than 2 hours.

Lamb bourguignon
Prepare the meat, blanch the onions and fry the mushrooms. The lamb can be cooked completely in advance and then reheated in a preheated moderate oven (160°C/325°F, Gas Mark 3) for 1 hour.

Chocolate and orange ice cream
Chill the evaporated milk. Make the ice cream and freeze.

AVOCADO-STUFFED TOMATOES

Metric	Imperial
1 avocado, peeled, stoned and diced	1 avocado, peeled, stoned and diced
2 x 5 ml spoons lemon juice	2 teaspoons lemon juice
1 x 15 ml spoon mayonnaise	1 tablespoon mayonnaise
100 g cream cheese	4 oz cream cheese
1 x 5 ml spoon snipped fresh chives	1 teaspoon snipped fresh chives
Salt	Salt
Freshly ground black pepper	Freshly ground black pepper
6 large ripe tomatoes	6 large ripe tomatoes

Push the avocado flesh through a nylon sieve and beat in the lemon juice, mayonnaise, cream cheese and chives. When smooth, turn into a bowl and adjust the seasoning.

Cut the tops from the tomatoes, scoop out the seeds and membrane, and fill with the avocado mixture. Chill before serving.

LAMB BOURGUIGNON

Metric	Imperial
1.25 kg boned lean leg of lamb (boned weight)	2½ lb boned lean leg of lamb (boned weight)
225 g small onions	8 oz small onions
3 x 15 ml spoons corn oil	3 tablespoons corn oil
50 g margarine	2 oz margarine
225 g button mushrooms	8 oz button mushrooms
225 ml red wine	8 fl oz red wine
300 ml brown stock	½ pint brown stock
1 x 2.5 ml spoon salt	½ teaspoon salt
Freshly ground black pepper	Freshly ground black pepper
1 x 15 ml spoon arrowroot	1 tablespoon arrowroot
1 x 15 ml spoon water	1 tablespoon water
Chopped fresh parsley and fried croûtons to garnish	Chopped fresh parsley and fried croûtons to garnish

Discard all skin and fat from the lamb. Cut into large fork-size pieces. Blanch the onions in boiling water for 2 minutes, then drain and peel them.

Heat the oil in a deep frying pan. Add the margarine and, when frothing, put in the meat to seal on all sides. Remove the meat cubes from the pan as they brown. Add the onions and brown evenly. Drain and add to the meat. Finally, lightly fry the mushrooms.

Replace the meat and vegetables in the pan and stir in the wine, stock and seasoning. Bring to the boil, then transfer to a flameproof casserole. Cover and cook in a preheated moderate oven (160°C/325°F, Gas Mark 3) for about 1½ hours or until the meat is tender.

Dissolve the arrowroot in the water. When the lamb is cooked, put the casserole on top of the cooker and stir in the arrowroot. Cook until clear and thickened – about 2 minutes. Serve the lamb garnished with parsley and croûtons.

Avocado-stuffed tomatoes.

Lamb bourguignon; Glazed carrots; Rice.

GLAZED CARROTS

Metric	Imperial
1 kg carrots, peeled and cut into thin strips	2 lb carrots, peeled and cut into thin strips
300 ml water	½ pint water
50 g butter	2 oz butter
4 x 15 ml spoons demerara sugar	4 tablespoons demerara sugar

Put the carrots in an ovenproof dish with the water, butter and sugar. Cover loosely with foil and cook in a preheated moderate oven (160°C/325°F, Gas Mark 3) for 1½ hours, with the Lamb bourguigon.

CHOCOLATE AND ORANGE ICE CREAM

Metric	Imperial
1 small can evaporated milk, chilled	1 small can evaporated milk, chilled
150 ml double cream	¼ pint double cream
75 g plain chocolate-flavoured cake covering, finely grated	3 oz plain chocolate-flavoured cake covering, finely grated
Finely grated rind and juice of 1 large orange	Finely grated rind and juice of 1 large orange
1 x 15 ml spoon orange-flavoured liqueur	1 tablespoon orange-flavoured liqueur
3 x 15 ml spoons icing sugar	3 tablespoons icing sugar
Ice cream wafers to serve	Ice cream wafers to serve

Whip the evaporated milk as thickly as possible. Whip the cream to the same consistency and fold into the evaporated milk. Fold in the grated chocolate and orange rind, strained orange juice and liqueur.

Sift in the icing sugar. Stir well to mix. Pour into a rigid container and freeze until mushy. Remove from the freezer and whisk with a fork to break down any ice crystals. Freeze until firm. Allow to come to cool room temperature before serving with ice cream wafers.

Chocolate and orange ice cream.

SIMPLE DINNER PARTIES

The subtle flavours belie the simplicity of preparation of these dinners for six, and the main courses are chosen to avoid last minute attention. The Southern Beef and Bean Pot is a wonderfully warming dish for a chilly evening and will not spoil if your guests are late arriving. Sage and Bacon Stuffed Pork can be kept waiting, too. Summer calls for lighter but equally flavourful fare, using fresh fruit and vegetables. You can add an extra-delicious touch to the new potatoes by grinding coarse sea salt over them at the table.

WINTER DINNER PARTY FOR SIX

Prawn cauliflower salad, Brown bread and butter / Sage and bacon stuffed pork, Baked jacket potatoes, Brussels sprouts with Brazil nuts / Mandarin vacherin

BEFOREHAND

Prawn cauliflower salad
In the morning, prepare, cover and refrigerate. Prepare bread and butter, cling-wrap and refrigerate.
Sage and bacon stuffed pork
In the morning, open out the joint, stuff and tie; refrigerate.
Brussels sprouts with Brazil nuts
Prepare sprouts, breadcrumbs and nuts and keep in separate polythene bags in refrigerator.
Mandarin vacherin
Make the meringue well ahead – several days if convenient – and keep in airtight tin, unfilled.

BRUSSELS SPROUTS WITH BRAZIL NUTS

Metric	Imperial
750 g Brussels sprouts	1½ lb Brussels sprouts
75 g butter	3 oz butter
100 g Brazil nuts, shelled and chopped	4 oz Brazil nuts, shelled and chopped
75 g fresh white breadcrumbs	3 oz fresh white breadcrumbs
Salt	Salt
Freshly ground black pepper	Freshly ground black pepper

Trim the Brussels sprouts and cut a cross in the base of each. Cook in boiling salted water for 10 to 15 minutes until tender. Drain.

Melt the butter in a pan, add the Brazil nuts and cook over a gentle heat until golden. Add the breadcrumbs and continue cooking until they have absorbed the butter and are crisp and golden. Add the Brussels sprouts and salt and pepper to taste. Heat through, stirring.

PRAWN CAULIFLOWER SALAD

Metric	Imperial
6 x 15 ml spoons thick mayonnaise	6 tablespoons thick mayonnaise
1 x 15 ml spoon tomato paste	1 tablespoon tomato paste
1 x 15 ml spoon medium sherry	1 tablespoon medium sherry
2 x 15 ml spoons lemon juice	2 tablespoons lemon juice
Salt	Salt
Freshly ground black pepper	Freshly ground black pepper
1 small cauliflower, about 500 g trimmed weight, broken into tiny florets	1 small cauliflower, about 1 lb trimmed weight, broken into tiny florets
100 g cucumber, diced	4 oz cucumber, diced
100 g frozen shelled prawns, thawed	4 oz frozen shelled prawns, thawed
1 small endive, broken into leaves	1 small endive, broken into leaves
Chopped fresh parsley to garnish	Chopped fresh parsley to garnish

In a large bowl, mix the mayonnaise with the tomato paste, sherry, lemon juice and seasoning. Blanch the cauliflower florets in boiling salted water for 2 to 3 minutes, then drain them well. While warm, stir into the mayonnaise mixture and allow to cool.

Sprinkle the cucumber dice lightly with salt and leave for about 20 minutes. Drain. Fold through the cauliflower with the prawns. Cover and chill.

To serve, line six natural scallop shells or small dishes with endive leaves. Pile on the cauliflower mixture and garnish with parsley.

SAGE AND BACON STUFFED PORK

Metric	Imperial
1 kg boned loin of pork, well scored	2¼ lb boned loin of pork, well scored
225 g back bacon rashers, rinds removed	8 oz back bacon rashers, rinds removed
12 fresh or dried sage leaves	12 fresh or dried sage leaves
Cooking oil and salt	Cooking oil and salt

Ask the butcher to bone the pork and score the rind deeply and evenly. Place the joint on a flat surface, fat side down, and cut the flesh at intervals to open it out a little. Lay the rashers over the flesh and place the sage leaves at intervals. Roll up carefully and secure firmly with string, parcel fashion. Put in a roasting tin. Rub the rind well with oil and salt and roast in a preheated moderately hot oven (190°C/375°F, Gas Mark 5) for about 2 hours. Remove the strings and place the meat on a serving dish.

Prawn cauliflower salad.

Sage and bacon stuffed pork; Brussels sprouts with Brazil nuts; Mandarin vacherin.

MANDARIN VACHERIN

Metric	Imperial
For the meringues:	**For the meringues:**
3 egg whites	3 egg whites
175 g caster sugar	6 oz caster sugar
75 g toasted ground hazelnuts	3 oz toasted ground hazelnuts
For the filling:	**For the filling:**
300 ml double cream	½ pint double cream
Icing sugar	Icing sugar
2 x 312 g cans mandarins, drained	2 x 11 oz cans mandarins, drained

To make the meringues, beat the egg whites until stiff. Gradually beat in the sugar, keeping the mixture stiff. Fold in the ground nuts. Draw two 20 cm (8 inch) circles on non-stick paper. Divide one into six wedge shapes. Pipe a good half of the mixture onto the plain circle, using a 1 cm (½ inch) plain nozzle. Pipe the remaining mixture into six separated triangles within the circle area on the other sheet of paper, allowing room between them for spreading. Bake in a preheated moderately hot oven (190°C/375°F, Gas Mark 5) for 30 to 35 minutes or until crisp and golden. Cool, then peel off the paper.

To complete the vacherin, stiffly whip the cream with icing sugar to taste. Reserve a few mandarins for the decoration. Fold the remaining mandarins into half the cream and pile onto the meringue circle. Place the wedges on top. Decorate with the rest of the whipped cream. Just before serving, dust with icing sugar and add the reserved mandarins.

WINTER DINNER PARTY FOR SIX

Artichoke and pepper gratin/Southern beef and bean pot, Jacket potatoes, Chicory, tomato and chive salad/Apple fig snow

BEFOREHAND

Artichoke and pepper gratin
Complete, but do not cook, on the morning of the party.
Southern beef and bean pot
This can be made a day ahead and reheated in a preheated
moderate oven (180°C/350°F, Gas Mark 4) for 1 hour when
required. But remember that the beans must be soaked
overnight before you use them.
Jacket potatoes
Scrub the day before.
Chicory, tomato and chive salad
Make just before the party.
Apple fig snow
Make on the morning of the party. (The apples can be stewed,
and then the figs added, on the day before.)

ARTICHOKE AND PEPPER GRATIN

Metric	Imperial
25 g margarine	1 oz margarine
50 g onion, peeled and finely chopped	2 oz onion, peeled and finely chopped
1 medium green pepper, cored, seeded and finely chopped	1 medium green pepper, cored, seeded and finely chopped
2 x 312 g cans artichoke fronds, drained	2 x 11 oz cans artichoke fronds, drained
50 g Edam cheese, grated	2 oz Edam cheese, grated
50 g fresh white breadcrumbs	2 oz fresh white breadcrumbs
1 x 2.5 ml spoon paprika	½ teaspoon paprika

Melt the margarine in a frying pan. Add the onion and green pepper
and fry until softened. Place 2 or 3 artichoke fronds in six well-
greased individual ovenproof dishes and pile the pepper mixture on
top. Combine the cheese, breadcrumbs and paprika and scatter a
little over each serving. Bake in a preheated very hot oven
(230°C/450°F, Gas Mark 8) for 10 minutes.

SOUTHERN BEEF AND BEAN POT

Metric	Imperial
1 kg lean chuck steak	2 lb lean chuck steak
3 x 15 ml spoons seasoned flour	3 tablespoons seasoned flour
3 x 15 ml spoons corn oil	3 tablespoons corn oil
175 g onions, peeled and sliced	6 oz onions, peeled and sliced
450 ml beef stock	¾ pint beef stock
100 g dried red kidney beans, soaked overnight and drained	4 oz dried red kidney beans, soaked overnight and drained
8 juniper berries	8 juniper berries
1 bay leaf	1 bay leaf
Thinly pared rind of ½ orange	Thinly pared rind of ½ orange
Salt	Salt
Freshly ground black pepper	Freshly ground black pepper
Parsley sprigs to garnish	Parsley sprigs to garnish

Trim all fat from the meat and cut it into large fork-size pieces. Coat
in the seasoned flour. Heat the oil in a saucepan and fry the meat
with the onions until evenly browned, stirring occasionally. Add the
stock, beans and berries. Tie the bay leaf and orange rind in a piece of
muslin and add. Season. Boil for 10 minutes. Cover, reduce the heat

*Above: Artichoke and pepper gratin. Right: Southern beef and bean
pot; Chicory, tomato and chive salad; Apple fig snow.*

and simmer for 2 to 2½ hours, stirring from time to time. Alternatively, place in a casserole and cook in the bottom of a preheated
moderate oven (180°C/350°F, Gas Mark 4) for 2 to 2½ hours. Stir
occasionally and add more stock if necessary. Discard the orange
rind and bay leaf. Serve garnished with parsley.

APPLE FIG SNOW

Metric	Imperial
1 kg cooking apples, peeled, cored and sliced	2 lb cooking apples, peeled, cored and sliced
Grated rind and juice of 1 lemon	Grated rind and juice of 1 lemon
3 x 15 ml spoons water	3 tablespoons water
25 g margarine	1 oz margarine
25 g soft brown sugar	1 oz soft brown sugar
75 g honeyed dessert figs, finely chopped	3 oz honeyed dessert figs, finely chopped
3 egg whites	3 egg whites

Put the apple slices, lemon rind and juice, water, margarine and sugar
in a saucepan. Cover and stew gently until really soft, being careful
that the fruit does not stick and burn in the pan.

Remove the pan from the heat and beat the apple mixture until
smooth. Then, while still warm, add the figs. Leave to cool.

Whisk the egg whites until stiff. Beat 2 x 15 ml spoons (2 tablespoons) into the apple to lighten the mixture, then fold in the rest
carefully. Pile into a glass dish and chill well. Serve decorated with a
piece of fresh fig, if available.

SUMMER DINNER PARTY FOR SIX

Mushroom quiches/Veal escalopes with tomatoes and cucumber, New potatoes in their jackets, Buttered mange-tout/
Gooseberry almond crush

BEFOREHAND

Mushroom quiches

Make the pastry the day before. Line the tins, cover tightly and keep in a cool place. On the morning of the dinner, soak the anchovies in milk and slice and fry the mushrooms. Cool. Start baking the unfilled pastry cases about 45 minutes before dinner. Finish the quiche mixture.

Veal escalopes with tomatoes and cucumber

The escalopes can be beaten out on the day before; keep them in the refrigerator, loosely covered. Prepare the vegetables on the morning of the dinner; keep covered. Reduce the wine if wished.

Potatoes and mange-tout

Wash and store – separately – in polythene bags in refrigerator.

Gooseberry almond crush

Prepare this on the morning of the dinner party.

MUSHROOM QUICHES

Metric	Imperial
6 anchovy fillets, drained	6 anchovy fillets, drained
Milk	Milk
100 g plain flour	4 oz plain flour
1 x 2.5 ml spoon salt	½ teaspoon salt
1 x 1.25 ml spoon paprika	¼ teaspoon paprika
75 g block margarine	3 oz block margarine
25 g mature Cheddar cheese, finely grated	1 oz mature Cheddar cheese, finely grated
About 1 x 15 ml spoon water	About 1 tablespoon water
25 g butter	1 oz butter
175 g button mushrooms, sliced	6 oz button mushrooms, sliced
2 small eggs, beaten	2 small eggs, beaten
200 ml single cream	⅓ pint single cream
Freshly ground black pepper	Freshly ground black pepper

Soak the anchovies in a little milk for about 1 hour.

Sift together the flour, salt and half the paprika. Rub in the margarine until the mixture resembles breadcrumbs. Stir in the cheese and enough water to bind. Knead lightly and roll out thinly

Mushroom quiches.

on a floured surface. Cut out six circles with a 12.5 cm (5 inch) cutter – use a saucer or a saucepan lid – and press gently into six 11.5 cm (4½ inch) individual loose-bottomed flan tins. Prick the bottoms and bake blind in a preheated moderately hot oven (200°/400°F, Gas Mark 6) for 10 minutes.

Melt the butter in a frying pan and quickly fry the mushrooms. Divide between the cases. Drain the anchovies and pound to a paste in a small bowl. Beat in the eggs and cream, and season with black pepper. Spoon into the pastry cases. Dust lightly with the remaining paprika and return to the oven to bake for a further 20 minutes or until lightly set and slightly browned on top. Serve at once.

VEAL ESCALOPES WITH TOMATOES AND CUCUMBER

Metric	Imperial
6 veal escalopes, about 75 g each	6 veal escalopes, about 3 oz each
Salt	Salt
Freshly ground black pepper	Freshly ground black pepper
25 g butter	1 oz butter
2 x 15 ml spoons corn oil	2 tablespoons corn oil
100 g onion, peeled and sliced	4 oz onion, peeled and sliced
1 garlic clove, crushed	1 garlic clove, crushed
150 ml dry white wine	¼ pint dry white wine
½ cucumber, peeled, halved, seeded and sliced	½ cucumber, peeled, halved, seeded and sliced
500 g firm tomatoes, skinned, quartered and seeded	1 lb firm tomatoes, skinned, quartered and seeded
1 x 15 ml spoon lemon juice	1 tablespoon lemon juice
4 x 15 ml spoons finely chopped fresh parsley	4 tablespoons finely chopped fresh parsley

Trim the escalopes and bat them out between sheets of non-stick paper, then season. Heat the butter and oil in a large frying pan and brown the escalopes, two at a time. Keep on one side. Add the onion and fry until golden. Stir in the garlic, wine and seasoning. Replace the veal, with any juices, in the pan and simmer gently, uncovered, for 10 minutes. Arrange the escalopes in a large warmed serving dish and keep warm.

Boil the liquid in the frying pan to reduce to 4 x 15 ml spoons (4 tablespoons). Add the cucumber and cook, stirring, for 5 minutes. Add the tomatoes and lemon juice, stir gently and adjust the seasoning. Cook for 2 minutes. Spoon over the escalopes and garnish with the parsley.

Note: To give more depth of flavour to the wine for cooking, start with 300 ml (½ pint) and boil to reduce by half in an open pan.

NEW POTATOES IN THEIR JACKETS

Metric	Imperial
1 kg walnut-sized new potatoes	2 lb walnut-sized new potatoes
Salt	Salt
50 g butter	2 oz butter
Freshly ground black pepper	Freshly ground black pepper

Wash the potatoes carefully, put into cold salted water and bring to the boil. Cover and simmer for 15 to 20 minutes or until just tender. Drain well and return to the pan. Add the butter and plenty of pepper. Stir over a low heat until the potatoes are covered with melted butter. Transfer to a serving dish and serve hot.

Veal escalopes with tomatoes and cucumber; Buttered mange-tout; New potatoes in their jackets.

BUTTERED MANGE-TOUT (SUGAR PEAS)

Metric	Imperial
750 g mange-tout, topped and tailed	1½ lb mange-tout, topped and tailed
Salt	Salt
25 g butter	1 oz butter
Freshly ground black pepper	Freshly ground black pepper

Put the mange-tout in a pan containing 1 cm (½ inch) boiling salted water. Bring back to the boil, cover and simmer for 5 minutes or until just tender. Drain well and toss in the butter, adding plenty of freshly ground pepper.

GOOSEBERRY ALMOND CRUSH

Metric	Imperial
500 g gooseberries, topped and tailed	1 lb gooseberries, topped and tailed
2 x 15 ml spoons water	2 tablespoons water
100-125 g caster sugar	4 oz caster sugar
2 x 15 ml spoons Kirsch	2 tablespoons Kirsch
100 g French almond macaroons, crumbled	4 oz French almond macaroons, crumbled
150 ml whipping cream	¼ pint whipping cream
3 macaroons to decorate	3 macaroons to decorate

Cook the gooseberries with the water and sugar until the fruit is soft and well reduced, then sieve it. Stir in the Kirsch. Arrange the macaroon crumbs and gooseberry purée in alternate layers in six tall glasses. Leave in a cool place for several hours.

Whip the cream until it barely holds its shape. Spoon some of the soft cream over each serving and top each with a halved macaroon.

Gooseberry almond crush.

EXOTIC DINNER PARTIES

If you want to give an unusual and enjoyable party without putting too much of a strain on the budget, organise a meal with an exotic flavour. There are several here, all adapted when necessary to the foods available in this country.

Follow the specific menus through with a careful choice of drinks and table settings. Serve the Chinese food, for example, the Chinese way, from small bowls grouped in the centre of the table. Provide chop-sticks; even though you and your guests may not be very good at eating with them, you'll enjoy having a try.

Before the Indian dinner party, serve hot samosas as appetisers with pre-dinner drinks. Serve them with segmented limes for squeezing over them (lemons make an acceptable substitute if limes aren't available). With the curries, serve poppadums and a few side dishes such as desiccated coconut, raisins, sliced tomatoes, diced cucumber, mango chutney and sliced bananas (prepared just before they are needed).

CHINESE PARTY FOR SIX

Almond soup/Chicken with cashews, Crispy noodles with pork and water chestnuts, Prawns with bean sprouts, Boiled rice, Prawn crackers/Canned litchis in syrup, or Fruit-filled melon

BEFOREHAND

Almond soup
Make this early in the day and reheat in pan when needed.

Chicken with cashews
The day before, cube the chicken and cut up the vegetables. Keep the chicken and vegetables covered (separately) in the refrigerator. Fry the cashews. One hour before required, mix the ingredients for the sauce and make the sauce; keep it warm, preferably in a double saucepan. Fry the chicken and vegetables and keep warm, having removed them from the pan. When required, return to the pan, pour over the sauce and complete preparation.

Crispy noodles with pork and water chestnuts
The day before, boil and drain the noodles. Refrigerate, covered. Dice the pork; refrigerate. Prepare the vegetables; keep in polythene bag in refrigerator.

Prawns with bean sprouts
In the morning of the party, soak the prawns.

Fruit-filled melon
Prepare early in the day. Chill thoroughly in the refrigerator.

Rice
Boil the day before and heat when required, as indicated in the recipe.

ALMOND SOUP

Metric	Imperial
3 x 15 ml spoons olive oil	3 tablespoons olive oil
175 g blanched almonds, finely chopped	6 oz blanched almonds, finely chopped
1.5 x 15 ml spoons chopped onion	1½ tablespoons chopped onion
1 x 5 ml spoon crushed garlic	1 teaspoon crushed garlic
1.5 x 5 ml spoons chopped fresh parsley	1½ teaspoons chopped fresh parsley
10 x 15 ml spoons fresh white breadcrumbs	10 tablespoons fresh white breadcrumbs
1.8 litres chicken stock	3 pints chicken stock
Salt	Salt
Freshly ground black pepper	Freshly ground black pepper
Spring onion fans to garnish	Spring onion fans to garnish

Heat the oil in a saucepan and gently cook the almonds, onion, garlic and parsley, stirring all the time. Do not brown. Stir in the breadcrumbs and cook slowly for a further 3 minutes. Pour on the stock, season and cover. Simmer for 15 minutes. Serve garnished with spring onion fans.

Almond soup.

Chicken with cashews; Crispy noodles with pork and water chestnuts; Rice.

CHICKEN WITH CASHEWS

Metric	Imperial
4 x 15 ml spoons cooking oil	4 tablespoons cooking oil
100 g cashews, blanched	4 oz cashews, blanched
1 onion, peeled and chopped	1 onion, peeled and chopped
350 g chicken meat, cut into small cubes	12 oz chicken meat, cut into small cubes
50 g mushrooms, chopped	2 oz mushrooms, chopped
1 green pepper, cored, seeded and chopped	1 green pepper, cored, seeded and chopped
1 carrot, peeled and sliced	1 carrot, peeled and sliced
1 canned bamboo shoot, chopped	1 canned bamboo shoot, chopped
Salt	Salt
2 x 5 ml spoons cornflour	2 teaspoons cornflour
2 x 5 ml spoons sugar	2 teaspoons sugar
1 x 15 ml spoon soy sauce	1 tablespoon soy sauce
2 x 5 ml spoons dry sherry	2 teaspoons dry sherry
300 ml water	½ pint water

Heat 1 x 15 ml spoon (1 tablespoon) of the oil in a frying pan and fry the cashews until golden brown. Remove from the pan. Add 2 x 15 ml spoons (2 tablespoons) of the oil to the pan. Heat and fry the onion until it is transparent. Remove it from the pan. Fry the chicken until it begins to brown. Add the remaining oil, the vegetables, including the onion, and salt to taste and cook, stirring occasionally, for 5 to 6 minutes.

Mix together the cornflour, a little salt, the sugar, soy sauce, sherry and water in a saucepan. Bring to the boil, stirring all the time, and pour over the chicken. Add the nuts and cook until very hot. Serve at once in warmed bowls.

CRISPY NOODLES WITH PORK AND WATER CHESTNUTS

Metric	Imperial
175 g packet Chinese egg noodles	6 oz packet Chinese egg noodles
Oil for deep frying	Oil for deep frying
100 g boneless pork, finely diced	4 oz boneless pork, finely diced
Salt	Salt
Freshly ground black pepper	Freshly ground black pepper
50 g canned water chestnuts, shredded	2 oz canned water chestnuts, shredded
50 g mushrooms, finely chopped	2 oz mushrooms, finely chopped
50 g onion, peeled and finely chopped	2 oz onion, peeled and finely chopped
175 g bean sprouts	6 oz bean sprouts
1 x 5 ml spoon cornflour	1 teaspoon cornflour
2 x 5 ml spoons soy sauce	2 teaspoons soy sauce
Few drops of sesame oil (optional)	Few drops of sesame oil (optional)

Cook the noodles in boiling water for 5 minutes, then rinse under cold running water and drain. Heat the oil to 190°C/375°F. Arrange the noodles in a frying basket in the shape of six nests and deep fry for 5 minutes, until crisp and golden.

Oil a large frying pan and heat it. Fry the pork for 2 minutes, stirring. Season to taste. Add the vegetables and cook for 2 minutes. Dissolve the cornflour in the soy sauce and enough water to make a thin paste. Add to the pan and cook for 1 minute. Sprinkle with the sesame oil, if used, and serve in the noodle nests.

PRAWNS WITH BEAN SPROUTS

Metric	Imperial
500 g shelled prawns	1 lb shelled prawns
120 ml dry sherry	4 fl oz dry sherry
150 ml oil	¼ pint oil
1.5 x 5 ml spoons salt	1½ teaspoons salt
500 g bean sprouts	1 lb bean sprouts
4.5 x 15 ml spoons light soy sauce	4½ tablespoons light soy sauce
1.5 x 5 ml spoons sugar	1½ teaspoons sugar

Soak the prawns in the sherry for 1½ hours. Drain. Heat the oil in a large saucepan or frying pan. Add the prawns and salt and fry for 2 minutes. Add the bean sprouts and fry for 2 minutes. Add the soy sauce and sugar and mix well. Heat thoroughly. Serve in warmed bowls.

BOILED RICE

Metric	Imperial
350 g long-grain rice	12 oz long-grain rice
1.5 x 5 ml spoons salt	1½ teaspoons salt
25 g butter	1 oz butter

Cook the rice in boiling salted water for 11 minutes. Drain, rinse and drain again thoroughly. Place in a lightly greased baking dish, dot with butter and cover with foil. Reheat when required in a preheated moderate oven (180°C/350°F, Gas Mark 4) for 30 to 40 minutes.

Prawns with bean sprouts.

Fruit-filled melon.

FRUIT-FILLED MELON

Metric	Imperial
1 medium firm ripe watermelon	1 medium firm ripe watermelon
Canned litchis, loquats, kumquats and/or Chinese gooseberries as available, drained	Canned litchis, loquats, kumquats and/or Chinese gooseberries as available, drained

Cut the melon in half crossways. Scoop out the pulp with a melon baller or scoop into balls. Discard the seeds. Alternatively cut the pulp into cubes with a knife. Mix with the rest of the fruit and spoon back into the watermelon shells. Chill thoroughly.

Note: Canned drained apricots, orange sections, apple wedges and/or canned or fresh pineapple wedges can be added to or substituted for the fruits mentioned.

36

INDIAN DINNER PARTY FOR EIGHT

Samosas (deep-fried savoury pastries) /Lamb biryani or Fish curry, Rice, Avial (vegetable curry), Chappatis, Raita/Fresh fruit

BEFOREHAND

Samosas
Make these the day before, or on the morning of the party, and reheat them later. Or prepare them, without frying, and complete this process 30 minutes before your guests are due. Keep them warm.

Lamb biryani
Make the day before, then, when required, reheat it in a preheated moderate oven (180°C/350°F, Gas Mark 4) for 1 hour. Sauté the almonds and sultanas for the garnish while the biryani is reheating.

Fish curry
Make the sauce the day before. One hour before the curry is required, reheat it gently in a large pan. When it is simmering, add the fish. Put into a casserole and cook in a preheated moderate oven (180°C/350°F, Gas Mark 4) for 45 minutes or until the fish is tender. (Or cook on top of the stove as indicated in the recipe.)

Avial
Prepare the vegetables and keep in a covered container in the refrigerator until needed. (They can be prepared the day before or early on the day of the party.)

Rice
Measure and place in dish ready for the addition of water when required.

Chappatis
Cook earlier in the day and reheat when required.

Raita
Make during the afternoon and keep chilled.

SAMOSAS

Metric	Imperial
For the pastry:	**For the pastry:**
225 g plain flour	8 oz plain flour
1 x 2.5 ml spoon salt	½ teaspoon salt
25 g butter	1 oz butter
4-6 x 15 ml spoons water	4-6 tablespoons water
Oil for deep frying	Oil for deep frying
For the filling:	**For the filling:**
25 g butter	1 oz butter
1 onion, peeled and finely chopped	1 onion, peeled and finely chopped
2 garlic cloves, crushed	2 garlic cloves, crushed
1 green chilli, seeded and finely chopped	1 green chilli, seeded and finely chopped
2.5 cm piece of fresh root ginger, peeled and chopped	1 inch piece of fresh root ginger, peeled and chopped
1 x 2.5 ml spoon ground turmeric	½ teaspoon ground turmeric
1 x 2.5 ml spoon mild chilli powder	½ teaspoon mild chilli powder
1 x 5 ml spoon salt	1 teaspoon salt
2 x 5 ml spoons garam masala	2 teaspoons garam masala
350 g lean minced meat	12 oz lean minced meat

These deep-fried pastries contain a spicy filling which can be meat or vegetable; they are delicious as appetizers or snacks.

Sift the flour and salt into a bowl, then rub in the butter until the mixture resembles breadcrumbs. Mix in enough water to bind to a dough. Knead for about 5 minutes or until smooth and elastic. Leave covered with a damp cloth while you make the filling.

Melt the butter in a frying pan and gently fry the onion, garlic, chilli and ginger for 5 minutes. Stir in the seasonings and the meat and fry for 15 minutes longer. Remove from the heat and allow to cool while shaping the dough.

Divide the dough into 15 equal pieces. Roll each piece out to form a 10 cm (4 inch) round. Cut each round in half and lightly dampen the edges of the semi-circles. Shape each to form a cone and fill each with some of the filling. Seal the edges well and set aside in a cool place for 30 minutes.

Heat the oil in a deep-frying pan to 190°C/375°F. Deep-fry the samosas, a few at a time, for 2 to 3 minutes or until golden brown. Drain and serve hot. Makes 30

Right: Samosas.

LAMB BIRYANI

Metric

700 g long-grain rice
2 x 5 ml spoons saffron fronds or
    1.56 grain packet of saffron
    powder
120 ml hot water
120 ml oil
4 garlic cloves, crushed
5 cm piece of fresh root ginger,
    peeled and chopped
1.5 kg boned lean lamb, cubed
1 x 2.5 ml spoon cayenne pepper
2 x 5 ml spoons ground cumin
2 x 5 ml spoons ground
    coriander
2 x 5 ml spoons ground cloves
2 x 5 ml spoons ground
    cinnamon
2 x 5 ml spoons salt
2 x 5 ml spoons freshly ground
    black pepper
600 ml unsweetened natural
    yogurt
4 onions, peeled and thinly
    sliced
50 g flaked almonds
50 g sultanas, cleaned
50 g butter

Imperial

1½ lb long-grain rice
2 teaspoons saffron fronds or
    1.56 grain packet of saffron
    powder
4 fl oz hot water
4 fl oz oil
4 garlic cloves, crushed
2 inch piece of fresh root ginger,
    peeled and chopped
3 lb boned lean lamb, cubed
½ teaspoon cayenne pepper
2 teaspoons ground cumin
2 teaspoons ground coriander
2 teaspoons ground cloves
2 teaspoons ground cinnamon
2 teaspoons salt
2 teaspoons freshly ground black
    pepper
1 pint unsweetened natural
    yogurt
4 onions, peeled and thinly
    sliced
2 oz flaked almonds
2 oz sultanas, cleaned
2 oz butter

This dish from the Moglai area traditionally layers rice with spiced meat and onions. It was originally made with lamb, but chicken pieces can equally well be used. Biryani can also be served without the meat as a vegetable dish.

Soak the rice in cold water to cover for 30 minutes. Put the saffron to soak in the hot water for 30 minutes (powdered saffron does not need soaking). Meanwhile, heat the oil in a frying pan and lightly fry the garlic and ginger. Add the meat and fry for 5 minutes. Stir in the spices and seasoning and the yogurt. Mix well together and simmer for about 35 minutes.

Bring a large saucepan of lightly salted water to the boil. Drain the rice and plunge it into the boiling water. Bring back to the boil and boil for 2 minutes. Drain well and divide the rice into three portions. Place one portion of rice in a 2.75 litre (5 pint) casserole dish. Soak another portion of rice in the saffron water to colour it yellow. Place half of the lamb mixture on top of the rice in the casserole and top with half the onions. Add the drained saffron rice. Cover with the rest of the lamb, then onions, then third portion of rice as the top layer. Cover the casserole with aluminium foil and then the lid and bake in a preheated moderate oven (180°C/350°F, Gas Mark 4) for 1 hour.

Sauté the almonds and sultanas in the butter and sprinkle on top of the biryani to garnish.

Below: Fish curry; Lamb biryani; Avial.

FISH CURRY

Metric	Imperial
50 g butter	2 oz butter
2 large onions, peeled and chopped	2 large onions, peeled and chopped
2 x 15 ml spoons curry powder	2 tablespoons curry powder
50 g plain flour	2 oz plain flour
600 ml chicken stock	1 pint chicken stock
600 ml milk	1 pint milk
2 small apples, peeled, cored and chopped	2 small apples, peeled, cored and chopped
4 tomatoes, skinned and chopped	4 tomatoes, skinned and chopped
50-100 g sultanas	2-4 oz sultanas
Salt	Salt
Freshly ground black pepper	Freshly ground black pepper
1.5 kg filleted cod, haddock, or similar white fish, skinned and cut into 2.5 cm cubes	3 lb filleted cod, haddock, or similar white fish, skinned and cut into 1 inch cubes

Melt the butter in a saucepan and fry the onions gently for 5 minutes without browning. Stir in the curry powder and fry it for 2 to 3 minutes, then add the flour and cook for a further 2 to 3 minutes. Remove the pan from the heat and gradually stir in the stock and milk. Bring to the boil, stirring, and simmer until the sauce thickens.

Add the apples, tomatoes, sultanas and salt and pepper to taste. Cover and simmer for 15 minutes. Add the fish, stir well and simmer for a further 10 minutes or until the fish is tender. Add more salt and pepper if necessary and serve with boiled rice. (For oven-cooking, see "Beforehand".)

AVIAL

Metric	Imperial
4 x 15 ml spoons oil	4 tablespoons oil
1 x 5 ml spoon mustard seeds	1 teaspoon mustard seeds
1 onion, peeled and finely chopped	1 onion, peeled and finely chopped
1 green chilli, seeded and finely chopped	1 green chilli, seeded and finely chopped
1 x 5 ml spoon ground turmeric	1 teaspoon ground turmeric
1 x 15 ml spoon ground coriander	1 tablespoon ground coriander
500 g mixed vegetables, prepared and sliced – choose from aubergine, carrots, beans, cauliflower, green pepper, okra, potatoes and tomatoes	1 lb mixed vegetables, prepared and sliced – choose from aubergine, carrots, beans, cauliflower, green pepper, okra, potatoes and tomatoes
1 x 5 ml spoon salt	1 teaspoon salt
100 g grated fresh coconut	4 oz grated fresh coconut
120 ml unsweetened natural yogurt	4 fl oz unsweetened natural yogurt
25 g butter, melted	1 oz butter, melted

A mild vegetable curry with coconut and yogurt, this includes a variety of vegetables. Indians include okra ('ladies' fingers') in this and other vegetable dishes whenever possible.

Heat the oil in a saucepan and gently fry the mustard seeds, onion, chilli and spices. Toss in the prepared vegetables. Season with the salt, and simmer with just enough water to keep the vegetables moist until they are cooked through but still crunchy. (The time will depend on the choice of vegetables used; those needing a little longer cooking can be started first.)

Stir in the coconut and simmer for a further 5 minutes. Remove from the heat, stir in the yogurt and melted butter and serve.

RICE (OVEN-COOKED)

Metric	Imperial
350 g long-grain rice	12 oz long-grain rice
900 ml water	1½ pints water
1.5 x 5 ml spoons salt	1½ teaspoons salt

Put the rice in an ovenproof dish. Bring the water to the boil with the salt, pour it over the rice and stir well. Cover tightly with a lid or with foil. Bake in a preheated moderate oven (180°C/350°F, Gas Mark 4) for 35 to 40 minutes or until the grains are just soft and the cooking liquid has all been absorbed by the rice.

Chappatis; Raita.

CHAPPATIS

Metric	Imperial
350 g plain wholewheat flour	12 oz plain wholewheat flour
1 x 5 ml spoon salt	1 teaspoon salt
200-300 ml water	7-10 fl oz water

Sift the flour and salt into a bowl. Add enough of the water to make a soft dough and knit together with your fingertips. Knead well for 10 minutes. Leave, covered with a damp cloth, for at least 1 hour.

Knead well again, then divide into eight pieces. Roll out each piece on a generously floured surface to make 10 to 12 cm (4 to 5 inch) rounds. Heat a very lightly greased griddle or a heavy based frying pan. Cook two chappatis at a time until pale brown on each side. Serve hot, brushed with butter, as an accompaniment to the main dishes. Makes 8

RAITA

Metric	Imperial
1 cucumber (about 500 g), finely diced	1 cucumber (about 1 lb), finely diced
2 onions, peeled and finely chopped	2 onions, peeled and finely chopped
2 garlic cloves, crushed	2 garlic cloves, crushed
600 ml unsweetened natural yogurt	1 pint unsweetened natural yogurt
1 x 5 ml spoon salt	1 teaspoon salt
1 x 2.5 ml spoon freshly ground black pepper	½ teaspoon freshly ground black pepper

A cool, fresh-tasting accompaniment to Indian dishes, Raita can be made from a variety of fresh raw vegetables. Combine all the ingredients and chill for 1 hour before serving.

ITALIAN DINNER FOR SIX

Pasta hors d'oeuvre/Saltimbocca alla romana, Courgettes with tomatoes, Green salad/Fresh peaches in wine

BEFOREHAND

Pasta hors d'oeuvre
The day before, cook the pasta shells and refrigerate them, covered. Make the mayonnaise. Cut the meats into strips; keep covered in refrigerator. Chop the parsley and keep in refrigerator. Cube the bread for croûtons.

Saltimbocca alla romana
Early in the day, prepare the veal rolls; keep, covered, in the refrigerator. Cube the bread for croûtons.

Courgettes with tomatoes
Early in the day, skin and chop the tomatoes. Chop the parsley and crush the garlic; keep wrapped until required. Slice the courgettes and sprinkle with salt an hour before cooking. (Drain before cooking.)

Green salad
The day before, prepare the vegetables and refrigerate in polythene bags. Make the dressing.

Fresh peaches in wine
Prepare an hour beforehand and chill thoroughly.

PASTA HORS D'OEUVRE

Metric	Imperial
175 g pasta shells	6 oz pasta shells
100 g garlic sausage, cut into strips	4 oz garlic sausage, cut into strips
100 g cooked tongue, cut into strips	4 oz cooked tongue, cut into strips
225 g crisp green apples, cored and finely diced	8 oz crisp green apples, cored and finely diced
1 egg yolk	1 egg yolk
Pinch of sugar	Pinch of sugar
1 x 2.5 ml spoon dry mustard	½ teaspoon dry mustard
Salt	Salt
Freshly ground black pepper	Freshly ground black pepper
225 ml corn oil	7½ fl oz corn oil
1.5 x 15 ml spoons vinegar	1½ tablespoons vinegar
1 x 15 ml spoon top of the milk	1 tablespoon top of the milk
50 g onion, peeled and finely chopped	2 oz onion, peeled and finely chopped
2 x 5 ml spoons tomato paste	2 teaspoons tomato paste
Chopped fresh parsley to garnish	Chopped fresh parsley to garnish

Cook the pasta shells in boiling salted water until tender. Drain and rinse under cold running water. Add the garlic sausage, tongue and apples to the pasta shells and toss together.

Put the egg yolk, sugar, mustard and salt and pepper to taste in a bowl and mix well. Gradually add the oil in drops, whisking well. When half the oil is incorporated, the remainder may be added in a thin stream. If the mayonnaise becomes too thick to work, add a little of the vinegar. Mix in the top of the milk, onion, tomato paste and remaining vinegar.

Fork the mayonnaise through the pasta mixture. Serve on individual plates garnished with chopped parsley.

SALTIMBOCCA ALLA ROMANA

Metric	Imperial
12 thin slices of veal	12 thin slices of veal
Lemon juice	Lemon juice
Freshly ground black pepper	Freshly ground black pepper
12 fresh sage or basil leaves or 2 x 5 ml spoons dried marjoram	12 fresh sage or basil leaves or 2 teaspoons dried majoram
12 thin slices of prosciutto or boiled ham	12 thin slices of prosciutto or boiled ham
75 g butter	3 oz butter
3 x 15 ml spoons Marsala	3 tablespoons Marsala
1 cm squares day-old bread, fried as croûtons	½ inch squares day-old bread, fried as croûtons

Ask the butcher to bat out the veal to pieces about 10 x 12.5 cm (4 x 5 inches). Season with lemon juice and pepper. Place a sage or basil leaf or a little marjoram in the centre of each slice of veal and cover with a slice of ham. Roll up and fix firmly with a wooden cocktail stick.

Melt the butter in a frying pan just large enough to take the rolls in a single layer, packed fairly tightly to keep the rolls a good shape. Gently fry the veal rolls until golden brown. Do not overheat the butter. Add the Marsala. Bring to simmering point, cover the pan and simmer gently until the veal rolls are tender. Serve hot, garnished with fried croûtons.

Left: Pasta hors d'oeuvre.

Above: Saltimbocca alla romana; Green salad; Courgettes with tomatoes. Below: Fresh peaches in wine.

COURGETTES WITH TOMATOES

Metric	Imperial
750 g courgettes, cut into 1 cm slices	1½ lb courgettes, cut into ½ inch slices
Salt	Salt
100 g butter	4 oz butter
225 g tomatoes, skinned and chopped	8 oz tomatoes, skinned and chopped
4 x 15 ml spoons chopped fresh parsley	4 tablespoons chopped fresh parsley
1 small garlic clove, crushed	1 small garlic clove, crushed
Freshly ground black pepper	Freshly ground black pepper
1 x 5 ml spoon sugar	1 teaspoon sugar

Put the courgette slices into a colander, sprinkle them with salt and allow to drain for about 1 hour. Dry them well. Melt 75 g (3 oz) of the butter in a frying pan. Add the courgettes and cook them gently until soft and slightly transparent. Put in a serving dish; keep warm.

Melt the remaining butter in the pan and cook the tomatoes, the parsley, the garlic, pepper to taste and sugar until a thickish purée forms. Adjust the seasoning if necessary and pour the purée over the courgettes in the serving dish.

FRESH PEACHES IN WINE

Metric	Imperial
6 ripe yellow peaches, peeled	6 ripe yellow peaches, peeled
6 x 5 ml spoons caster sugar	6 teaspoons caster sugar
175 ml sweet white wine (such as Orvieto)	6 fl oz sweet white wine (such as Orvieto)

Put one peach into each of six wine glasses and sprinkle with the sugar. Pour over the wine. Chill. The peach is eaten first, then the wine is drunk.

AMERICAN PARTY FOR EIGHT

Tomato jelly rings, Bread sticks/Chilli con carne, Baked jacket potatoes with soured cream and chives, Tossed green salad/Baked Alaska

BEFOREHAND

Tomato jelly rings
Make the day before.
Chilli con carne
Prepare and cook the day before, except for the beans. Cool before putting in the refrigerator. On the day, bring back to the boil, stirring, before adding the beans.
Potatoes
Scrub the day before.
Tossed green salad
Prepare the ingredients the day before and keep in separate polythene bags in the refrigerator.
Baked Alaska
The day before make or buy the sponge cake for the base.

TOMATO JELLY RINGS

Metric	Imperial
1 kg firm ripe tomatoes, skinned and quartered	2 lb firm ripe tomatoes, skinned and quartered
4 small onions, peeled and chopped	4 small onions, peeled and chopped
2 small garlic cloves, crushed	2 small garlic cloves, crushed
2 x 5 ml spoons sugar	2 teaspoons sugar
1 x 5 ml spoon salt	1 teaspoon salt
Pinch of celery salt	Pinch of celery salt
Pinch of grated nutmeg	Pinch of grated nutmeg
2 bay leaves	2 bay leaves
2 x 5 ml spoons peppercorns	2 teaspoons peppercorns
2 x 15 ml spoons powdered gelatine	2 tablespoons powdered gelatine
4 x 15 ml spoons water	4 tablespoons water
2 x 15 ml spoons tarragon vinegar	2 tablespoons tarragon vinegar
6 x 15 ml spoons lemon juice	6 tablespoons lemon juice
Watercress to garnish	Watercress to garnish

Above: Chilli con carne; Green salad; Baked potatoes.
Right: Baked Alaska.

Remove the centres from the tomatoes if they are tough. Put the tomatoes, onions, garlic, sugar, salts and nutmeg in a saucepan. Add the bay leaves and peppercorns, tied in muslin, and cook over a low heat until the onion is tender. Remove the muslin bag.

Dissolve the gelatine in the water in a small heatproof bowl over hot water. Purée the tomato mixture in an electric blender, then rub it through a sieve and pour it into a measuring jug. Add the vinegar and lemon juice and, if necessary, make up to 1 litre (1¾ pints) with water. Stir in the dissolved gelatine. Pour into eight dampened individual ring moulds and leave to set. To serve, turn out of the moulds and garnish with watercress.

CHILLI CON CARNE

Metric	Imperial
1.5 kg minced beef	3 lb minced beef
2 x 15 ml spoons fat or oil	2 tablespoons fat or oil
2 large onions, peeled and chopped	2 large onions, peeled and chopped
2 green peppers, cored, seeded and chopped (optional)	2 green peppers, cored, seeded and chopped (optional)
1 x 900 g can tomatoes	1 x 30 oz can tomatoes
Salt	Salt
Freshly ground black pepper	Freshly ground black pepper
2 x 15 ml spoons chilli powder	2 tablespoons chilli powder
2 x 15 ml spoons vinegar	2 tablespoons vinegar
2 x 5 ml spoons sugar	2 teaspoons sugar
4 x 15 ml spoons tomato paste	4 tablespoons tomato paste
2 x 425 g cans red kidney beans, drained	2 x 15 oz cans red kidney beans, drained

Fry the beef in the fat or oil in a saucepan until lightly browned. Add the onions and peppers, if using, and fry for 5 minutes or until soft. Drain off any excess fat. Stir in the tomatoes. Mix together seasoning, the chilli powder, vinegar, sugar and tomato paste and add to the pan. Mix well. Cover and simmer for 30 to 40 minutes. Ten minutes before the cooking time is completed, add the kidney beans.
Note: Add the chilli powder very judiciously; some of it is very hot. American chilli powder is usually a milder, pre-mixed seasoning, based on ground Mexican chilli peppers, so look for this kind.

Tomato jelly rings.

BAKED ALASKA

Metric
1 x 22.5 cm round sponge cake
1 x 566 g can fruit, e.g.
    raspberries, drained (syrup
    reserved)
1 litre block vanilla ice cream
6 egg whites
275 g caster sugar

Imperial
1 x 9 inch round sponge cake
1 x 20 oz can fruit, e.g.
    raspberries, drained (syrup
    reserved)
35¼ fl oz block vanilla ice cream
6 egg whites
10 oz caster sugar

Put the sponge cake on a flat ovenproof dish and spoon over just enough fruit syrup to moisten it. Put the ice cream in the centre of the cake and pile the fruit on top. Whisk the egg whites until stiff. Whisk in half the sugar, then fold in the remaining sugar. Pile this meringue mixture on the cake, covering the cake, ice cream and fruit completely, and taking the meringue down to the dish. Bake in a preheated very hot oven (230°C/450°F, Gas Mark 8) for 2 to 3 minutes, or until the outside of the meringue just begins to brown. Serve at once.

Variations: Use fresh crushed fruit, e.g. strawberries, when in season. Or sprinkle 2 to 4 x 15 ml spoons (2 to 4 tablespoons) sherry or rum over the cake before the ice cream is added.

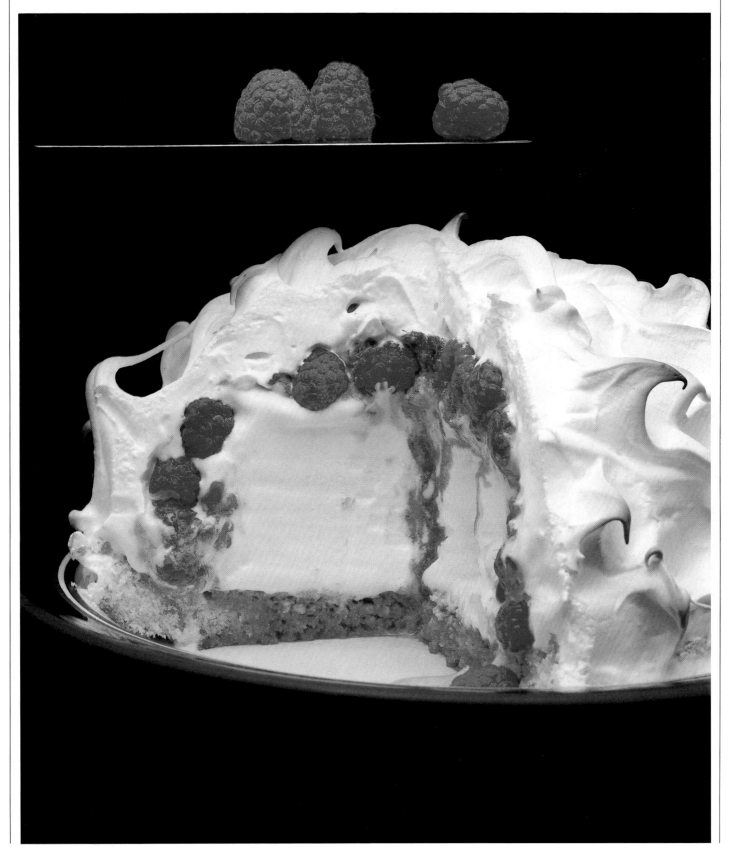

CELEBRATION DINNER PARTIES

Get out your best linen and china; dress up the table with a centrepiece of flowers, set low so that you can see your guests as well as hear them, and light the candles. Both these menus are perfect for a special celebration, whether for a summer or winter occasion.

Vermouth, used for the chicken in the winter menu, is a valuable cookery ingredient at any time of the year; keep it in the refrigerator and use it, if possible, within a month. This recipe also calls for tarragon. Use fresh tarragon if you can; if not use dried tarragon (half the quantity) but make sure it's a fresh supply and not something that's been crumbling away for months in the kitchen cupboard.

Make the most of summer foods in the second menu with a dinner party planned around a spectacular stuffed crown roast of lamb. Order the lamb a few days ahead and ask the butcher to prepare it. Make these celebration parties a memorable occasion by choosing special wines to go with them.

WINTER DINNER PARTY FOR SIX

Marinated kipper fillets, Toast triangles/Chicken with vermouth and mushrooms, Potato and chicory duchesse, Green peas/Pineapple sorbet, Almond tuiles/Coffee, Peppermint creams

BEFOREHAND

Marinated kipper fillets
Prepare and marinate overnight.
Chicken with vermouth and mushrooms
Wipe and trim chicken; keep in the refrigerator. Prepare mushrooms and watercress; refrigerate in polythene bags.
Potato and chicory duchesse
Prepare chicory; refrigerate in polythene bags. Peel potatoes; keep covered with water.
Pineapple sorbet
Can be made a week ahead and kept in freezer.
Almond tuiles
Make one day ahead; store in airtight tin.
Peppermint creams
Can be made several days ahead; store as indicated in recipe.

Marinated kipper fillets.

MARINATED KIPPER FILLETS

Metric	Imperial
500 g kipper fillets, skinned and cut into very thin strips	1 lb kipper fillets, skinned and cut into very thin strips
75 g onion, peeled and thinly sliced	3 oz onion, peeled and thinly sliced
100 g celery heart, thinly sliced	4 oz celery heart, thinly sliced
150 ml white wine vinegar	$\frac{1}{4}$ pint white wine vinegar
5 x 15 ml spoons soft brown sugar	5 tablespoons soft brown sugar
1 x 15 ml spoon snipped fresh or 1 x 5 ml spoon dried chives	1 tablespoon snipped fresh or 1 teaspoon dried chives
Freshly ground black pepper	Freshly ground black pepper
Tomato wedges and lettuce to garnish	Tomato wedges and lettuce to garnish

Layer the fish strips, onion and celery heart in a shallow serving dish. Mix the vinegar, sugar, chives and pepper to taste together and spoon over the fish. Cover the dish tightly and leave to marinate in the refrigerator for at least 12 hours, longer if possible. Remove from the refrigerator about 30 minutes before serving with fingers of toast. Garnish the fish with tomato wedges and lettuce.

POTATO AND CHICORY DUCHESSE

Metric	Imperial
225 g chicory	8 oz chicory
1 kg potatoes, peeled	2 lb potatoes, peeled
50 g butter	2 oz butter
1 garlic clove, crushed	1 garlic clove, crushed
6 x 15 ml spoons double cream	6 tablespoons double cream
3 eggs, separated	3 eggs, separated
Salt	Salt
Freshly ground black pepper	Freshly ground black pepper

Remove any damaged leaves from the chicory. Halve lengthways, then slice across into thin strips. Cook the potatoes in boiling water. Meanwhile, melt half of the butter in a frying pan. Add the garlic and chicory and cook gently for 10 minutes.

Drain the potatoes and mash until smooth. Beat in the chicory mixture, cream, egg yolks and seasoning. Beat the egg whites until stiff and fold into the potato mixture. Spoon into a well-buttered shallow oval ovenproof dish, and rough up with a fork. Dot with pieces of the remaining butter and bake in a preheated moderate oven (180°C/350°F, Gas Mark 4) for 35 to 40 minutes or until well risen and golden brown. Serve as soon as possible. If necessary, keep warm in a low oven.

CHICKEN WITH VERMOUTH AND MUSHROOMS

Metric
6 x 275 g chicken wing portions
25 g butter
2 x 15 ml spoons vegetable oil
6 x 15 ml spoons dry vermouth
450 ml chicken stock
1 x 15 ml spoon chopped fresh or
  1 x 5 ml spoon dried tarragon
Salt
Freshly ground black pepper
350 g small button mushrooms
3 x 15 ml spoons cornflour
4 x 15 ml spoons water
Watercress sprigs to garnish

Imperial
6 x 10 oz chicken wing portions
1 oz butter
2 tablespoons vegetable oil
6 tablespoons dry vermouth
¾ pint chicken stock
1 tablespoon chopped fresh or
  1 teaspoon dried tarragon
Salt
Freshly ground black pepper
12 oz small button mushrooms
3 tablespoons cornflour
4 tablespoons water
Watercress sprigs to garnish

Wipe and trim the joints (remove the skin, if you wish). Melt the butter with the oil in a flameproof casserole. Add the chicken joints and fry for 15 minutes or until browned all over. Warm the vermouth, pour into the casserole and set alight. Shake the pan gently until the flames subside. Stir in the stock, tarragon and seasoning and bring to the boil. Cover tightly and transfer to a preheated moderate oven (180°C/350°F, Gas Mark 4). Cook for about 40 minutes.

Add the mushrooms to the casserole, pushing them under the surface of the liquid. Cover and cook for a further 10 minutes, or until clear liquid runs from the joints when pierced with a skewer.

Remove the chicken from the casserole and place on a large warmed serving platter. Cover with foil and keep warm. Dissolve the cornflour in the water. Stir into the casserole juices and simmer on top of the stove for a few minutes, stirring until thickened. Spoon a little sauce over the chicken and pour the rest into a warmed sauceboat. Garnish the chicken with watercress sprigs and serve.

Chicken with vermouth and mushrooms; Potato and chicory duchesse.

Peppermint creams; Pineapple sorbet; Almond tuiles.

PINEAPPLE SORBET

Metric	Imperial
1 x 375 g can pineapple rings or chunks	1 x 13 oz can pineapple rings or chunks
50 g sugar	2 oz sugar
3 x 15 ml spoons lemon juice	3 tablespoons lemon juice
1 egg white	1 egg white

Put the undrained pineapple, sugar and lemon juice in an electric blender goblet and blend until a smooth purée. Pour into a freezer container and freeze until mushy.

Turn the pineapple mixture into a chilled bowl and beat well until the ice crystals are broken down. Whisk the egg white until stiff and fold into the pineapple mixture. Spoon into six freezerproof serving dishes, cover and freeze.

Allow to 'come to' for 15 minutes in the refrigerator before serving with Almond tuiles.

ALMOND TUILES

Metric	Imperial
3 egg whites	3 egg whites
175 g caster sugar	6 oz caster sugar
75 g plain flour	3 oz plain flour
75 g flaked or nibbed almonds	3 oz flaked or nibbed almonds
75 g butter, melted	3 oz butter, melted

Using a rotary whisk and a large bowl, whisk the egg whites until stiff. Fold in the caster sugar, sifted flour and almonds. Mix well. Fold in the cooled melted butter. Place very small spoonsful of the mixture on a baking sheet lined with non-stick paper, keeping them well apart. Smooth each one out thinly with the back of the spoon, retaining the circular shape. Bake in a preheated moderately hot oven (190°C/375°F, Gas Mark 5) for 8 to 10 minutes or until lightly browned.

Use a palette knife to lift each biscuit from the baking sheet and place it over the handle of a wooden spoon so that it sets in a curled shape. Allow a moment or two for the biscuit to harden, then remove it to a wire rack to cool. Store in an airtight tin. Makes about 30

PEPPERMINT CREAMS

Metric	Imperial
225 g icing sugar, sifted	8 oz icing sugar, sifted
1 x 15 ml spoon beaten egg white (approx)	1 tablespoon beaten egg white (approx)
Few drops of peppermint essence	Few drops of peppermint essence
25 g plain chocolate, melted (optional)	1 oz plain chocolate, melted (optional)

In a bowl, mix the icing sugar to a stiff paste with the egg white. Add a few drops of peppermint essence to taste. Roll out the peppermint dough to 6 mm ($\frac{1}{4}$ inch) thick between sheets of non-stick kitchen or wax paper. Stamp out 2.5 cm (1 inch) rounds with a plain cutter. Leave for at least 24 hours to firm. Coat half the peppermint creams with melted chocolate, to give a fifty-fifty effect. Place on wax paper to dry.

Store both plain and chocolate creams in an airtight container, with paper between each of the layers. Makes about 28

SUMMER DINNER PARTY FOR SIX

Cream of prawn soup or Croûtes aux tomates/Stuffed crown roast of lamb, Château potatoes, Carrots in orange butter/Strawberry and orange mousse, Meringue twists

BEFOREHAND

Cream of prawn soup
This can be made earlier in the day, but don't add the prawns until you reheat the soup for serving.

Stuffed crown roast of lamb
A few days ahead, order the lamb – most butchers will prepare a crown roast and may also supply the cutlet frills. The day before, make the stuffing and stuff the lamb; weigh the completed joint in order to calculate cooking time. Refrigerate, covered. Make sure you have redcurrant jelly in the storecupboard.

Potatoes
Scrape and keep covered in cold water.

Carrots
Trim and scrub and keep refrigerated in a polythene bag.

Strawberry and orange mousse
Make the day before (even earlier if you have a freezer).

Meringue twists
Make several days ahead; store in an airtight tin.

Croûtes aux tomates
Prepare the rounds of bread, grate the cheese, and skin and slice the tomatoes several hours ahead; keep refrigerated, separately, in polythene bags or containers. Fry the croûtes about 2 hours before the meal; add toppings and leave on a baking sheet ready for the oven.

Melt the margarine in a heavy-based pan. Add the vegetables and cook gently, covered, for about 15 minutes or until they are soft. Stir in the flour and cook for 1 minute. Remove from the heat and stir in the milk and stock.

Return to the heat and bring to the boil, stirring. Add seasoning and the bay leaf. Cover and simmer gently for 30 minutes, stirring occasionally. Cool slightly, then remove the bay leaf and liquidise the soup. Return to the rinsed-out pan and reheat.

Reserve a few prawns for garnish and roughly chop the rest. Add the chopped prawns to the soup and heat through gently. Adjust the seasoning and garnish with chives and the reserved prawns.

CROÛTES AUX TOMATES

Metric	Imperial
2 large slices of medium cut bread	2 large slices of medium cut bread
Oil for frying	Oil for frying
25 g Gruyère cheese, finely grated	1 oz Gruyère cheese, finely grated
2 medium tomatoes, skinned and sliced	2 medium tomatoes, skinned and sliced
1 x 275 g can asparagus tips, drained	1 x 10 oz can asparagus tips, drained

Using a 3 cm (1½ inch) plain round or oval cutter, stamp out six rounds or ovals from the bread. Fry in a little oil until golden brown on both sides. Remove and drain on absorbent kitchen paper, then arrange on a baking sheet. Top each croûte with a little cheese, using half of it, and a tomato slice. Cut the asparagus tips to fit the croûtes. (The remaining stalks can be used for a soup or casserole.) Arrange the asparagus tips on top of the tomatoes in pairs. Sprinkle the remaining cheese over the stalk ends of the asparagus.

Bake in a preheated moderately hot oven (190°C/375°F, Gas Mark 5) at the lowest shelf position, for 20 minutes. Transfer to a warmed serving dish and serve immediately.

Note: If fresh asparagus is available and not too expensive, cook it and use instead of the canned asparagus. These croûtes may also be served as a savoury.

Cream of prawn soup.

CREAM OF PRAWN SOUP

Metric	Imperial
75 g margarine	3 oz margarine
175 g onions, peeled and thinly sliced	6 oz onions, peeled and thinly sliced
175 g celery, trimmed and thinly sliced	6 oz celery, trimmed and thinly sliced
5 x 15 ml spoons plain flour	5 tablespoons plain flour
900 ml milk	1½ pints milk
450 ml light stock	¾ pint light stock
Salt	Salt
Freshly ground black pepper	Freshly ground black pepper
1 bay leaf	1 bay leaf
175 g frozen shelled prawns, thawed	6 oz frozen shelled prawns, thawed
Snipped fresh chives to garnish	Snipped fresh chives to garnish

Croûtes aux tomates.

STUFFED CROWN ROAST OF LAMB

Metric	Imperial
50 g butter or margarine	2 oz butter or margarine
100 g onion, peeled and chopped	4 oz onion, peeled and chopped
100 g streaky bacon rashers, rinds removed, diced	4 oz streaky bacon rashers, rinds removed, diced
225 g dessert apples, peeled, cored and finely chopped	8 oz dessert apples, peeled, cored and finely chopped
225 g celery, trimmed and chopped	8 oz celery, trimmed and chopped
Finely grated rind and juice of 1 lemon	Finely grated rind and juice of 1 lemon
50 g walnuts, chopped	2 oz walnuts, chopped
2 x 15 ml spoons chopped fresh parsley	2 tablespoons chopped fresh parsley
225 g fresh white breadcrumbs	8 oz fresh white breadcrumbs
Salt	Salt
Freshly ground black pepper	Freshly ground black pepper
Beaten egg, to bind	Beaten egg, to bind
1 x 12-bone crown roast of lamb	1 x 12-bone crown roast of lamb
Lard or dripping for roasting	Lard or dripping for roasting
Parsley sprigs to garnish	Parsley sprigs to garnish

The 'crown' is formed by joining two best ends of neck, and is stuffed with a savoury filling. Melt the butter or margarine and lightly brown the onion and bacon. Remove from the heat and mix in the apples, celery, lemon rind and juice, walnuts, parsley, breadcrumbs and seasoning. Add sufficient beaten egg to bind.

Place the crown roast in a roasting tin greased with lard or dripping and spoon the stuffing into the hollow. (If there is too much stuffing, form the excess into balls and place around the meat.) Weigh the roast. Wrap foil around the tips of the bones to prevent them burning. Roast in a preheated moderate oven (180°C/350°F, Gas Mark 4), allowing 30 minutes per 450 g (1 lb) plus 30 minutes over.

Remove the foil for serving and replace with small cutlet frills. Garnish with parsley. Serve with gravy made from the pan drippings and redcurrant jelly.

CHÂTEAU POTATOES

Metric	Imperial
75 g butter	3 oz butter
1 kg new potatoes, scraped	2 lb new potatoes, scraped
Salt	Salt
Freshly ground black pepper	Freshly ground black pepper
Fresh parsley sprigs to garnish	Fresh parsley sprigs to garnish

Melt the butter in a frying pan and add the potatoes. Cover and cook over a gentle heat, shaking the pan occasionally, for 15 to 20 minutes, until golden brown.

If the potatoes are fairly large, pour the butter and potatoes into an ovenproof dish, cover and cook in the oven with the crown roast (in a preheated moderate oven 180°C/350°F, Gas Mark 4) for 20 to 25 minutes, until cooked. Season well and serve garnished with parsley.

Below: Stuffed crown roast of lamb; Château potatoes; Carrots in orange butter.

CARROTS IN ORANGE BUTTER

Metric	Imperial
1 kg new carrots, scrubbed or scraped	2 lb new carrots, scrubbed or scraped
Salt	Salt
50 g butter	2 oz butter
4 x 15 ml spoons brown sugar	4 tablespoons brown sugar
Grated rind and juice of 2 oranges	Grated rind and juice of 2 oranges
Orange slices to garnish	Orange slices to garnish

Cook the carrots in boiling salted water for 10 minutes until just tender but still crisp. Drain well. Return the carrots to the saucepan and stir in the butter, sugar and orange rind and juice. Heat gently to dissolve the sugar and melt the butter, then bring to the boil and simmer gently for 5 minutes. Turn into a warmed serving dish and garnish with orange slices.

STRAWBERRY AND ORANGE MOUSSE

Metric	Imperial
500 g ripe strawberries, hulled and sliced	1 lb ripe strawberries, hulled and sliced
5 x 15 ml spoons icing sugar	5 tablespoons icing sugar
2 x 15 ml spoons orange-flavoured liqueur	2 tablespoons orange-flavoured liqueur
Finely grated rind of 1 orange	Finely grated rind of 1 orange
1 small can evaporated milk	1 small can evaporated milk
4 x 5 ml spoons powdered gelatine	4 teaspoons powdered gelatine
4 x 15 ml spoons orange juice	4 tablespoons orange juice
120 ml double cream, whipped	4 fl oz double cream, whipped
1 egg white	1 egg white
Red food colouring (optional)	Red food colouring (optional)

Strawberry and orange mousse; Meringue twists.

Put the strawberries into a shallow dish and spoon on the sugar, liqueur and orange rind. Marinate for several hours, covered. Mix with the evaporated milk and rub through a nylon sieve, or use an electric blender, to form a purée.

Sprinkle the gelatine over the orange juice in a small heatproof bowl. When the juice is absorbed, dissolve the gelatine by standing the bowl in a pan of simmering water. Stir into the fruit purée with the cream. Beat the egg white until stiff, then fold into the fruit mixture with food colouring, if used.

Turn into a well-oiled 1 litre (1¾ pint) non-stick brioche tin and refrigerate until set. Turn out when required and decorate with meringue twists. (If using a metal tin, turn out the mousse as soon as it has set in order to prevent metallic tainting.)

MERINGUE TWISTS

Metric	Imperial
1 egg white	1 egg white
50 g caster sugar	2 oz caster sugar

Whisk the egg white until it is fairly stiff and looks like cottonwool. Whisk in half the sugar until the texture is smooth and close and the meringue stands in stiff peaks when the whisk is lifted. Lightly but evenly fold in the remaining sugar.

Pipe the meringue into small figures of eight on non-stick paper and dry in a preheated very cool oven (120°C/250°F, Gas Mark ½) for about 1 hour.

CHILDREN'S PARTIES

Lots of colour, lots of individual, tasty mouthfuls – savoury and sweet – make a children's party fun for the guests and help to guarantee success for the hostess. Young children like easy-to-eat food that looks inviting, such as savoury sandwiches with familiar fillings but cut in fancy shapes, for instance. Slightly older children love bridge rolls topped with savoury spreads. All children enjoy little sausages, crisps and cheesy savouries.

Pipe initials or names, in icing, on little iced cakes or biscuits and use them as place markers. Jellies and ice creams in individual waxed containers are always popular.

For young children, unbreakable or disposable tableware is advisable. You can get delightful coordinated sets of plates, cups, dishes, serviettes and cloths.

Keep the party happily short rather than boringly long; specify exact times of arrival and departure on the invitations.

Decorate the room with balloons to be given to the guests when they go. Have a list of games ready and be sure that everyone gets a prize at the end.

PARTY FOR 8 TO 12 GUESTS, 4 TO 6 YEARS OLD

Chocolate train, Cheese shorties, Sausage kebabs, Crisps, Jammy faces, Traffic lights

BEFOREHAND

Chocolate train
Make the slab cake several days ahead, the Swiss roll two days ahead. Two days ahead cut the cakes as shown in the diagram, and as described in the recipe. The day before, continue construction of the cake and decorate it.

Cheese shorties
These can be made one or two days ahead, stored in an airtight tin and refreshed in the oven when needed.

Sausage kebabs
Roll up the bacon, twist the sausages, and cut up the cheese the day before; keep in polythene bags in the refrigerator. About 1 hour before serving, cook the kebabs and finish making the arrangement.

Jammy faces and Traffic lights
Make the biscuits several days ahead and keep in airtight tins. Put together with jam the day before the party.

Coating the cake sections with glacé icing.

CHOCOLATE TRAIN

Metric	Imperial
For the slab cake:	**For the slab cake:**
275 g butter	10 oz butter
275 g caster sugar	10 oz caster sugar
5 eggs	5 eggs
275 g self-raising flour	10 oz self-raising flour
For the Swiss roll:	**For the Swiss roll:**
3 eggs	3 eggs
100 g caster sugar	4 oz caster sugar
100 g plain flour	4 oz plain flour
1 x 15 ml spoon hot water	1 tablespoon hot water
Caster sugar to dredge	Caster sugar to dredge
Warmed raspberry jam	Warmed raspberry jam
For the glacé icing:	**For the glacé icing:**
175 g plain chocolate or chocolate dots	6 oz plain chocolate or chocolate dots
About 150 ml water	About $\frac{1}{4}$ pint water
15 g butter	$\frac{1}{2}$ oz butter
450 g icing sugar, sifted	1 lb icing sugar, sifted
Vanilla essence	Vanilla essence
For the buttercream:	**For the buttercream:**
100 g butter	4 oz butter
225 g icing sugar, sifted	8 oz icing sugar, sifted
Cottonwool, small candles and 1 box of Smarties to decorate	Cottonwool, small candles and 1 box of Smarties to decorate

Spread the making of the cake over several days.

For the slab cake, grease and line a 30 by 25 cm (12 by 10 inch) baking tin. Cream the butter and sugar together until pale and fluffy. Add the eggs a little at a time, beating well after each addition. Fold in half the sifted flour using a metal spoon, then fold in the rest. Place the mixture in the tin and level it with a knife. Bake in the centre of a preheated moderate oven (180°C/350°F, Gas Mark 4) for 40 to 50 minutes. Cool on a wire rack.

To make the Swiss roll, line a 30 by 23 cm (12 by 9 inch) Swiss roll tin with non-stick paper. Put the eggs and sugar in a large heatproof bowl placed over a pan of hot water and whisk until light and creamy; the mixture should be stiff enough to retain the impression of the whisk for a few seconds. Remove the bowl from the heat and whisk until cool. Sift half the flour over the mixture and fold in very lightly, using a metal spoon. Add the remaining flour in the same way, then lightly stir in the hot water. Pour the mixture into the prepared tin.

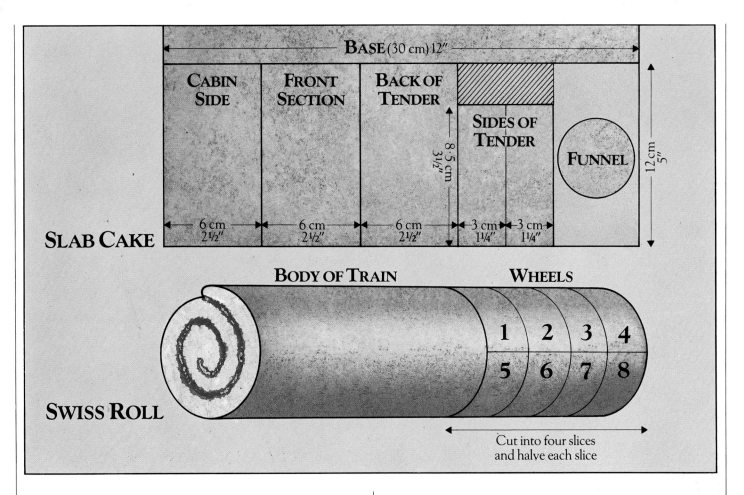

BASE (30 cm) 12"

| CABIN SIDE | FRONT SECTION | BACK OF TENDER | SIDES OF TENDER | FUNNEL |

8·5 cm 3½"

12 cm 5"

6 cm 2½" 6 cm 2½" 6 cm 2½" 3 cm 1¼" 3 cm 1¼"

SLAB CAKE

BODY OF TRAIN **WHEELS**

| 1 | 2 | 3 | 4 |
| 5 | 6 | 7 | 8 |

SWISS ROLL

Cut into four slices
and halve each slice

Tilt the tin backwards and forwards so the mixture spreads over the whole surface. Bake in a preheated hot oven (220°C/425°F, Gas Mark 7) for 7 to 9 minutes or until golden brown and well risen.

Meanwhile, sprinkle a sheet of greaseproof paper liberally with caster sugar. To help make the sponge pliable, place the paper on a teatowel lightly wrung out in hot water.

Turn the cake quickly out onto the paper. Trim off the crusty edges with a sharp knife and spread the surface with warmed jam. Roll up with the aid of the paper. Make the first turn firmly so that the whole cake will roll evenly and have a good shape when finished, but roll more lightly after this turn. Cool on a wire rack.

To make the rich chocolate glacé icing, cut the chocolate into small pieces and put them in a pan with the water. Melt slowly over a gentle heat. Remove from the heat and allow to cool slightly, then beat in the butter. Gradually add the icing sugar, with a little vanilla essence, and beat until the mixture is glossy. If necessary, add more tepid water or more sifted icing sugar to give the correct consistency. If the icing contains many air bubbles after it has been beaten, warm it slightly and stir very gently.

For the buttercream, cream the butter until soft, then gradually beat in the icing sugar.

To assemble the cake, two days ahead, cut the slab cake in half lengthways and cut the pieces from one-half as shown in the diagram. Cut up the Swiss roll as shown. Split the cabin side and the front section to make four pieces. Cut a strip 3.5 cm (1½ inches) deep from either the top or the bottom of the tender sides. From the remaining section cut out a round funnel. Coat all these cut sections, including the other half of the slab cake (the train's base), with the rich chocolate glacé icing and leave to set on a wire rack.

The day before, cover an oblong board or a piece of thick card measuring 36 by 15 cm (14 by 6 inches) with kitchen foil. Place the large base, iced side uppermost, on the board. Spread a little buttercream on the underside of the body of the train and place it on the base. Spread more buttercream over the cabin end of the body and join one of the front sections in an upright position to this. Spread buttercream over the narrow ends and top of the front sections and fix the cabin sides to it, supported on the board. Use the other front sections as a roof.

To make the tender, cover the back section lengthways. Buttercream one long edge and end of each side and place in position on top of the base. Fix the wheels and funnel with buttercream.

Give the funnel a plume of cottonwool steam. Pipe with buttercream. Fill the tender with Smarties and insert the candles at the back of the tender.

The finished Chocolate train.

55

CHEESE SHORTIES

Metric	Imperial
175 g plain flour	6 oz plain flour
Salt	Salt
Freshly ground pepper	Freshly ground pepper
175 g Cheddar cheese, grated	6 oz Cheddar cheese, grated
175 g butter	6 oz butter
2 x 15 ml spoons top of the milk	2 tablespoons top of the milk

Sift the flour and a little salt and pepper into a mixing bowl. Stir in the cheese, then work in the butter and milk by kneading and squeezing the butter and flour with the fingers. When the mixture has formed a smooth dough, roll out to 6 mm (¼ inch) thick on a lightly floured surface. Stamp out shapes with fancy cutters and place on a lightly greased baking sheet. Bake in a preheated moderately hot oven (190°C/375°F, Gas Mark 5) for about 15 minutes, until golden. Cool and serve piled on a plate.

SAUSAGE KEBABS

Metric	Imperial
500 g pork chipolatas	1 lb pork chipolatas
500 g streaky bacon rashers, rinds removed	1 lb streaky bacon rashers, rinds removed
500 g Cheddar cheese, cubed	1 lb Cheddar cheese, cubed

Twist each sausage in half and cut into two small sausages. Place these in a baking tin and cook in a preheated moderately hot oven (200°C/400°F, Gas Mark 6) for about 30 minutes.

Meanwhile, stretch the rashers on a flat surface with the back of a knife. Cut each in half crossways and form into rolls. Place in a tin and cook in the oven with the sausages until beginning to colour.

Spear the cheese cubes on cocktail sticks. Spear the sausages and bacon rolls on sticks. Stick all the cheese cubes, sausages and bacon rolls into a cabbage, large apples or a long French loaf. The sausages and bacon are best eaten just warm. Surround the cabbage, apples or loaf with potato crisps.

SHREWSBURY BISCUITS

Metric	Imperial
125 g butter or margarine	4 oz butter or margarine
150 g caster sugar	5 oz caster sugar
1 egg yolk	1 egg yolk
225 g plain flour	8 oz plain flour
Grated rind of 1 lemon	Grated rind of 1 lemon

Cream the fat and sugar together until pale and fluffy. Add the egg yolk and beat well. Stir in the sifted flour and lemon rind and mix to a fairly firm dough. Knead lightly and roll out to about 6 mm (¼ inch) thick on a lightly floured surface. Cut into rounds with a 6 cm (2½ inch) fluted cutter and put on greased baking sheets. Bake in a preheated moderate oven (180°C/350°F, Gas Mark 4) for about 15 minutes, until firm and a very light brown colour.
Makes 20 to 24

Jammy faces
Roll out the Shrewsbury biscuit mixture and cut it into 6 cm (2½ inch) rounds with a plain or fluted cutter. From half the biscuits remove two holes with a small round cutter, to represent eyes, and make a slit to represent a mouth. Bake. When the biscuits are cool, spread the plain rounds with jam and cover with the 'faces.'
Makes 10 to 12

Traffic lights
Roll out the Shrewsbury biscuit mixture and cut it into fingers. Using a small round cutter, cut out three holes, one above the other, from half the fingers. Bake. When the biscuits are cool, place a little raspberry, apricot and greengage jam on each of the plain biscuits and cover with the others, dredged with icing sugar. (Apricot jam, tinted with a little green food colouring, can be used instead of greengage jam.) Makes 12

Below: Traffic lights; Jammy faces; Cheese shorties; Sausage kebabs.

Clock birthday cake, Chicken puffs, Egg boats, Pinwheel sandwiches, Lollipop biscuits, Banana and honey ice cream

BEFOREHAND

Clock birthday cake
Can be made and iced two or three days ahead.
Chicken puffs
Prepare and cook the day before the party. Just before tea, reheat them in a preheated moderate oven (180°C/350°F, Gas Mark 4) for about 15 minutes.
Egg boats
Hard-boil the eggs.
Pinwheel sandwiches
Make these on the morning of the party and refrigerate, wrapped in polythene or foil. Cut across in slices just before serving.
Lollipop biscuits
Bake these several days ahead. Complete, with icing, the day before the party.
Banana and honey ice cream
Make several days ahead. Keep in the freezer compartment of the refrigerator, but remove it 1 hour before serving and allow it to 'come to' in the refrigerator.

CLOCK BIRTHDAY CAKE

Metric	Imperial
225 g margarine	8 oz margarine
225 g caster sugar	8 oz caster sugar
4 eggs, beaten	4 eggs, beaten
225 g self-raising flour	8 oz self-raising flour
For the buttercream:	**For the buttercream:**
50 g butter or margarine	2 oz butter or margarine
75 g icing sugar	3 oz icing sugar
25 g cocoa powder	1 oz cocoa powder
Little milk	Little milk
For the glacé icing and decoration:	**For the glacé icing and decoration:**
250 g icing sugar	9 oz icing sugar
2 x 5 ml spoons cocoa powder	2 teaspoons cocoa powder
100 g almond paste (bought or see page 77)	4 oz almond paste (bought or see page 77)
Edible flower decorations	Edible flower decorations
Candles	Candles

Grease and bottom line two 20.5 to 23 cm (8 to 9 inch) sandwich tins. Cream the margarine and sugar together until fluffy. Beat in the eggs a little at a time, then sift in the flour. Fold in lightly and divide the mixture between the tins. Smooth the tops and bake in a preheated moderate oven (180°C/350°F, Gas Mark 4) for 25 to 30 minutes. Cool, then split each cake into two layers.

To make the buttercream, cream together the butter or margarine and sifted icing sugar until soft. Gradually beat in the cocoa, adding a little milk if necessary. Use the buttercream to sandwich the cake layers together. Place the cake on a 25 to 28 cm (10 to 11 inch) cake board.

Add enough warm water to the icing sugar to make a smooth glacé icing. Use to coat the cake. Allow to set.

Knead the cocoa powder into the almond paste to make chocolate coloured paste. Cut or shape two-thirds of it into rabbits and place round the side of the cake, securing with a little icing. Between them place the edible flowers. Roll out the remaining paste and cut out the numerals for the clock face. Place around the top of the cake. From the trimmings, cut out clock hands and place them to show the child's age, adding the correct number of candles opposite the age.

As an alternative use chocolate rabbits round the edge and pipe chocolate icing numbers and hands on the cake.

Below: Clock birthday cake.

CHICKEN PUFFS

Metric	Imperial
50 g butter or margarine	2 oz butter or margarine
100 g onion, peeled and finely chopped	4 oz onion, peeled and finely chopped
50 g plain flour	2 oz plain flour
300 ml milk	½ pint milk
450 g cooked chicken meat, cut into 1 cm pieces	1 lb cooked chicken meat, cut into ½ inch pieces
Lemon juice	Lemon juice
Salt	Salt
Freshly ground black pepper	Freshly ground black pepper
1 x 368 g packet frozen puff pastry, thawed	1 x 13 oz packet frozen puff pastry, thawed
Beaten egg to glaze	Beaten egg to glaze

Melt the butter or margarine in a saucepan. Add the onion and fry until soft but not coloured. Stir in the flour and cook for 2 minutes. Off the heat add the milk, stirring. Bring to the boil, stirring, then reduce the heat and cook for 3 minutes. Add the chicken, lemon juice and seasoning. Turn into a bowl, cover closely with damp greaseproof paper and leave to cool.

Roll out the dough very thinly, then cut out twenty-four 10 cm (4 inch) rounds. Brush the edge of each with egg. Put a small spoonful of the chicken mixture in the centre of each, fold over the dough, seal and glaze with egg. Bake on a baking sheet in a preheated moderately hot oven (200°C/400°F, Gas Mark 6) for about 20 minutes until puffed and golden. Serve warm, not hot. Makes 24

EGG BOATS

Metric	Imperial
12 small bread rolls	12 small bread rolls
3 eggs, hard-boiled and chopped	3 eggs, hard-boiled and chopped
1.5 x 15 ml spoons mayonnaise	1½ tablespoons mayonnaise
Butter	Butter
3 medium tomatoes, quartered and seeded	3 medium tomatoes, quartered and seeded

Left: Pinwheel sandwiches; Chicken puffs; Egg boats; Lollipop biscuits. Above: Banana and honey ice cream.

Cut the tops off the bread rolls and scoop out some of the crumb. Mix with the chopped hard-boiled eggs and mayonnaise. Butter the rolls and fill with the egg mixture. Push a cocktail stick through each tomato quarter and use to represent a sail. Makes 12

PINWHEEL SANDWICHES

Metric	Imperial
1 large uncut sandwich loaf	1 large uncut sandwich loaf
175-225 g butter, softened	6-8 oz butter, softened
Marmite	Marmite
Cream cheese and chopped tomatoes	Cream cheese and chopped tomatoes

Cut the loaf into slices lengthways and trim off the crusts. Butter right to the edges. Spread one slice with Marmite. Roll up like a Swiss roll. Spread another slice with cream cheese and chopped tomatoes and roll up. Cover the remaining slices in this way. Wrap the rolls in cling film or aluminium foil and put in a cool place or refrigerator for several hours. Just before serving, cut across in slices.

LOLLIPOP BISCUITS

Metric	Imperial
175 g block margarine	6 oz block margarine
Grated rind of 1 lemon	Grated rind of 1 lemon
175 g caster sugar	6 oz caster sugar
1 egg, beaten	1 egg, beaten
175 g plain flour	6 oz plain flour
50 g rice flour	2 oz rice flour
Smarties and iced lolly sticks to decorate	Smarties and iced lolly sticks to decorate
Lemon glacé icing:	**Lemon glacé icing:**
225 g icing sugar, sifted	8 oz icing sugar, sifted
2 x 15 ml spoons lemon juice	2 tablespoons lemon juice

Cream together the margarine, lemon rind and sugar, then beat in the egg gradually. Sift in the flours and mix evenly. Knead lightly to a smooth mixture. Roll out to about 3 mm (⅛ inch) thick on a well-floured surface. Stamp out into rounds, using a 5 cm (2 inch) plain cutter. Re-roll the trimmings as necessary. Bake in rotation on greased baking sheets in a preheated moderate oven (180°C/350°F, Gas Mark 4) for 10 to 15 minutes. Cool for a few minutes on the sheets, then transfer to wire racks.

Mix together the icing sugar and lemon juice for the icing and use to sandwich together pairs of biscuits. Decorate with coloured Smarties held in place with a little icing, or thicken the icing, using more icing sugar, and pipe a child's name on each lollipop. Insert an iced lolly stick between the two biscuits. Makes about 35

BANANA AND HONEY ICE CREAM

Metric	Imperial
500 g bananas	1 lb bananas
150 ml double cream	¼ pint double cream
150 ml unsweetened natural yogurt	¼ pint unsweetened natural yogurt
Juice of 1 large lemon	Juice of 1 large lemon
5 x 15 ml spoons thick honey	5 tablespoons thick honey
2 egg whites	2 egg whites

Mash the bananas in a large bowl using a fork. Add the unwhipped cream, yogurt, lemon juice and honey. Beat well to combine. Turn into a rigid plastic container – not too deep. Cover and half-freeze, to the mushy stage.

Whisk the egg whites until stiff. Fold them into the banana mixture and finish freezing. Allow to 'come to' in the refrigerator for 1 hour before serving with fan wafers.

PARTY FOR 8 TO 12 GUESTS, 6 TO 8 YEARS OLD

Birthday house, Cheese scones with butter, Windmill thins with butter and Marmite, Cheese and sausage toasts, Twiglets, salted nuts, various crisps, Fairy fingers, Orange fizz

BEFOREHAND

Birthday house
Make the cakes several days ahead; store in airtight containers. Make up the house and decorate it the day before the party.

Cheese scones
Make on the morning of the party.

Windmill thins
Make a day or two before; keep in an airtight container.

Cheese and sausage toasts
Can be made up the day before and browned when needed.

Fairy fingers
Make several days ahead and store in an airtight tin.

Orange fizz
Make this on the morning of the party, without the addition of the lemonade, cucumber and orange slices; add these just before serving.

BIRTHDAY HOUSE

Metric	Imperial
550 g butter or margarine	1¼ lb butter or margarine
550 g caster sugar	1¼ lb caster sugar
10 eggs, beaten	10 eggs, beaten
550 g self-raising flour	1¼ lb self-raising flour
2 x 15 ml spoons cocoa powder	2 tablespoons cocoa powder
5 x 15 ml spoons water	5 tablespoons water
Cochineal	Cochineal
For the buttercream:	**For the buttercream:**
175 g butter	6 oz butter
350 g icing sugar, sifted	12 oz icing sugar, sifted
For the decoration:	**For the decoration:**
1 x 30.5 cm square cake board	1 x 12 inch square cake board
700 g royal icing, made with 700 g icing sugar (see page 77)	1½ lb royal icing, made with 1½ lb icing sugar (see page 77)
Green food colouring	Green food colouring
Coffee essence	Coffee essence
225 g milk chocolate finger biscuits	8 oz milk chocolate finger biscuits
17 chocolate sticks	17 chocolate sticks
Ice cream wafers	Ice cream wafers
1 packet jelly sweets	1 packet jelly sweets
1 piece of nougat	1 piece of nougat
Polka dots	Polka dots
2 round ice cream cones	2 round ice cream cones

Grease and line two 20.5 x 15 cm (8 x 6 inch) cake tins that are 10 cm (4 inches) deep. Cream the butter or margarine and sugar together, then beat in the eggs one at a time. Fold in the flour. Halve the mixture. Dissolve the cocoa in the water and beat it into one half of the cake mixture. Turn it into one of the tins. Colour the other half of the mixture pink with cochineal and turn it into the second tin. Bake in the centre of a preheated moderate oven (180°C/350°F, Gas Mark 4) for about 70 minutes. Turn out and cool on a wire rack.

When cold, level off the cakes and split each into two layers.

To make the buttercream, cream the butter and icing sugar together. Using one pink cake layer as a base, sandwich alternate coloured layers with the buttercream.

Make up the royal icing to the "peak" stage. Colour about 1 x 15 ml spoon (1 tablespoon) icing green and put it in a paper icing bag without a nozzle. Keep 4 x 15 ml spoons (4 tablespoons) of the remaining icing white and colour the rest to resemble stone with coffee essence.

Cut away two wedges from the top quarter of the cake and use these to make the point of the roof. Cover the whole house with the stone-coloured icing. Tile the roof with finger biscuits. Spread 2 x 15 ml spoons (2 tablespoons) of the white icing over the board and rough up with a palette knife. Place the cake on the board.

From the cake trimmings cut out a door, doorstep and lintel. Place on the long side of cake. Using whole and halved chocolate sticks, make one large window on the same side as the door, two windows, one above the other, on each of the two ends and one window on the back wall. Keep 2 chocolate sticks for the chimney. Cut the wafers to fit the windows for shutters and place round the roof. Fix jelly sweets on the door with a little icing, and use the rest to decorate the front and back of the cake.

Attach the piece of nougat to the side of the roof with a little white icing. Cut each remaining chocolate stick in half. Stick two halves together with a little icing and place on the nougat, as chimneys, with a little icing. Use white icing on the roof to resemble snow.

Make a pathway with polka dots. Cover the two ice cream cones with the green icing and rough up to resemble trees. Place on the board to each side of the path. Attach to the board with a little icing.

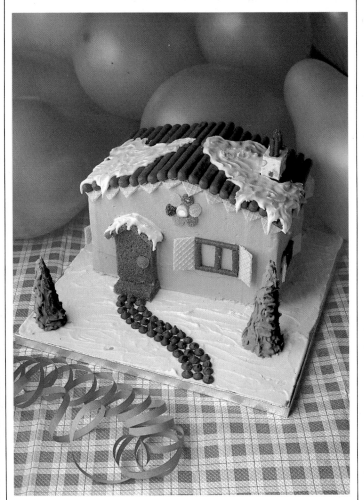

Birthday house.

60

CHEESE SCONES

Metric	Imperial
450 g self-raising flour	1 lb self-raising flour
Pinch of salt	Pinch of salt
2 x 5 ml spoons dry mustard	2 teaspoons dry mustard
150-200 g Cheddar cheese, grated	6-8 oz Cheddar cheese, grated
6 x 15 ml spoons corn oil	6 tablespoons corn oil
About 200 ml cold milk	About 8 fl oz cold milk

Sift together the flour, salt and mustard. Stir in the remaining ingredients and knead lightly to a manageable dough. On a lightly floured board, roll out the dough to 2 cm (¾ inch) thick and stamp out 5 cm (2 inch) diameter rounds. Place on a lightly greased baking sheet. Bake in a preheated hot oven (220°C/425°F, Gas Mark 7) for about 10 minutes. Cool on a wire rack. Makes 16

WINDMILL THINS

Metric	Imperial
225 g plain flour	8 oz plain flour
1 x 2.5 ml spoon salt	½ teaspoon salt
1 x 5 ml spoon baking powder	1 teaspoon baking powder
50 g butter or block margarine	2 oz butter or block margarine
5-6 x 15 ml spoons water	5-6 tablespoons water
Beaten egg to glaze	Beaten egg to glaze
Rock salt	Rock salt

Sift the flour, salt and baking powder into a bowl. Rub in the fat until the mixture resembles fine crumbs. Bind to a soft but manageable dough with cold water. Roll out *very* thinly and stamp out 7.5 cm (3 inch) plain rounds. Prick well with a fork. Place on a greased baking sheet. Brush with beaten egg and sprinkle with salt. Bake in a preheated moderate oven (180°C/350°F, Gas Mark 4) for 15 to 20 minutes until golden. Cool on a wire rack. Spread these crisp salted savoury crackers with butter and Marmite to serve. Makes about 20

CHEESE AND SAUSAGE TOASTS

Metric	Imperial
24 small squares of toast	24 small squares of toast
Butter	Butter
French mustard	French mustard
6 cooked sausages, thinly sliced	6 cooked sausages, thinly sliced
100 g cheese, finely grated	4 oz cheese, finely grated

Spread the toast squares with butter and a thin layer of mustard. Top each with a few slices of sausage, then sprinkle with grated cheese. Either brown in a preheated moderate oven (180°C/350°F, Gas Mark 4) or under the grill. (The toasts can be made in advance and browned when needed.) Makes 24

Cheese scones; Windmill thins; Cheese and sausage toasts.

Fairy fingers; Orange fizz.

FAIRY FINGERS

Metric	Imperial
50 g butter	2 oz butter
40 g caster sugar	1½ oz caster sugar
2 x 15 ml spoons single cream	2 tablespoons single cream
50 g plain flour	2 oz plain flour
2 x 15 ml spoons cornflour	2 tablespoons cornflour
1 x 2.5 ml spoon baking powder	½ teaspoon baking powder

These are bite-size, crisp and not too sweet. Cream the butter and sugar together until soft. Beat in the cream. Sift the flour, cornflour and baking powder over the creamed ingredients and mix well together. Place the mixture in a piping bag fitted with a 1 cm (½ inch) plain nozzle. Pipe into 5 cm (2 inch) fingers on non-stick paper-lined baking sheets, leaving room for the biscuits to spread. Bake in a preheated moderate oven (190°C/375°F, Gas Mark 5) for about 12 minutes, or until firm to the touch and golden brown around the edges. Cool on a wire rack and store in an airtight tin. Serve dredged with icing sugar, if you like. Makes about 20

ORANGE FIZZ

Metric	Imperial
2 x 190 ml cans frozen orange juice, thawed	2 x 6½ fl oz cans frozen orange juice, thawed
150 ml blackcurrant syrup	¼ pint blackcurrant syrup
2 x 700 ml bottles fizzy lemonade	2 x 25 fl oz bottles fizzy lemonade
Cucumber slices	Cucumber slices
Orange slices	Orange slices

Make up the concentrated orange juice to 1.2 litres (2 pints) with water and add the blackcurrant syrup. Just before serving, stir in the lemonade and cucumber and orange slices. Serve in glasses, with straws. Makes about 2 litres (3½ pints)

THE YOUNG SET

Lots of food, plenty of soft drinks and enough room to enjoy both the food and the music – those are necessary ingredients for a successful teenage party. Here are lots of ideas which are calculated to make it go with a swing. The youngsters may not feel up to coping with *all* the preparations, but they can help to prepare some of the dishes. If you have an attic or spare room which can house the party, the young people will enjoy decorating it for the occasion. If there aren't enough chairs, provide cushions and nobody will mind as long as there's enough food to eat. For safety's sake, ban candles but see the lights are dim by using low wattage bulbs.

The menus include a panic-free party for ten, French farmhouse style, with everything prepared the day before. Provide sturdy rustic pottery and bright cloths and table napkins. Choose warmer fare for colder days like the hot punch and pancakes party, served in the kitchen on a 'come-and-get-it-while-it's-hot' basis.

PÂTÉ AND POT LUCK FOR TEN

Sardine and anchovy pâté, Toast/Beef and bean pot, Tomato and cucumber salad/Iced lemon pie

BEFOREHAND

Sardine and anchovy pâté
Make two or three days ahead and refrigerate. (Or make the day before and keep in a cool place.) Make the toast for the pâté just before serving.

Beef and bean pot
Cook the day before; cool quickly and refrigerate.

Tomato and cucumber salad
Put dressing ingredients in a lidded container – avoid a metal lid. Put the salad together 1 hour before serving.

Iced lemon pie
The day before, make as far as the lemon filling stage and freeze. On the day, add the ice cream topping and return to the freezer compartment for about 1 hour. (Or freeze the finished pie, uncovered, in the freezer and take out a short time before serving. If to be left for more than a day in the freezer, keep in a freezer bag.)

SARDINE AND ANCHOVY PÂTÉ

Metric	Imperial
3 x 140 g cans sardines in tomato sauce	3 x 4⅜ oz cans sardines in tomato sauce
225 g curd or cream cheese	8 oz curd or cream cheese
50 g butter, melted	2 oz butter, melted
1 x 15 ml spoon lemon juice	1 tablespoon lemon juice
2 x 15 ml spoons anchovy essence	2 tablespoons anchovy essence
Freshly ground black pepper	Freshly ground black pepper
10 lemon slices	10 lemon slices

Put the sardines, cheese, butter, lemon juice and anchovy essence in a bowl and beat with an electric mixer until smooth and creamy. Season to taste with pepper. Divide between ten individual ramekin dishes and fork up the tops. Place a lemon slice on top of each. Cover and chill for at least 30 minutes before serving with toast.

BEEF AND BEAN POT

Metric	Imperial
1.5 kg lean minced beef	3 lb lean minced beef
2 eggs	2 eggs
50 g fresh white breadcrumbs	2 oz fresh white breadcrumbs
50 g onion, peeled and finely chopped	2 oz onion, peeled and finely chopped
Salt	Salt
Freshly ground black pepper	Freshly ground black pepper
2 x 15 ml spoons oil	2 tablespoons oil
3 x 432 g cans red kidney beans	3 x 15¼ oz cans red kidney beans
2 x 400 g cans tomatoes	2 x 14 oz cans tomatoes
300 ml beef stock	½ pint beef stock
1 x 141 g can tomato paste	1 x 5 oz can tomato paste
2 garlic cloves, crushed	2 garlic cloves, crushed
3 x 15 ml spoons chilli seasoning	3 tablespoons chilli seasoning

In a bowl, combine the minced beef, eggs, breadcrumbs, onion, 1 x 5 ml spoon (1 teaspoon) salt and pepper to taste. Shape into about 100 small balls the size of a walnut, with floured hands.

Heat the oil in a frying pan. Add a single layer of beef balls and cook over medium heat for 5 minutes until browned on all sides to seal the surface. Repeat until all the meatballs are browned. Drain well on absorbent kitchen paper.

In a large saucepan or flameproof casserole, combine the rest of the ingredients, including the bean can juices. Season with salt and pepper. Add the meat balls. Cover and cook over medium heat for 30 minutes. Uncover and continue to cook for a further 30 minutes, until the juices have thickened. Stir occasionally to prevent burning on the bottom.

Left: Sardine and anchovy pâté.

Beef and bean pot; Iced lemon pie; Tomato and cucumber salad.

TOMATO AND CUCUMBER SALAD

Metric
8 large tomatoes, sliced
2 cucumbers, sliced
225 g onions, peeled and cut into rings
For the dressing:
150 ml salad oil
4 x 15 ml spoons garlic vinegar
1 x 2.5 ml spoon salt
1 x 2.5 ml spoon sugar
1 x 2.5 ml spoon dry mustard
Freshly ground black pepper

Imperial
8 large tomatoes, sliced
2 cucumbers, sliced
8 oz onions, peeled and cut into rings
For the dressing:
¼ pint salad oil
4 tablespoons garlic vinegar
½ teaspoon salt
½ teaspoon sugar
½ teaspoon dry mustard
Freshly ground black pepper

Arrange alternate layers of tomato slices, cucumber slices and onion rings on a serving plate.

Shake the dressing ingredients together with pepper to taste in a screwtop jar. Pour evenly over the salad. Leave to marinate for at least 2 hours to infuse the flavours.

ICED LEMON PIE

Metric
100 g butter
225 g digestive biscuits, crushed
25 g demerara sugar
3 eggs, separated
200 ml condensed milk
Grated rind of 2 lemons
9 x 15 ml spoons lemon juice
4 x 15 ml spoons caster sugar
2.3 litres vanilla ice cream
Lemon slices to garnish

Imperial
4 oz butter
8 oz digestive biscuits, crushed
1 oz demerara sugar
3 eggs, separated
⅓ pint condensed milk
Grated rind of 2 lemons
9 tablespoons lemon juice
4 tablespoons caster sugar
½ gallon vanilla ice cream
Lemon slices to garnish

Melt the butter in a saucepan and add the biscuits and demerara sugar. Mix well. Divide the crumb mixture between two 20 cm (8 inch) pie plates, reserving about 3 x 15 ml spoons (3 tablespoons) crumbs. Press the crumbs onto the bottoms and sides of the pans.

Beat the egg yolks until thick and creamy. Stir in the condensed milk, lemon rind and juice and continue stirring until thick. Whisk the egg whites until stiff, then whisk in the sugar until the mixture stands in peaks. Fold into the lemon mixture and divide between the crumb cases. Freeze until firm.

Scoop out small balls of ice cream and arrange on top of the pies. Decorate with the reserved crumb mixture. Freeze for about 1 hour. Allow a short while to 'come to' before serving. Garnish with halved lemon slices. Makes 2 pies, each to serve 5 to 6

HOT PUNCH AND PANCAKES FOR EIGHT TO TEN

Non-alcoholic punch (see pages 180-1), Salted twisters and Cheese crescents/Curried beef pancakes, Gouda cheese and prawn pancakes/Hazelnut meringues, Chocolate fudge sauce

BEFOREHAND

Salted twisters and Cheese crescents
Bake the day before and when cold store in an airtight tin. Refresh in the oven when needed for about 10 minutes, along with the reheated pancakes.

Pancakes
Make the day before and layer up in packs of 10 with greaseproof paper between each. Foil-wrap and refrigerate. Make the fillings; store in covered containers in the refrigerator. Fill the pancakes early on the day of the party, ready for reheating.

Hazelnut meringues with Chocolate fudge sauce
Make the meringues several days ahead and keep in airtight containers. Make the sauce the day before the party.

SALTED TWISTERS AND CHEESE CRESCENTS

Metric	Imperial
1 x 368 g packet frozen puff pastry, thawed	1 x 13 oz packet frozen puff pastry, thawed
Beaten egg	Beaten egg
Coarse sea salt	Coarse sea salt
25 g cheese, finely grated	1 oz cheese, finely grated
Poppy seeds	Poppy seeds

Divide the pastry dough in half. For the twisters, roll out one portion to a rectangle about 38 by 12.5 cm (15 by 5 inches). Cut into 1 cm (½ inch) strips along the length, and cut each strip into two, widthways. To shape, wrap the end of a dough strip round the loop end of a plain round skewer, but do not take in the loop itself. Press the dough to secure, then continue to spiral the strip around the skewer, leaving a space between each turn. Place join side down on a

baking sheet. Twist each strip of dough in the same way. Brush with beaten egg and sprinkle lightly with salt. Bake in a preheated moderately hot oven (200°C/400°F, Gas Mark 6) for 10 to 15 minutes. Remove from the skewers while warm.

For the crescents, roll out the rest of the dough to an oblong 40 by 20 cm (16 by 8 inches). Cut into eight equal sized squares. Cut each square in half diagonally to make 16 triangles. Brush with beaten egg. Scatter with cheese. Roll up from the long edges and shape into crescents. Brush again with egg and sprinkle with poppy seeds. Bake as for the twisters. Serve warm. Makes 20 twisters and 16 crescents

CURRIED BEEF PANCAKES

Metric	Imperial
For the pancakes:	**For the pancakes:**
175 g plain flour	6 oz plain flour
Pinch of salt	Pinch of salt
2 eggs	2 eggs
450 ml milk	¾ pint milk
Oil for frying	Oil for frying
For the filling:	**For the filling:**
100 g butter	4 oz butter
350 g onions, peeled and chopped	12 oz onions, peeled and chopped
225 g cooking apples, peeled, cored and chopped	8 oz cooking apples, peeled, cored and chopped
1 x 15 ml spoon mild curry powder	1 tablespoon mild curry powder
75 g plain flour	3 oz plain flour
1 x 350 g can corned beef, chopped	1 x 12 oz can corned beef, chopped
1 x 198 g can corned beef, chopped	1 x 7 oz can corned beef, chopped
300 ml beef stock	½ pint beef stock
2 x 5 ml spoons lemon juice	2 teaspoons lemon juice
Salt	Salt
Freshly ground black pepper	Freshly ground black pepper
Flaked almonds and strips of canned pimiento to garnish	Flaked almonds and strips of canned pimiento to garnish

Sift the flour and salt into a bowl. Make a well in the centre and add the eggs and half the milk. Mix well until smooth, then beat in the remaining milk. Pour this batter into a jug. Heat a little oil in an 18 cm (7 inch) diameter frying pan. Pour in a little batter, just enough to cover the bottom of the pan. Fry until the underside of the pancake is golden brown, then, with the help of a palette knife, turn it and brown the other side. Turn out onto kitchen paper. Make 15 pancakes stacking them with greaseproof paper between them.

For the filling, melt 75 g (3 oz) of the butter in a large saucepan and fry the onions and apples until golden. Stir in the curry powder and flour and cook for 2 minutes. Add the corned beef and stock and bring to the boil, stirring. Reduce the heat, cover and simmer for 30 minutes. Season with lemon juice, salt and pepper.

Divide the filling between the pancakes and roll up. Place side by side in an ovenproof dish. Garnish with almonds and pimiento and brush with the remaining butter, melted. Reheat in a preheated moderate oven (160°C/325°F, Gas Mark 3) for 20 minutes. Makes 15
Note: Stuffed pancakes take about 1 hour to reheat from cold.

Left: Salted twisters; Cheese crescents.

Pasta Party for Twelve

Curried chicken lasagne, or Spaghetti with bacon ragu, Tossed green salad, Blue cheese dressing, Country herb soda bread/Fruit and hazelnut shortcake

BEFOREHAND

Curried chicken lasagne
Prepare completely the day before, but do not bake; keep refrigerated, lightly covered. Reheat in a preheated moderate oven (180°C/350°F, Gas Mark 4) for 1 to 1½ hours when needed.

Bacon ragu
Prepare and cook the ragu the day before; keep refrigerated, lightly covered. Reheat thoroughly on the top of the stove over a low heat, stirring occasionally to prevent sticking.

Salad and dressing
The day before, choose salad ingredients in season; prepare, put in polythene bags and refrigerate. Crumble enough blue cheese into French dressing for personal taste.

Country herb soda bread
Make completely the day before; when cold, foil-wrap. Refresh next day.

Fruit and hazelnut shortcake
Make the shortcake bases the day before; when cold store in airtight container.

CURRIED CHICKEN LASAGNE

Metric	Imperial
2 x 2 kg oven-ready chickens, skinned	2 x 4½ lb oven-ready chickens, skinned
100 g butter	4 oz butter
4 x 15 ml spoons plain flour	4 tablespoons plain flour
6 x 15 ml spoons hot (Madras) curry powder	6 tablespoons hot (Madras) curry powder
2.4 litres milk	4 pints milk
Salt	Salt
Freshly ground black pepper	Freshly ground black pepper
75 g desiccated coconut	3 oz desiccated coconut
750 g lasagne	1½ lb lasagne
2 x 15 ml spoons fresh breadcrumbs	2 tablespoons fresh breadcrumbs

Remove all the meat from the chicken carcasses with a small sharp knife. Trim off any fat and cut the meat into 1 cm (½ inch) chunks.

Melt the butter in a large heavy-based saucepan. Stir in the flour and curry powder and cook for 2 minutes. Off the heat, gradually stir in the milk and seasoning, then bring to the boil, stirring all the time. Simmer for 5 minutes, then stir in 50 g (2 oz) of the coconut. Spoon some of the sauce over the bottoms of two 2.3 litre (4 pint) shallow ovenproof dishes. Layer the lasagne and the chicken in the oven-proof dishes, spooning a little sauce over each layer. Finish with a layer of lasagne, covered with the remaining sauce. Sprinkle over the remaining coconut and the breadcrumbs. Bake in a preheated moderate oven (180°C/350°F, Gas Mark 4) for 1 to 1¼ hours until the lasagne is tender and the top browned. Serve with chutney, chopped hard-boiled egg and cucumber, etc. Makes 2 batches, each to serve 6
Note: The lasagne sheets are not first cooked in boiling water as they cook very well in the made-up dish with the sauce to moisten them.

SPAGHETTI WITH BACON RAGU

Metric	Imperial
120 ml oil	4 fl oz oil
500 g onions, peeled and sliced	1 lb onions, peeled and sliced
2 garlic cloves, crushed	2 garlic cloves, crushed
1.5 kg lean collar bacon, very finely chopped	3 lb lean collar bacon, very finely chopped
4 x 15 ml spoons plain flour	4 tablespoons plain flour
1 x 142 g can concentrated tomato purée	1 x 5 oz can concentrated tomato purée
1 x 15 ml spoon dried sage	1 tablespoon dried sage
1 kg tomatoes, skinned, seeded and quartered	2 lb tomatoes, skinned, seeded and quartered
120 ml dry white wine	4 fl oz dry white wine
900 ml unseasoned stock	1½ pints unseasoned stock
Freshly ground black pepper	Freshly ground black pepper
750 g spaghetti	1½ lb spaghetti
Salt	Salt
50 g butter, melted	2 oz butter, melted
Grated Parmesan cheese to serve	Grated Parmesan cheese to serve

Heat the oil in a large heavy-based saucepan. Add the onions and fry until golden brown. Add the garlic and cook for a further 1 minute. Stir in the bacon and fry, stirring, for 5 minutes.

Sprinkle over the flour and cook, stirring, for 1 minute. Add the tomato purée, sage and tomatoes and mix well, then stir in the wine and stock. Bring to the boil, stirring. Season well with pepper and simmer, uncovered, for about 1¼ hours or until the mixture is reduced by half and the meat is tender.

Fifteen minutes before the ragu is ready, cook the spaghetti in plenty of boiling salted water until it is just tender. Drain well and return to the saucepan. Add the melted butter and toss until all the spaghetti strands are coated.

Pile the spaghetti in a warmed serving dish and pour over the bacon ragu. Serve sprinkled with grated Parmesan.

Left: Curried chicken lasagne. Right: Country herb soda bread; Spaghetti with bacon ragu.

COUNTRY HERB SODA BREAD

Metric	Imperial
225 g plain flour	8 oz plain flour
225 g plain wholemeal flour	8 oz plain wholemeal flour
1.5 x 5 ml spoons salt	1½ teaspoons salt
1 x 5 ml spoon bicarbonate of soda	1 teaspoon bicarbonate of soda
25 g butter	1 oz butter
225 g onions, peeled and minced	8 oz onions, peeled and minced
100 g celery, trimmed and minced	4 oz celery, trimmed and minced
1 x 2.5 ml spoon dried mixed herbs	½ teaspoon dried mixed herbs
2 x 15 ml spoons chopped parsley	2 tablespoons chopped parsley
175 ml milk	6 fl oz milk
2 x 5 ml spoons lemon juice	2 teaspoons lemon juice
Milk to glaze	Milk to glaze
50 g mature Cheddar cheese, grated	2 oz mature Cheddar cheese, grated

Fruit and hazelnut shortcake.

Place the flours, salt and bicarbonate of soda in a large bowl and mix well together. Rub in the butter. Stir in the onions, celery and herbs. Mix the milk and lemon juice together and stir into the dry ingredients. Knead lightly on a floured surface to a smooth dough. Pat out to a 23 cm (9 inch) round on a floured baking sheet. Brush with milk and sprinkle with the grated cheese. Score the top into 12 portions and bake in a preheated moderately hot oven (200°C/400°F, Gas Mark 6) for about 35 minutes, or until golden brown. Serve warm or cold.

FRUIT AND HAZELNUT SHORTCAKE

Metric	Imperial
225 g shelled hazelnuts	8 oz shelled hazelnuts
300 g butter, softened	10 oz butter, softened
175 g caster sugar	6 oz caster sugar
350 g plain flour	12 oz plain flour
600 ml whipping cream, lightly whipped	1 pint whipping cream, lightly whipped
3 x 412 g cans guavas or passion fruit, drained	3 x 14½ oz cans guavas or passion fruit, drained
Icing sugar	Icing sugar

Roast the hazelnuts in a preheated hot oven (220°C/425°F, Gas Mark 7) until dark, then rub in a cloth to remove the skins. Grind. Cream the butter and sugar together until light and fluffy and work in the sifted flour and ground nuts. Knead lightly to form a dough and leave to rest for 15 minutes.

Divide the dough into six equal pieces. Shape each piece into a 20 cm (8 inch) round in a flan ring on a non-stick paper-lined baking sheet. Press the dough into the shape of the ring, then remove the ring and roll the surface of the round lightly with a rolling pin to smooth it. Bake each round in rotation in a preheated moderate oven (180°C/350°F, Gas Mark 4) for 12 to 15 minutes or until pale golden. Cut two of the rounds into 12 sections each and leave on the sheets to become crisp – about 5 minutes. Transfer to wire racks to cool.

About 2 hours before they are needed, assemble the two cakes, sandwiching two lots of rounds together with half the cream and fruit. Spoon the rest of the cream on the tops and arrange the cut triangles on their edges. Slice the remaining fruit and pile in the centre. Sift icing sugar over the cakes just before serving.
Makes 2 cakes, each to serve 6

SEASONAL CELEBRATIONS

Appropriate decorations can help to create the right atmosphere for a seasonal celebration, but something special in the way of food is needed, too. Christmas and Easter aren't the only occasions for traditional fare; events such as those commemorating Guy Fawkes and Hallowe'en for instance, coming at rather bleak times of the year, provide good excuses for celebrations and special food.

When seasonal celebrations are also family get-togethers, it's important to cater for the very young and very old too, providing them with something familiar and not too elaborate in the way of traditional fare.

Although winter parties call for warming food, cool starters and puddings provide a refreshing balance; it often makes life easier for the hostess if there's only one hot course to dish up and serve. While chilled soup is an ideal starter for a summer party, lashings of hot coffee, in good-sized cups, will be more than welcome as the evening grows cooler.

CHRISTMAS DINNER FOR SIX TO EIGHT

Roast turkey, Chestnut stuffing, Sausagemeat stuffing, Chipolatas, Bacon rolls, Bread sauce, Cranberry sauce, Pickled prunes, Roast potatoes, Brussels sprouts, Parsnips/Brandy butter, Apricot mincemeat flan, Christmas pudding, Light Christmas cake

BEFOREHAND

Weeks ahead
Make the Christmas cake, the pudding and preserves.

Early in December
Decide on the meat and/or poultry you're going to have and order it, if necessary. When ordering a turkey, allow about 350 g (12 oz) oven-ready weight per person; a good, fleshy 4.5 to 5.4 kg (10 to 12 lb) oven-ready bird should give 6 to 8 hot helpings, 8 cold cut helpings and some leftover.

Mid-December
Almond-paste the cake. Royal ice the cake one week before Christmas. Make and refrigerate brandy butter.

December 23
Prepare crumbs for bread sauce. Make dry stuffing mix; store in the refrigerator. Prepare the giblet stock for the gravy: simmer the giblets – gizzard, heart and neck – with 1.2 litres (2 pints) water, seasoning, flavouring vegetables and a few bacon rinds for about 2 hours. Cook the liver separately; mince. Refrigerate.

Christmas Eve
If you're having a bacon joint, soak it and cook it. Prepare the potatoes and leave in cold water. Trim the sprouts, put into polythene bags and store in a cool place. Have the giblet gravy ready, a little thicker than required, so that it will take the de-fatted turkey juices. Make the Apricot mincemeat flan.

Christmas Day
Times based on a 4.5 to 5.4 kg (10 to 12 lb) stuffed turkey in foil, fast roasting method. For other times, see chart.

Three and a half hours before: switch on oven; stuff and truss the bird.

Three hours before: put pudding to steam.

Two and a half hours before: lay the table; put out the cranberry sauce and prepare the wines. Put the bread sauce to infuse.

One and a half hours before: boil potatoes for roasting in salted water for 7 minutes; drain. Heat 2.5 cm (1 inch) dripping in a baking tin; put the potatoes in the hot fat, spoon it over and place it in the oven.

One hour before: grill the chipolatas and bacon rolls, turning them to brown evenly; cover with foil to keep warm. Cook the Brussels sprouts and gravy. Finish the gravy, having poured off into it the juices from the bird. Add the liver.

Just before required, simmer the bread sauce for 5 minutes; remove the onion and add 25 g (1 oz) butter. Drain the sprouts and dish them. Turn out the pudding; leave the upturned basin over it to keep it warm. When the bird is cooked, remove the trussing and dish up on a serving platter.

CHOOSING AND COOKING THE TURKEY

Approx thawing times at room temp 21°C/70°F	Weight	Quick method: 230°C/450°F, Gas Mark 8	Slow method: 160°C/325°F, Gas Mark 3
12 hrs	2.7-3.6 kg (6-8 lb)	2¼-2½ hrs	3-3½ hrs
14 hrs	3.6-4.5 kg (8-10 lb)	2½-2¾ hrs	3½-3¾ hrs
15-17 hrs	4.5-5.4 kg (10-12 lb)	2¾-2 hrs 50 mins	3¾-4 hrs
17 hrs	5.4-6.4 kg (12-14 lb)	2 hrs 50 mins-3 hrs	4-4¼ hrs
17-20 hrs	6.4-7.2 kg (14-16 lb)	3-3¼ hrs	4¼-4½ hrs
24 hrs	7.2-8.1 kg (16-18 lb)	3¼-3½ hrs	4½-4 hrs 50 mins

PICKLED PRUNES

Metric	Imperial
1 kg prunes, soaked overnight and drained	2 lb prunes, soaked overnight and drained
450 g sugar	1 lb sugar
450 ml vinegar	¾ pint vinegar
Thinly pared rind of ¼ lemon	Thinly pared rind of ¼ lemon
2 whole cloves	2 whole cloves
1 x 15 ml spoon whole allspice	1 tablespoon whole allspice
Small piece of root ginger	Small piece of root ginger
Piece of cinnamon stick	Piece of cinnamon stick

These are delicious with roast pork or turkey. Prick the skins of the prunes with a pin. Dissolve the sugar in the vinegar in a saucepan, then add the flavouring ingredients. Add the prunes and boil gently for about 15 minutes.

Pack the prunes into hot jars. Discard the flavourings from the vinegar mixture and boil until syrupy. Pour over the prunes to fill the jars. Seal at once with vinegar-proof preserving skin. If jars with cork stoppers are used, cover the base and sides of the stoppers with cling film.

CHESTNUT STUFFING

Metric	Imperial
50 g bacon, rinds removed, chopped	2 oz bacon, rinds removed, chopped
100 g fresh white breadcrumbs	4 oz fresh white breadcrumbs
1 x 5 ml spoon chopped parsley	1 teaspoon chopped parsley
25 g butter, melted	1 oz butter, melted
Grated rind of 1 lemon	Grated rind of 1 lemon
225 g chestnut purée (see note)	8 oz chestnut purée (see note)
Salt	Salt
Freshly ground black pepper	Freshly ground black pepper
1 egg, beaten	1 egg, beaten

Ingredients for stuffings.

Pickled prunes.

Fry the bacon gently in its own fat for 3 to 5 minutes, until crisp. Drain and add the rest of the ingredients, binding with the beaten egg. Makes enough for a 4.5 kg (10 lb) oven-ready turkey.

Note: Chestnut purée may be made from fresh, canned or dried chestnuts – or use unsweetened canned chestnut purée. If using fresh chestnuts, snip or cut the brown outer skins across the top with a pair of scissors or a sharp knife. Blanch the chestnuts in boiling water for 3 to 5 minutes. Lift them out, a few at a time, and peel off both the brown and inner skins. To cook, simmer them gently in a little chicken stock until tender; they will take 35 to 40 minutes. 450 g (1 lb) fresh chestnuts gives 350 g (12 oz) peeled. When cooked and puréed the yield is about 400 g (14 oz) unsweetened purée.

Whole canned, unsweetened chestnuts may be used as fresh cooked chestnuts and puréed for this stuffing.

Dried chestnuts should be soaked overnight in cold water. Drain and simmer in stock or milk until tender – about 40 minutes. 450 g (1 lb) dried chestnuts gives 900 g (2 lb) whole chestnuts, which may be used as fresh cooked chestnuts.

SAUSAGE MEAT STUFFING

Metric	Imperial
1 large onion, peeled and chopped	1 large onion, peeled and chopped
500 g pork sausage meat	1 lb pork sausage meat
2 x 5 ml spoons chopped parsley	2 teaspoons chopped parsley
1 x 5 ml spoon dried mixed herbs	1 teaspoon dried mixed herbs
25 g fresh white breadcrumbs	1 oz fresh white breadcrumbs
Salt	Salt
Freshly ground black pepper	Freshly ground black pepper

Mix all the ingredients together. Use with chicken or turkey, adapting the quantities as necessary.
Enough for a 4 to 4.5 kg (9 to 10 lb) oven-ready turkey

Bread Sauce

Metric	Imperial
2 cloves	2 cloves
1 medium onion, peeled	1 medium onion, peeled
450 ml milk	$\frac{3}{4}$ pint milk
Salt	Salt
Few peppercorns	Few peppercorns
$\frac{1}{2}$ small bay leaf	$\frac{1}{2}$ small bay leaf
Knob of butter	Knob of butter
75 g fresh white breadcrumbs	3 oz fresh white breadcrumbs

Stick the cloves into the onion and put it in a saucepan with the milk, salt, peppercorns and bay leaf. Bring almost to boiling point, then remove from the heat and leave in a warm place for about 20 minutes to infuse.

Remove the peppercorns and bay leaf. Add the butter and breadcrumbs. Mix well and allow to cook very gently for about 15 minutes. Remove the onion.

If you prefer, remove the onion before adding the breadcrumbs; however, a better flavour is obtained by cooking it with the crumbs, as this allows the taste of the onion to penetrate them.

Makes about 600 ml (1 pint)

Apricot Mincemeat Flan

Metric	Imperial
For the pastry:	**For the pastry:**
175 g plain flour	6 oz plain flour
Pinch of salt	Pinch of salt
2 x 5 ml spoons caster sugar	2 teaspoons caster sugar
100 g butter or block margarine	4 oz butter or block margarine
1 egg yolk	1 egg yolk
1 x 15 ml spoon water	1 tablespoon water
For the filling:	**For the filling:**
50 g dried apricots, soaked overnight, drained and chopped	2 oz dried apricots, soaked overnight, drained and chopped
1 x 410 g jar mincemeat	1 x 14$\frac{1}{2}$ oz jar mincemeat
100 g ground almonds	4 oz ground almonds
75 g caster sugar	3 oz caster sugar
2 egg whites	2 egg whites
Few drops of almond essence	Few drops of almond essence
To decorate:	**To decorate:**
Icing sugar	Icing sugar
Glacé cherries	Glacé cherries
Candied angelica	Candied angelica

Apricot mincemeat flan.

Christmas pudding.

Sift the flour and salt into a bowl. Stir in the sugar, then rub in the fat until the mixture resembles breadcrumbs. Bind to a dough with the egg yolk and water. Roll out and use to line a 23 cm (9 inch) fluted flan tin. Prick and chill for 20 minutes, then bake blind in a preheated moderately hot oven (190°C/375°F, Gas Mark 5) for about 20 minutes. Cool in the tin.

Mix together the apricots and mincemeat and spoon into the flan case. Sift together the ground almonds and caster sugar. Whisk the egg whites until stiff, then fold in the almond mixture with the essence. Using a large star vegetable nozzle, pipe the mixture onto the mincemeat mixture, leaving a star shape uncovered in the centre. Bake in a preheated moderate oven (180°C/350°F, Gas Mark 4) for 30 to 40 minutes. Dust with icing sugar and decorate with glacé cherries and angelica while hot. Serve slightly warm or cold. Serves 6 to 8

Brandy Butter

Metric	Imperial
175 g butter	6 oz butter
175 g caster sugar	6 oz caster sugar
4-6 x 15 ml spoons brandy	4-6 tablespoons brandy

Cream the butter until pale and soft. Beat in the sugar gradually and add the brandy a few drops at a time, taking care not to allow the mixture to curdle. The finished sauce should be pale and frothy. Pile it up in a small dish and leave to harden before serving.

For a less granular texture, use sifted icing sugar, or half icing and half caster sugar. Serves 8

CHRISTMAS PUDDING

Metric	Imperial
450 g fresh white breadcrumbs	1 lb fresh white breadcrumbs
1 x 5 ml spoon ground ginger	1 teaspoon ground ginger
1 x 5 ml spoon mixed spice	1 teaspoon mixed spice
1 x 5 ml spoon salt	1 teaspoon salt
225 g shredded suet	8 oz shredded suet
225 g soft brown sugar	8 oz soft brown sugar
100 g chopped mixed peel	4 oz chopped mixed peel
100 g currants, cleaned	4 oz currants, cleaned
100 g sultanas, cleaned	4 oz sultanas, cleaned
450 g seedless raisins, cleaned	1 lb seedless raisins, cleaned
75 g carrots, peeled and grated	3 oz carrots, peeled and grated
2 eggs, beaten	2 eggs, beaten
5 x 15 ml spoons milk	5 tablespoons milk
2 x 15 ml spoons golden syrup	2 tablespoons golden syrup

This is a light-textured pudding, delicious served with brandy or orange-flavoured chilled whipped cream, brandy butter, rum butter or dairy ice cream.

Grease two 1.2 litre (2 pint) pudding basins. Mix together all the dry ingredients. Mix the eggs, milk and syrup together and stir into the dry ingredients. Let the mixture stand for 1 hour.

Stir again and divide between the basins. Cover with greased greaseproof paper and then kitchen foil and secure with string. Steam for 8 hours, topping up the pan with water as necessary.

Take the puddings from the pan and allow to cool. Remove the covering and replace with fresh greaseproof paper. Store in a cool dry place for at least 1 month. To use, steam for a further 2 to 3 hours.
Makes 2 puddings, each to serve 6 to 8

LIGHT CHRISTMAS CAKE

Metric	Imperial
125 g glacé cherries	4 oz glacé cherries
50 g glacé pineapple, diced	2 oz glacé pineapple, diced
225 g currants, cleaned	8 oz currants, cleaned
225 g sultanas, cleaned	8 oz sultanas, cleaned
125 g chopped mixed peel	4 oz chopped mixed peel
125 g plain flour, sifted	4 oz plain flour, sifted
225 g butter or block margarine	8 oz butter or block margarine
Finely grated rind of 1 lemon	Finely grated rind of 1 lemon
Finely grated rind of 1 orange	Finely grated rind of 1 orange
225 g light soft brown sugar	8 oz light soft brown sugar
50 g ground almonds	2 oz ground almonds
4 eggs, beaten	4 eggs, beaten
100 g self-raising flour, sifted	4 oz self-raising flour, sifted
2 x 15 ml spoons lemon juice	2 tablespoons lemon juice
3 x 15 ml spoons brandy	3 tablespoons brandy

Wash the cherries if syrupy and dry them well, then quarter. Mix all the fruit well together with 3 x 15 ml spoons (3 tablespoons) of the plain flour. Cream the fat with the lemon and orange rinds, then add the sugar and continue to cream until light and fluffy. Stir in the almonds. Beat in the eggs little by little and lastly fold in the remaining plain flour, the self-raising flour, fruit, strained lemon juice and brandy. Turn into a greased and lined 20 cm (8 inch) round cake tin.

Bake in a preheated moderate oven (160°C/325°F, Gas Mark 3) for 2½ to 3 hours, covering with double greaseproof paper after 2 hours if necessary. Cool in the tin.

You will need 550 g (1¼ lb) Almond paste and 750 g (1½ lb) Royal icing to finish the cake. Makes a 20 cm (8 inch) cake

Light Christmas cake.

ALMOND PASTE

Metric	Imperial
225 g icing sugar	8 oz icing sugar
225 g caster sugar	8 oz caster sugar
450 g ground almonds	1 lb ground almonds
1 x 5 ml spoon vanilla essence	1 teaspoon vanilla essence
2 standard eggs, lightly beaten	2 standard eggs, lightly beaten
Lemon juice	Lemon juice

Sift the icing sugar into a bowl and mix with the caster sugar and almonds. Add the essence, with sufficient egg and lemon juice to mix to a stiff dough. Form into a ball and knead lightly.

Any almond paste left over after covering the cake can be used for stuffing dates and making other marzipan sweets. Makes 900 g (2 lb)

ROYAL ICING

Metric	Imperial
900 g icing sugar	2 lb icing sugar
4 egg whites	4 egg whites
1 x 15 ml spoon glycerine (optional)	1 tablespoon glycerine (optional)

Sift the sugar twice. Put the egg whites in a bowl and stir slightly – just sufficiently to break up the albumen, but without causing too many air bubbles. Add half the icing sugar and stir until well mixed, using a wooden spoon. Beat for about 5 to 10 minutes, or until the icing is smooth, glossy and white. Cover the bowl with a damp cloth or dampened greaseproof paper and leave for at least 30 minutes to allow any air bubbles to rise to the surface.

Gradually add the remaining icing sugar until the required consistency is obtained. When the icing is intended for flat work, stand a wooden spoon upright in it – if the consistency is correct it will fall slowly to one side. For rough icing, the mixture should be stiff enough for peaks to be easily formed on the surface when you 'pull' it up with the spoon. Add any desired colouring and the glycerine for a softer texture. If possible, leave the icing overnight in an airtight container in a cool place before use.

To obtain a really smooth result, just before using the icing, remove 1 x 15 ml spoon (1 tablespoon) of it and mix to a coating consistency with water. Return it to the rest and mix until smooth. Makes 900 g (2 lb) quantity

GUY FAWKES OR HALLOWE'EN PARTY FOR EIGHT

Curried chicken pilaf, Sambals/or Lamb and cider hotpot/Cauliflower with fried walnuts/Baked fruit flambé

BEFOREHAND

Curried chicken pilaf
Prepare ingredients (and keep in polythene bags or containers in the refrigerator) on the day before. Don't cook until the evening of the party.
Lamb and cider hotpot
Make a day ahead, then cool quickly and store in refrigerator. Reheat for about 1 hour in a preheated moderate oven (180°C/350°F, Gas Mark 4).
Baked fruit flambé
Prepare the fruit and arrange in the ovenproof dish, with the syrup poured over (but don't bake).

CURRIED CHICKEN PILAF

Metric	Imperial
4 x 15 ml spoons chicken fat	4 tablespoons chicken fat
350 g onions, peeled and sliced	12 oz onions, peeled and sliced
350 g leeks, trimmed and sliced	12 oz leeks, trimmed and sliced
2 x 15 ml spoons hot (Madras) curry powder	2 tablespoons hot (Madras) curry powder
450 g long-grain rice	1 lb long-grain rice
1.2 litres chicken stock	2 pints chicken stock
50 g sultanas, cleaned	2 oz sultanas, cleaned
Salt	Salt
Freshly ground black pepper	Freshly ground black pepper
1 kg cooked chicken meat, chopped	2 lb cooked chicken meat, chopped
Chopped parsley to garnish	Chopped parsley to garnish

Heat the fat in a flameproof casserole or heavy pan and fry the onions and leeks with the curry powder for 1 minute. Add the rice and cook gently for 2 minutes, stirring. Gradually add the stock, then the sultanas and seasoning. Bring to the boil, cover and simmer for 10 minutes.

Add the chicken and simmer for another 5 minutes or until the rice is cooked and the liquid is absorbed. Adjust the seasoning and serve sprinkled with parsley.

Curried chicken pilaf, sambals of bananas, cucumber and salted peanuts.

LAMB AND CIDER HOTPOT

Metric	Imperial
2 kg shoulder of lamb, boned and cut into 5 cm pieces	4 lb shoulder of lamb, boned and cut into 2 inch pieces
50 g plain flour	2 oz plain flour
90 g butter	3½ oz butter
6 x 15 ml spoons vegetable oil	6 tablespoons vegetable oil
225 g onions, peeled and sliced	8 oz onions, peeled and sliced
350 g celery, trimmed and sliced	12 oz celery, trimmed and sliced
500 g cooking apples, peeled, cored and sliced	1 lb cooking apples, peeled, cored and sliced
600 ml light stock	1 pint light stock
300 ml cider	½ pint cider
Salt	Salt
Freshly ground black pepper	Freshly ground black pepper
750 g potatoes, peeled and thinly sliced	1½ lb potatoes, peeled and thinly sliced

Toss the meat in the flour. Melt 50 g (2 oz) of the butter with the oil in a frying pan and brown the meat on all sides. Drain and put in a 3 litre (5 pint) capacity pie dish. Sprinkle in any excess flour.

Add the onions, celery and apples to the frying pan and brown lightly. Spoon on top of the meat. Pour in the stock and cider and add plenty of seasoning. Top with the sliced potatoes and dot with the remaining butter. Stand the dish on a baking sheet and bake in a preheated moderate oven (180°C/350°F, Gas Mark 4) for about 1½ hours or until the meat is tender and the potatoes crisp.

Left: Lamb and cider hotpot. Right: Baked fruit flambé.

BAKED FRUIT FLAMBÉ

Metric

1 small fresh pineapple
4 x 15 ml spoons thick honey
1 x 2.5 ml spoon ground
  cinnamon
50 g butter
150 ml water
4 oranges, peeled and
  segmented
350 g fresh apricots, halved and
  stoned (see note)
4 x 15 ml spoons rum or vodka

Imperial

1 small fresh pineapple
4 tablespoons thick honey
½ teaspoon ground cinnamon
2 oz butter
¼ pint water
4 oranges, peeled and
  segmented
12 oz fresh apricots, halved and
  stoned (see note)
4 tablespoons rum or vodka

Trim off both ends of the pineapple, then cut it into 1 cm (½ inch) slices. Remove the skin with a sharp knife and the centre core with an apple corer. Cut the rings into 6 to 8 segments each.

Heat the honey, cinnamon, butter and water until well mixed. Arrange the fruit in a shallow ovenproof dish and pour over the honey mixture. Cover and bake in a preheated moderate oven (180°C/350°F, Gas Mark 4) for 50 minutes, until the apricots are tender. Transfer to a pre-heated chafing dish, over a lighted burner.

Heat the rum or vodka in a small pan. Pour it over the fruit, set alight and serve immediately, flaming. Serve with thick pouring cream.

Note: Instead of fresh apricots, a drained 439 g (15 oz) can of apricot halves can be used. Cook for 25 minutes only.

EASTER PARTY FOR SIX

Coloured Easter eggs / Egg and watercress mousse / Barbecued shoulder of lamb, Roast potatoes, Broccoli amandine / Sherry trifle

BEFOREHAND

Coloured Easter eggs
Any children in the house might like to do these for themselves.
Egg and watercress mousse
Make the day before; keep in the refrigerator.
Barbecued shoulder of lamb
Prepare the sauce ingredients the day before.
Roast potatoes
Peel the potatoes and keep in water.
Sherry trifle
Prepare the day before up to the addition of cream; keep in the refrigerator, covered with cling film. Decorate with cream, cherries, etc. just before serving.

COLOURED EASTER EGGS

You can decorate hard-boiled eggs with wax crayons, non-toxic felt-tipped pens, vegetable dyes, water colours or oil paints – but it's more fun if you colour them as they cook.

Only use white-shelled eggs. Hard-boiled with onion or shallot skins tied around them with brown cotton, you'll get a mottled orangey-brown effect.

Stick narrow strips of masking tape onto eggs and add a few drops of vegetable dye or food colouring to the water. This will produce a white design on a coloured background – even initials can be produced in this way. Lightly brush with glue and roll in glitter for a frosted effect or stick on sequins with a touch of glue.

Once the eggs have been hard-boiled they can be polished with a little olive oil.

EGG AND WATERCRESS MOUSSE

Metric	Imperial
1 large bunch of watercress, trimmed	1 large bunch of watercress, trimmed
4 eggs, hard-boiled and finely chopped	4 eggs, hard-boiled and finely chopped
300 ml mayonnaise	½ pint mayonnaise
1 x 15 ml spoon powdered gelatine	1 tablespoon powdered gelatine
1 x 15 ml spoon lemon juice	1 tablespoon lemon juice
2 x 15 ml spoons water	2 tablespoons water
Salt	Salt
Freshly ground black pepper	Freshly ground black pepper
1 egg white	1 egg white

A light, creamy cool starter, this has a refreshing taste of watercress.

Reserve about six tiny watercress sprigs for the garnish and finely chop the remainder. Mix the chopped watercress with the eggs and mayonnaise.

Sprinkle the gelatine over the lemon juice and water in a small heatproof bowl. Dissolve by standing the bowl in a pan of simmering water. Cool a little, then fold into the other ingredients with seasoning to taste.

Whisk the egg white until stiff and fold it into the watercress mixture. Turn into a 1.2 litre (2 pint) soufflé dish (or six individual ones). Cover and refrigerate until set.

Serve well chilled, garnished with the reserved watercress sprigs and accompanied by crispbread.

Note: The watercress and eggs can be chopped together in the blender with the mayonnaise; put half the ingredients at a time into the goblet.

BARBECUED SHOULDER OF LAMB

Metric	Imperial
1 x 1.75 kg shoulder of lamb	1 x 3½ lb shoulder of lamb
1 x 5 ml spoon dry mustard	1 teaspoon dry mustard
1 x 5 ml spoon ground ginger	1 teaspoon ground ginger
1 x 5 ml spoon salt	1 teaspoon salt
1 x 5 ml spoon freshly ground black pepper	1 teaspoon freshly ground black pepper
2 garlic cloves, crushed	2 garlic cloves, crushed
Plain flour	Plain flour
For the barbecue sauce:	**For the barbecue sauce:**
4 x 15 ml spoons Worcestershire sauce	4 tablespoons Worcestershire sauce
4 x 15 ml spoons brown table sauce	4 tablespoons brown table sauce
4 x 15 ml spoons mushroom ketchup	4 tablespoons mushroom ketchup
2 x 5 ml spoons sugar	2 teaspoons sugar
1 x 15 ml spoon malt or white vinegar	1 tablespoon malt or white vinegar
3 x 15 ml spoons melted butter	3 tablespoons melted butter
Cayenne pepper	Cayenne pepper
Salt	Salt
150 ml water	¼ pint water
1 small onion, peeled and thinly sliced	1 small onion, peeled and thinly sliced

Trim off any excess fat from the shoulder of lamb. Score the skin in diamonds. Mix the mustard, ginger, salt, pepper and garlic well together and rub into the surface of the meat. Sprinkle the meat with flour and put it in a roasting tin.

Mix the sauce ingredients well together, adding the sliced onion last, and pour over the meat. Cook in a preheated hot oven (220°C/425°F, Gas Mark 7) for 30 minutes, then lower the heat to moderate (180°C/350°F, Gas Mark 4) and continue to cook for a further 1 hour 35 minutes. Baste the joint with the sauce two or three times during the cooking, adding a little more water to the sauce if needed.

BROCCOLI AMANDINE

Metric
1 kg broccoli, trimmed
Salt
50 g butter
50 g flaked almonds
2 x 15 ml spoons lemon juice
Freshly ground black pepper

Imperial
2 lb broccoli, trimmed
Salt
2 oz butter
2 oz flaked almonds
2 tablespoons lemon juice
Freshly ground black pepper

Cook the broccoli in boiling salted water for 10 to 15 minutes. Meanwhile, melt the butter in another pan. Add the almonds and cook over a gentle heat for about 5 minutes until golden brown. Stir in the lemon juice and seasoning.

Drain the broccoli well and turn into a warmed serving dish. Spoon over the almond mixture.

Below: Barbecued shoulder of lamb; Broccoli amandine; Egg and watercress mousse; Sherry trifle. Below left: Coloured Easter eggs.

SHERRY TRIFLE

Metric
8 trifle sponge cakes
Jam
150 ml medium sherry
6 macaroons, crushed
450 ml custard
300 ml double cream, whipped
Sugar
Flavouring
Glacé cherries and ratafias to
   decorate

Imperial
8 trifle sponge cakes
Jam
¼ pint medium sherry
6 macaroons, crushed
¾ pint custard
½ pint double cream, whipped
Sugar
Flavouring
Glacé cherries and ratafias to
   decorate

Split the sponge cakes in half. Spread them with jam and arrange them in a glass dish. Pour the sherry over and leave to soak for 30 minutes. Sprinkle the macaroons over the sponge cakes and pour on the warm, not hot, custard. Cover the dish with a plate to prevent a skin forming and leave until cold.

Sweeten and flavour the whipped cream to taste and spread most of it over the custard. Decorate with the rest of the cream, piped, the cherries and ratafias (or with angelica, almonds, etc.). Fruit juice, such as orange juice, may replace some or all of the sherry.

MIDSUMMER'S EVE PARTY FOR EIGHT

Chilled summer soup/Lemon-stuffed roast veal, or Chicken à la grecque, Avocado apple mayonnaise, crusty French bread/Syllabub trifle/Cheese board and crackers

BEFOREHAND

The day before:
Make the soup and cook the chicken; refrigerate. Prepare the fruit for the trifle and layer in the dish, topped with a single layer of macaroons; cling-film cover.
The morning of the party:
Prepare the veal, ready for cooking.
The afternoon of the party:
Complete the trifle without the decoration (of cream-filled ratafias and berries). Prepare the Avocado apple mayonnaise and cover with polythene; chill. Garnish just before serving.

CHILLED SUMMER SOUP

Metric	Imperial
1 large bunch of watercress, trimmed	1 large bunch of watercress, trimmed
75 g butter or margarine	3 oz butter or margarine
175 g onions, peeled and thinly sliced	6 oz onions, peeled and thinly sliced
1.8 litres milk	3 pints milk
1.5 kg peas, podded or 750 g frozen peas	3 lb peas, podded or 1½ lb frozen peas
Salt	Salt
Freshly ground black pepper	Freshly ground black pepper
225 ml single cream	8 fl oz single cream

Reserve a few watercress sprigs for the garnish and chop the remainder. Melt the fat in a saucepan. Add the chopped watercress and onions and cover. Cook gently for about 15 minutes, without browning. Off the heat, stir in the milk, peas and seasoning. Bring to the boil, stirring.

Cover and simmer gently for about 30 minutes, or until the peas are really soft. Cool slightly, then purée. Pour into a large bowl. Adjust the seasoning. Cool. Stir in the cream and chill well before serving, garnished with the reserved watercress sprigs.

LEMON-STUFFED ROAST VEAL

Metric	Imperial
1 x 1.5 kg boned breast of veal	1 x 3 lb boned breast of veal
Salt	Salt
Freshly ground black pepper	Freshly ground black pepper
3 x 15 ml spoons lemon juice	3 tablespoons lemon juice
25 g fresh white breadcrumbs, toasted	1 oz fresh white breadcrumbs, toasted
1 x 5 ml spoon dried rosemary	1 teaspoon dried rosemary
1 x 15 ml spoon chopped parsley	1 tablespoon chopped parsley
1 garlic clove, crushed	1 garlic clove, crushed
25 g butter, melted	1 oz butter, melted
1 egg, beaten	1 egg, beaten
4 thin lemon slices	4 thin lemon slices
4 streaky bacon rashers, rinds removed	4 streaky bacon rashers, rinds removed
1 x 15 ml spoon cooking oil	1 tablespoon cooking oil
Watercress and lemon wedges to garnish	Watercress and lemon wedges to garnish

Flatten out the meat and season with salt, pepper and 1 x 15 ml spoon (1 tablespoon) of the lemon juice. In a bowl, combine the breadcrumbs, rosemary, parsley, garlic, melted butter, 1 x 1.25 ml spoon (¼ teaspoon) salt, black pepper to taste and the egg. Using a palette knife, fill the pocket in the meat with this stuffing and spread any remaining stuffing over the meat. With scissors, remove the rind from the lemon slices and arrange them down the centre. Roll up the meat and secure it with string at intervals. Lay the bacon across the meat.

Put the oil and the rest of the lemon juice on the bottom of a casserole just large enough to take the joint. Place the meat on top, cover and roast in a preheated moderate oven (180°C/350°F, Gas Mark 4) for about 3½ hours, until tender. Baste occasionally.

Serve garnished with watercress and lemon wedges.

AVOCADO APPLE MAYONNAISE

Metric	Imperial
500 g green-skinned eating apples, cored and sliced	1 lb green-skinned eating apples, cored and sliced
3 x 15 ml spoons lemon juice	3 tablespoons lemon juice
200 ml mayonnaise	⅓ pint mayonnaise
4 x 15 ml spoons single cream	4 tablespoons single cream
Salt	Salt
Freshly ground black pepper	Freshly ground black pepper
2 large ripe avocados	2 large ripe avocados

Sprinkle one of the sliced apples with 1 x 15 ml spoon (1 tablespoon) of the lemon juice and reserve. Mix the mayonnaise with the remaining lemon juice and the cream. Season well. Halve the avocados and remove the stones. Peel off the skin, slice the flesh and fold through the mayonnaise immediately. Fold in the apple slices and adjust the seasoning to taste. Cover and chill well before piling into a salad bowl for serving. Garnish with the reserved apple slices. *Note:* Polish the apples with a clean dry cloth before slicing.

Left: Chilled summer soup.

Lemon-stuffed roast veal; Chicken à la grecque; Avocado apple mayonnaise.

CHICKEN À LA GRECQUE

Metric	Imperial
50 g butter	2 oz butter
2 x 1.5 kg oven-ready chickens	2 x 3 lb oven-ready chickens
450 ml chicken stock	¾ pint chicken stock
150 ml vegetable oil	¼ pint vegetable oil
2 x 15 ml spoons wine vinegar	2 tablespoons wine vinegar
4 x 5 ml spoons tomato paste	4 teaspoons tomato paste
1 large garlic clove, crushed	1 large garlic clove, crushed
1 x 15 ml spoon chopped fresh thyme or basil, or 1 x 5 ml spoon dried thyme or basil	1 tablespoon chopped fresh thyme or basil, or 1 teaspoon dried thyme or basil
Salt	Salt
Freshly ground black pepper	Freshly ground black pepper
350 g small button onions, peeled	12 oz small button onions, peeled
2 x 5 ml spoons caster sugar	2 teaspoons caster sugar
500 g button mushrooms, halved or quartered	1 lb button mushrooms, halved or quartered

Spread the butter over the chickens and place them in a roasting tin. Pour around the stock and roast in a preheated moderately hot oven (200°C/400°F, Gas Mark 6) for about 1¼ hours, basting frequently.

Meanwhile, mix 6 x 15 ml spoons (6 tablespoons) of the oil with the vinegar, tomato paste, garlic, herbs and seasoning. Blanch the onions in boiling water for 5 minutes. Drain them well, then fry in the remaining oil, sprinkled with the sugar. Add the mushrooms and toss over a high heat for a few seconds. Tip the contents of the pan into the dressing.

Joint each hot chicken into eight pieces and spoon the vegetables and dressing over them. Allow to cool, then chill well.

Syllabub trifle.

SYLLABUB TRIFLE

Metric	Imperial
500 g strawberries, hulled and halved	1 lb strawberries, hulled and halved
225 g green grapes, halved and pipped	8 oz green grapes, halved and pipped
175 g macaroons	6 oz macaroons
3 egg whites	3 egg whites
175 g caster sugar	6 oz caster sugar
150 ml dry white wine	$\frac{1}{4}$ pint dry white wine
Juice of $\frac{1}{2}$ lemon	Juice of $\frac{1}{2}$ lemon
2 x 15 ml spoons brandy	2 tablespoons brandy
300 ml double cream	$\frac{1}{2}$ pint double cream
Miniature ratafias to decorate	Miniature ratafias to decorate

Arrange the strawberries and grapes alternately round the bottom of a glass dish. Cover with a single layer of macaroons. Layer with the remaining fruit and macaroons, reserving 10 strawberries and grape halves for decoration.

Whisk the egg whites until stiff. Gradually add half the sugar and continue whisking until the meringue holds its shape. Fold in the remaining sugar. Pour the wine, lemon juice and brandy over and fold the liquids into the egg whites.

Whip the cream until it just holds its shape. Use a little to sandwich pairs of the ratafias and fold the remainder through the frothy meringue mixture. Pour over the fruit and allow to stand for several hours in a cool place, to let the macaroons become moistened. Just before serving, place the cream-filled ratafias and reserved strawberries and grapes on top.

New Year's Eve Party for Six

Dubonnet almond punch (or see pages 176-81) /Cock-a-leekie soup, Oatcakes /Spiced silverside, Bashed neeps and chappit tatties /Old English egg nog pie. Instead of the silverside, you could serve haggis — buy it ready made and serve it with the traditional neeps and tatties — and nips (of whisky)!

BEFOREHAND

Cock-a-leekie soup
Prepare the leeks the day before and keep in polythene bags in a cool place.

Spiced silverside
Soak overnight. Simmer in the morning and complete the oven-cooking in the evening.

Bashed neeps and chappit tatties
Peel the potatoes and swedes and keep covered in water.

Old English eggnog pie
Make the day before; decorate just before dinner.

DUBONNET ALMOND PUNCH

Metric	Imperial
1 x 75 cl bottle red Dubonnet	1 x 75 cl bottle red Dubonnet
150 ml Amaretto di Saronno	$\frac{1}{4}$ pint Amaretto di Saronno
12 allspice berries	12 allspice berries
6 cloves	6 cloves
3 thin-skinned oranges	3 thin-skinned oranges
600 ml boiling water	1 pint boiling water

Heat the Dubonnet and Amaretto with the allspice, cloves and one of the oranges, thinly sliced. Heat almost to boiling point. Squeeze the juice from the remaining oranges and add to the punch with the boiling water. Serve hot.

Dubonnet almond punch.

COCK-A-LEEKIE SOUP

Metric
15 g butter
275-350 g chicken (2 small or
  1 large portion)
350 g leeks, trimmed
1.2 litres chicken stock
1 bouquet garni
1 x 2.5 ml spoon salt
Freshly ground black pepper
6 prunes

Imperial
½ oz butter
10-12 oz chicken (2 small or
  1 large portion)
12 oz leeks, trimmed
2 pints chicken stock
1 bouquet garni
½ teaspoon salt
Freshly ground black pepper
6 prunes

Scotland's national soup, this is one of her oldest and most popular traditional dishes.

Melt the butter in a large saucepan and fry the chicken quickly until golden on all sides. Meanwhile, cut the white part of the leeks into four lengthways and chop into 2.5 cm (1 inch) pieces. Finely shred the green parts of the leeks. Add the white parts to the pan and fry for 5 minutes. Add the stock, bouquet garni and seasoning. Bring to the boil and simmer for about 30 minutes or until the chicken is tender.

Add the prunes and the shredded green of the leeks and simmer for a further 30 minutes.

To serve, remove the chicken, cut the meat into large pieces, discard the skin and bones and place the meat in a warmed soup tureen. Adjust the seasoning of the soup and pour over the meat. Serve with oatcakes.

Below: Cock-a-leekie soup.

SPICED SILVERSIDE

Metric	Imperial
2 kg piece of salted silverside	4 lb piece of salted silverside
1 onion, peeled and sliced	1 onion, peeled and sliced
2 carrots, peeled and sliced	2 carrots, peeled and sliced
1 small turnip, peeled and sliced	1 small turnip, peeled and sliced
1-2 celery stalks, trimmed and chopped	1-2 celery stalks, trimmed and chopped
8 cloves	8 cloves
100 g soft brown sugar	4 oz soft brown sugar
1 x 2.5 ml spoon dry mustard	½ teaspoon dry mustard
1 x 5 ml spoon ground cinnamon	1 teaspoon ground cinnamon
Juice of 1 orange	Juice of 1 orange

Order the joint well ahead, to enable the butcher to salt it for you. Soak the meat for several hours or overnight, then drain and rinse. Put it in a large pan with the vegetables, cover with water and bring slowly to the boil. Remove any scum, cover with a lid and simmer until tender, allowing about 3 to 4 hours. Allow to cool in the liquid.

Drain the meat, put into a roasting tin and stick the cloves into the fat. Mix together the remaining ingredients and spread them over the meat. Bake in a preheated moderate oven (180°C/350°F, Gas Mark 4) for 45 minutes to 1 hour, basting from time to time.

BASHED NEEPS AND CHAPPIT TATTIES

Metric	Imperial
1 kg potatoes, peeled	2 lb potatoes, peeled
1 kg swedes, peeled and diced	2 lb swedes, peeled and diced
50 g butter	2 oz butter
Salt	Salt
Freshly ground black pepper	Freshly ground black pepper
150 ml hot milk	¼ pint hot milk
Chopped parsley to garnish	Chopped parsley to garnish

Cook the potatoes and swedes separately. Drain. Purée the swedes with half the butter. Cook over high heat to drive off the moisture. Season. Mash and cream the potatoes with the milk and remaining butter. Season. Pile the vegetables side by side in a warmed dish and garnish with chopped parsley.

Spiced silverside; Bashed neeps and chappit tatties.

OLD ENGLISH EGG NOG PIE

Metric	Imperial
125 g butter or margarine	4 oz butter or margarine
175 g plain flour, sifted	6 oz plain flour, sifted
3 x 15 ml spoons ground almonds	3 tablespoons ground almonds
6 x 15 ml spoons caster sugar	6 tablespoons caster sugar
3 egg yolks	3 egg yolks
1 x 15 ml spoon water	1 tablespoon water
300 ml milk	½ pint milk
1 x 1.25 ml spoon grated nutmeg	¼ teaspoon grated nutmeg
1 x 15 ml spoon powdered gelatine	1 tablespoon powdered gelatine
3 x 15 ml spoons rum	3 tablespoons rum
6 x 15 ml spoons double cream, lightly whipped	6 tablespoons double cream, lightly whipped
1 egg white	1 egg white
Chocolate curls to decorate	Chocolate curls to decorate

Rub the fat into the flour. Stir in the ground almonds with 3 x 15 ml spoons (3 tablespoons) of the sugar. Bind to a soft dough with 1 egg yolk and the water. Roll out the dough and use to line a deep 20 cm (8 inch) loose-bottomed flan tin. Bake blind in a preheated moderately hot oven (200°C/400°F, Gas Mark 6) for 20 minutes. Cool.

Bring the milk to just below boiling point. Beat the remaining egg yolks and sugar together and gradually stir in the hot milk and the nutmeg. Return to the pan and cook gently until the custard thickens, without boiling. Soak the gelatine in the rum and stir into the hot custard to dissolve. Allow to cool.

Fold the whipped cream into the half-set custard. Whisk the egg white until stiff and fold into the mixture. Turn into the flan case. Refrigerate until set. Remove the flan ring and leave for 30 minutes at room temperature. Decorate with chocolate curls.

Old English egg nog pie.

EASY WEEKENDS

Weekend entertaining doesn't have to involve two whole days of work in the kitchen. By cooking as much as possible in advance you can enjoy the weekend with everyone else. To help things to run smoothly, go through the menus in advance and make a detailed shopping list. Make a list of the menus, pin it up in the kitchen with reheating and roasting times alongside as a quick reminder. Don't forget to lay in a stock of drink including beer and soft drinks.

Start on Friday evening with an appetising meal that can be kept waiting if your guests are late. Make Saturday breakfast a particularly good one, then keep Saturday lunch simple. Serve a more formal menu for Saturday evening.

If your guests rise late on Sunday, our ideas for brunch will probably see them through to teatime; but if children are involved you'll want to provide a traditional Sunday lunch.

And whether you serve afternoon tea at four o'clock or high tea at six or a snack supper on Sunday, you'll find lots of ideas in this chapter.

FRIDAY DINNER FOR SIX

Cream of potato and watercress soup, Bread sticks/Beef pies, Green salad bowl with French dressing/Fresh fruit, Lemon shorties

BEFOREHAND

Cream of potato and watercress soup
Make the day before, but don't reheat after puréeing. Cool and refrigerate. Reheat, with cream, when needed.
Beef pies
Make the filling a day ahead and refrigerate. Top with crust at reheating time.
Green salad bowl
Prepare vegetables and refrigerate in polythene bags, ready for tossing with dressing when needed. Make enough dressing for this and other salads during the weekend and keep in a screwtop jar.
Lemon shorties
Make early in the day.

Beef pies.

CREAM OF POTATO AND WATERCRESS SOUP

Metric	Imperial
1 large bunch of watercress, trimmed	1 large bunch of watercress, trimmed
50 g margarine	2 oz margarine
1 x 15 ml spoon plain flour	1 tablespoon plain flour
600 ml milk	1 pint milk
600 ml water	1 pint water
75 g instant mashed potato granules	3 oz instant mashed potato granules
2 x 5 ml spoons salt	2 teaspoons salt
Freshly ground black pepper	Freshly ground black pepper
150 ml single cream	$\frac{1}{4}$ pint single cream
Butter and grated Parmesan cheese to garnish	Butter and grated Parmesan cheese to garnish

Set aside a few watercress sprigs for the garnish and roughly chop the remainder. Melt the margarine in a saucepan and cook the chopped watercress, covered, for about 15 minutes. Stir in the flour, milk and water and bring to the boil. Add the potato granules and seasoning and simmer gently for 20 minutes, stirring occasionally.

Purée the soup in a blender. Reheat gently with the cream, making sure the soup doesn't boil, or it may curdle. Garnish with the reserved sprigs of watercress, dots of butter and Parmesan. Serves 6 to 8

Cream of potato and watercress soup.

BEEF PIES

Metric	Imperial
2 x 15 ml spoons red wine vinegar	2 tablespoons red wine vinegar
300 ml pale ale	½ pint pale ale
1 garlic clove, crushed (optional)	1 garlic clove, crushed (optional)
1.5 kg stewing steak, cut into 2.5 cm cubes	3½ lb stewing steak, cut into 1 inch cubes
4 x 15 ml spoons plain flour	4 tablespoons plain flour
2-3 x 15 ml spoons oil	2-3 tablespoons oil
175 g onions, peeled and sliced	6 oz onions, peeled and sliced
1 x 142 g can tomato paste	1 x 5 oz can tomato paste
Salt	Salt
Freshly ground black pepper	Freshly ground black pepper
1 x 368 g packet frozen puff pastry, thawed	1 x 13 oz packet frozen puff pastry, thawed
Beaten egg	Beaten egg
Paprika	Paprika
Parsley sprigs to garnish	Parsley sprigs to garnish

Below: Lemon shorties.

Mix together the vinegar, ale and crushed garlic if used. Add the meat cubes and turn to coat. Leave to marinate overnight.

Drain the meat and reserve the marinade. Dredge the meat with the flour. Heat the oil in a frying pan and fry the onions until softened. Remove from the pan. Add the meat cubes, in batches, and brown on all sides. Return the onions to the pan with the tomato paste, seasoning and marinade and stir well. Bring to the boil and simmer for 2 to 3 minutes, then turn into a casserole. Cook in a preheated cool oven (150°C/300°F, Gas Mark 2) for 2 hours. Cool.

Roll out the dough to a rectangle, 35 by 45 cm (14 by 18 inches). Cut in half widthways. Brush with egg, sprinkle with paprika and roll up from the long sides. Cut at an angle into 6 mm (¼ inch) slices.

Divide the meat mixture between six 450 to 600 ml (¾ to 1 pint) ovenproof dishes. Spoon over 1 to 2 x 15 ml spoons (1 to 2 tablespoons) of the juices. Arrange the dough slices around the edge, overlapping. Brush with egg.

Bake just above the centre in a preheated moderately hot oven (200°C/400°F, Gas Mark 6) for about 30 minutes. Garnish with parsley. Reheat the meat juices to serve separately.

FRENCH DRESSING

Metric	Imperial
1 x 5 ml spoon salt	1 teaspoon salt
Pinch of freshly ground black pepper	Pinch of freshly ground black pepper
1 x 5 ml spoon dry mustard	1 teaspoon dry mustard
1 x 5 ml spoon sugar	1 teaspoon sugar
5 x 15 ml spoons vinegar	5 tablespoons vinegar
150 ml salad oil	¼ pint salad oil

Put the salt, pepper, mustard, sugar and vinegar in a bowl and whisk together. Add the oil and whisk until thick and creamy. Alternatively, put all the ingredients in a screwtop jar and shake well until thickened. Makes scant 300 ml (½ pint)

LEMON SHORTIES

Metric	Imperial
For the dough:	**For the dough:**
250 g plain flour	10 oz plain flour
100 g caster sugar	4 oz caster sugar
150 g butter, softened	6 oz butter, softened
2 egg yolks	2 egg yolks
For the filling:	**For the filling:**
25 g butter	1 oz butter
300 ml single cream	½ pint single cream
25 g plain flour	1 oz plain flour
50 g caster sugar	2 oz caster sugar
2 egg yolks	2 egg yolks
Grated rind of ½ lemon	Grated rind of ½ lemon
1 x 2.5 ml spoon vanilla essence	½ teaspoon vanilla essence
Icing sugar	Icing sugar

Sift the flour onto a working surface. Make a well in the centre and put in the sugar, butter and egg yolks. Using the fingertips of one hand, mix together and knead lightly. Chill for 30 minutes.

For the filling, heat the butter and half the cream in a small pan. Mix together the flour and sugar and stir in the remaining cream. Add gradually to the mixture in the pan, beating well until smooth. Remove from the heat and beat in the egg yolks, lemon rind and essence. Return to the heat and cook gently for 5 minutes. Cool.

Roll out the dough on a floured surface. Cut out about 14 rounds with a 7.5 cm (3 inch) plain cutter and 14 rounds with a 6.25 cm (2½ inch) fluted cutter. Line 14 deep patty pans with the plain rounds. Divide the filling between the pastry cases. Place the fluted lids in position and press down lightly.

Bake in a preheated moderately hot oven (200°C/400°F, Gas Mark 6) for 15 to 18 minutes until lightly browned. Allow to cool in the tins before turning out. Serve dusted with icing sugar. Makes about 14

SATURDAY BREAKFAST FOR SIX

Orange wake-me-up/Swiss apple muesli/Eggs and bacon, Bran muffins

BEFOREHAND

Swiss apple muesli
Remember to mix oats and fruit juice on Friday night.
Bran muffins
Make on Friday and heat through when needed.

ORANGE WAKE-ME-UP

Metric	Imperial
Juice of 1 orange	Juice of 1 orange
1 x 15 ml spoon clear honey	1 tablespoon clear honey
1 egg	1 egg

Put all the ingredients in an electric blender and switch on for 30 seconds. Or whisk with a rotary whisk. Serves 1

SWISS APPLE MUESLI

Metric	Imperial
6 x 15 ml spoons rolled oats or medium oatmeal	6 tablespoons rolled oats or medium oatmeal
About 200 ml fruit juice or water	About ⅓ pint fruit juice or water
3 dessert apples, cored and chopped	3 dessert apples, cored and chopped
6 x 15 ml spoons cream or top of the milk	6 tablespoons cream or top of the milk
1.5 x 15 ml spoons honey	1½ tablespoons honey
Brown sugar	Brown sugar
75 g sultanas or seedless raisins, cleaned	3 oz sultanas or seedless raisins, cleaned
Chopped nuts	Chopped nuts

Put the oats and fruit juice or water in a bowl and leave overnight. The next day, mix in the apples, cream or milk, honey, a little brown sugar and the fruit. Put into bowls and sprinkle with the nuts.

BRAN MUFFINS

Metric	Imperial
200 g plain flour	7 oz plain flour
1 x 5 ml spoon salt	1 teaspoon salt
2 x 15 ml spoons baking powder	2 tablespoons baking powder
100-125 g ready-to-eat bran	4 oz ready-to-eat bran
450 ml milk	1 pint less 6 tablespoons milk
50 g butter, softened	2 oz butter, softened
4 x 15 ml spoons caster sugar	4 tablespoons caster sugar
2 eggs, beaten	2 eggs, beaten

Grease twenty 6.5 cm (2½ inch) diameter deep muffin tins. Sift the flour, salt and baking powder together. Soak the bran in the milk for 5 minutes. Meanwhile, cream the butter and sugar together until light. Add the eggs and stir until smooth. Stir in the bran mixture, then add the flour mixture and stir until just mixed, no longer. Fill the muffin tins two-thirds full and bake in the centre of a preheated moderately hot oven (200°C/400°F, Gas Mark 6) for 25 minutes, or until well browned. Turn out onto a wire rack. To serve, split rather than cut open, and butter. Makes 20

Top: Bran Muffins. Left: Orange wake-me-up; Swiss apple muesli.

SATURDAY LUNCH FOR SIX

Chilled tomato juice/Cold glazed bacon, Chutney, Jacket potatoes, Chicory salad/Lemon delight/Cheese board, Fresh fruit

BEFOREHAND

Cold glazed bacon
Cook the joint the day before.
Potatoes
Scrub and keep in water.
Lemon delight
Make the day before, but do not decorate.

COLD GLAZED BACON

Metric	Imperial
1 x 2 kg piece of collar or corner gammon bacon	1 x 4 lb piece of collar or corner gammon bacon
1 x 15 ml spoon clear honey	1 tablespoon clear honey
2 x 15 ml spoons white vinegar	2 tablespoons white vinegar
Demerara sugar	Demerara sugar

Soak the bacon joint, which should be tied securely into shape with string, overnight in cold water. Drain. Place, skin side down, in a large pan and cover with fresh cold water. Bring slowly to the boil, removing any scum. When boiling, reduce the heat, cover and simmer for 1 hour 10 minutes. Always keep the joint under water.

Drain the joint, strip off the rind, and, using a sharp knife, score the fat in a lattice pattern. Place in a roasting tin. Heat the honey and vinegar until combined, then brush this mixture over the joint. Dredge with sugar and pat well in. Crisp in a preheated moderate oven (180°C/350°F, Gas Mark 4) for 30 minutes until golden. Baste with any excess honey glaze. Leave until cold, then wrap in foil and refrigerate. Serves 6 with leftovers

Below: Cold glazed bacon; Lemon delight; Chicory salad.

CHICORY SALAD

Metric	Imperial
3 crisp eating apples, cored and diced	3 crisp eating apples, cored and diced
3 heads of chicory, thinly sliced	3 heads of chicory, thinly sliced
5-6 inner leaves of lettuce, torn into small pieces	5-6 inner leaves of lettuce, torn into small pieces
3 firm tomatoes, skinned, seeded and chopped	3 firm tomatoes, skinned, seeded and chopped
3 x 15 ml spoons French dressing (see page 91)	3 tablespoons French dressing (see page 91)

Toss all the ingredients together in the French dressing and chill for 30 minutes before serving.

LEMON DELIGHT

Metric	Imperial
$1\frac{1}{2}$ x 142 g lemon jelly tablet	$1\frac{1}{2}$ x 5 oz lemon jelly tablet
200 ml water	$\frac{1}{3}$ pint water
Grated rind and juice of 1 lemon	Grated rind and juice of 1 lemon
200 ml medium white wine	$\frac{1}{3}$ pint medium white wine
3 eggs	3 eggs
3 egg yolks	3 egg yolks
75 g caster sugar	3 oz caster sugar

In a small pan, dissolve the jelly squares in the water over a very low heat, stirring. Pour into a measure. Add the lemon rind, juice and wine, then make up to 900 ml ($1\frac{1}{2}$ pints) with water. Cool until on the point of setting.

In a deep heatproof bowl placed over a pan of hot but not boiling water, whisk together the eggs, egg yolks and sugar until really thick. Allow to cool, whisking occasionally, then whisk in the jelly mixture. Turn into a serving dish and chill. Decorate if wished with lightly whipped cream or chocolate curls.

SATURDAY DINNER FOR SIX

Kipper pâté, Melba toast/Roast duckling with grapefruit sauce, Broccoli, Sweetcorn, Duchesse potatoes/Apple and blackberry compôte, or Fresh fruit

BEFOREHAND

Kipper pâté
Make one or two days beforehand and refrigerate, covered.
Roast duckling with grapefruit sauce
Make the grapefruit sauce the day before.
Duchesse potatoes
Peel and keep in water.
Apple and blackberry compôte
Make the day before.

KIPPER PÂTÉ

Metric	Imperial
350 g kipper fillets, skinned	12 oz kipper fillets, skinned
6 x 15 ml spoons dry white wine	6 tablespoons dry white wine
2 x 15 ml spoons lemon juice	2 tablespoons lemon juice
100 g butter, softened	4 oz butter, softened
Freshly ground black pepper	Freshly ground black pepper
6 tomato slices	6 tomato slices
Melba toast to serve	Melba toast to serve

Put the kipper fillets in a shallow dish and spoon the wine over. Cover and leave to marinate in a cool place for 4 hours.

Work the fillets and marinade to a paste with a wooden spoon, or purée them in an electric blender until smooth, adding the lemon juice to make a softer mixture. Beat in the softened butter and season with black pepper. Divide between six 120 ml (4 fl oz) ramekin dishes. Smooth over the tops and mark with a fork. Top each with a tomato twist. Serve with Melba toast.

ROAST DUCKLING WITH GRAPEFRUIT SAUCE

Metric	Imperial
2 x 1.75 kg duckling or 12 duckling pieces, thawed if frozen	2 x 3½ lb ducklings or 12 duckling pieces, thawed if frozen
Salt	Salt
Freshly ground black pepper	Freshly ground black pepper
2 x 15 ml spoons plain flour	2 tablespoons plain flour
1 x 178 ml can frozen concentrated unsweetened grapefruit juice, thawed	1 x 6¼ fl oz can frozen concentrated unsweetened grapefruit juice, thawed
1 x 15 ml spoon arrowroot	1 tablespoon arrowroot
2 grapefruit, peeled and segmented	2 grapefruit, peeled and segmented
Watercress to garnish	Watercress to garnish

The grapefruit juice gives the duck a rich fruity flavour. Orange juice can be used instead if preferred, in which case add a squeeze of lemon juice to the orange sauce to sharpen the flavour.

Joint each duckling into six or ask the butcher to do this for you. Trim off excess fat. Wipe the joints and prick well. Season. Place the duckling joints, skin side up, on a wire rack in a roasting tin containing the giblets. Cook near the top of a preheated moderate oven (180°C/350°F, Gas Mark 4) for about 1½ hours. Baste with the pan juices twice during cooking. Twenty minutes before the end of the cooking time, sprinkle with the flour and baste again.

Make the grapefruit juice up to 450 ml (¾ pint) with water. Mix a little with the arrowroot in a small pan, then gradually stir in the remaining juice and bring to the boil, stirring.

Transfer the cooked duckling joints to a warmed serving dish. Arrange the fruit segments on top. Return to the oven to keep hot. Drain the fat from the roasting tin, leaving the duckling juices, and add the grapefruit sauce. Scrape the bottom of the roasting tin to loosen any sediment. Bring to the boil, stirring well. Adjust seasoning. Strain. Glaze the duckling with some of the sauce and serve the rest separately. Garnish with watercress.

DUCHESSE POTATOES

Metric	Imperial
1 kg potatoes, peeled	2 lb potatoes, peeled
Salt	Salt
100 g butter	4 oz butter
2 eggs, beaten	2 eggs, beaten
Freshly ground black pepper	Freshly ground black pepper
Pinch of grated nutmeg	Pinch of grated nutmeg

Cook the potatoes in boiling salted water for 15 to 20 minutes. Drain them well, then sieve or mash them. Beat in the butter, eggs, seasoning and nutmeg. Cool the mixture, then spoon it into a piping bag fitted with a large rosette nozzle. Pipe onto a greased baking sheet. Cook in a preheated moderately hot oven (200°C/400°F, Gas Mark 6) for about 25 minutes, until set and golden brown.
Note: If serving the potatoes with the duckling, allow 35 minutes cooking time in a moderate oven (180°C/350°F, Gas Mark 4).

Left: Kipper pâté. Right: Roast duckling with grapefruit sauce; Duchesse potatoes; Broccoli; Apple and blackberry compôte.

APPLE AND BLACKBERRY COMPÔTE

Metric
1.25 kg eating apples, peeled,
  cored and thinly sliced
450 ml water
Pared rind of $\frac{1}{2}$ lemon
75 g sugar
350 g blackberries
2 x 15 ml spoons Calvados or
  brandy

Imperial
2$\frac{1}{2}$ lb eating apples, peeled, cored
  and thinly sliced
$\frac{3}{4}$ pint water
Pared rind of $\frac{1}{2}$ lemon
3 oz sugar
12 oz blackberries
2 tablespoons Calvados or
  brandy

Poach the apple slices in the water with the lemon rind until transparent – about 7 minutes. Drain the apples and set aside to cool. Add the sugar to the cooking liquid. When dissolved, bring to the boil and continue boiling for 8 to 10 minutes or until reduced by half. Discard the lemon rind and pour this syrup over the apples.

Place half the apples in six individual dishes. Cover with half the blackberries. Add the Calvados or brandy to the remaining syrup and spoon it over the fruit. Fill up with layers of the remaining apples and blackberries. Chill well before serving with thick pouring cream.

SUNDAY BRUNCH FOR SIX

Melon/Kidney savouries, Floury baps

KIDNEY SAVOURIES

Metric	Imperial
6 small thick slices of white bread	6 small thick slices of white bread
40 g butter	1½ oz butter
3 x 15 ml spoons corn oil	3 tablespoons corn oil
3 streaky bacon rashers, rinds removed	3 streaky bacon rashers, rinds removed
6 lambs' kidneys, skinned, halved and cored	6 lambs' kidneys, skinned, halved and cored
12 pork chipolatas	12 pork chipolatas
3 tomatoes, halved	3 tomatoes, halved
Parsley sprigs to garnish	Parsley sprigs to garnish

Using an 8 cm (3¼ inch) plain pastry cutter, cut six rounds from the slices of bread. Heat 25 g (1 oz) of the butter and the oil in a frying pan and fry the bread rounds on both sides until crisp and golden. Drain on absorbent kitchen paper and keep warm. Stretch the bacon rashers with the back of a knife. Cut each in half. Roll up into six rolls and secure with half wooden cocktail sticks.

Melt the remaining butter in the pan and fry the kidneys for about 8 minutes. Meanwhile, grill the sausages and bacon rolls under a preheated moderate grill for 7 to 10 minutes, turning once. Grill the tomatoes for 4 minutes.

To assemble, place the fried bread rounds on a warmed platter. Place two sausages across each, then top with 2 kidney halves, a tomato half and finally a bacon roll and parsley sprig.

FLOURY BAPS

Metric	Imperial
15 g fresh yeast	½ oz fresh yeast
300 ml lukewarm milk and water mixed	½ pint lukewarm milk and water mixed
450 g strong plain flour	1 lb strong plain flour
1 x 5 ml spoon salt	1 teaspoon salt
50 g lard	2 oz lard

Mix the yeast with the liquid. Sift together the flour and salt and rub in the lard. Stir in the yeast liquid. Work the mixture to a firm dough, adding extra flour only if really needed, until the dough leaves the sides of the bowl clean. Knead on a floured surface for about 5 minutes. Place in a large bowl, cover with lightly oiled polythene and allow to rise until doubled in size.

Lightly knead the dough, then cut into eight or ten even-sized pieces. Shape each into a ball, place on a floured baking sheet and press down to flatten slightly. Cover with oiled polythene and allow to rise until doubled in size – 45 minutes at room temperature.

Dredge the tops lightly with flour and bake in a preheated moderately hot oven (200°C/400°F, Gas Mark 6) for 15 to 20 minutes. Cool on a wire rack. Makes 8 to 10

Kidney savouries; Floury baps.

Sunday Lunch for Six

Tomato bouillon/Rolled stuffed shoulder of lamb, Roast potatoes, Brussels sprouts/Rhubarb and apple snow

Beforehand

Rolled stuffed shoulder of lamb
The day before, stuff the joint and keep, loosely wrapped, in the refrigerator. Weigh to calculate cooking time.
Rhubarb and apple snow
Make the purée on Friday. Fold the stiffly whisked egg whites through the purée about 1 hour before the meal.

Tomato Bouillon

Mix equal amounts of canned beef consommé and tomato juice. Garnish with thinly sliced lemon.

Rolled Stuffed Shoulder of Lamb

Metric	Imperial
175 g streaky bacon rashers, rinds removed	6 oz streaky bacon rashers, rinds removed
25 g fresh white breadcrumbs	1 oz fresh white breadcrumbs
3 x 15 ml spoons chopped fresh mint	3 tablespoons chopped fresh mint
Salt	Salt
Freshly ground black pepper	Freshly ground black pepper
Beaten egg	Beaten egg
1 x 2-2.5 kg shoulder of lamb, boned	1 x 4-4½ lb shoulder of lamb, boned
1-2 x 15 ml spoons oil	1-2 tablespoons oil

Rhubarb and apple snow.

Finely scissor-snip the bacon and combine it with the breadcrumbs, mint and seasoning. Add sufficient beaten egg to bind the ingredients together. Spread out the lamb. Place the stuffing in the cavity where the bone was. Roll up the joint and secure with several bands of string. Weigh the joint.

Lightly grease a roasting tin with some of the oil. Place the joint in it and brush with the remaining oil. Cook in a preheated moderately hot oven (190°C/375°F, Gas Mark 5). Calculate the cooking time after stuffing by allowing 20 minutes per 450 g (1 lb) plus 30 minutes.

Rhubarb and Apple Snow

Metric	Imperial
500 g pink rhubarb, trimmed and cut into 2.5 cm pieces	1 lb pink rhubarb, trimmed and cut into 1 inch pieces
500 g cooking apples, peeled, cored and sliced	1 lb cooking apples, peeled, cored and sliced
75 g granulated sugar	3 oz granulated sugar
1 x 5 ml spoon ground cinnamon	1 teaspoon ground cinnamon
4 x 15 ml spoons water	4 tablespoons water
2 egg whites	2 egg whites

Put the rhubarb and apples in a heavy-based pan with the sugar, cinnamon and water. Cover and stew gently until the fruits are quite soft. Cool.

Purée the fruits in a blender until smooth. Whisk the egg whites until stiff and fold through the fruit purée. Turn into six individual glass dishes. Cover and refrigerate for about 1 hour before serving, with sponge fingers.

Rolled stuffed shoulder of lamb; Tomato bouillon.

HIGH TEA FOR SIX

Cheese and chive hotties/Eggs with tomato-pepper sauce/Dark chocolate swirl cake, Biscuits, teabreads and spreads (see pages 134-53)

BEFOREHAND

Cheese and chive hotties

Can be partly prepared on Friday. Make the rolls, but don't bake them. Refrigerate, wrapped, and bake as directed when needed.

Eggs with tomato-pepper sauce

The sauce can be made on Friday and kept in the refrigerator. Reheat it in a saucepan while the eggs are being boiled.

Cookies, cakes and spreads

Can be made two or three days ahead and kept in airtight containers.

CHEESE AND CHIVE HOTTIES

Metric
1 medium fresh uncut white sandwich loaf
Soft butter or margarine
225 g red Leicester cheese, grated
Snipped fresh chives
Salt
Freshly ground black pepper
Melted butter
Paprika

Imperial
1 medium fresh uncut white sandwich loaf
Soft butter or margarine
8 oz red Leicester cheese, grated
Snipped fresh chives
Salt
Freshly ground black pepper
Melted butter
Paprika

Chill the fresh loaf in the freezing compartment of the refrigerator for 30 minutes to make slicing easier. Cut and butter as many thin slices as possible along the whole length of the loaf. Remove crusts.

Sprinkle each slice with cheese, chives and seasoning. Roll up each slice from the shorter edge and wrap each roll in dampened grease-proof paper. Chill for 30 minutes longer.

Unwrap the rolls. Arrange them on baking sheets. Brush with melted butter, dust with paprika and bake in a preheated very hot oven (230°C/450°F, Gas Mark 8) for 5 to 10 minutes. Serve oven-fresh, with dill pickles.

EGGS WITH TOMATO-PEPPER SAUCE

Metric
25 g butter
50 g onion, peeled and finely chopped
100 g green pepper, cored, seeded and finely chopped
500 g ripe tomatoes, skinned and chopped
1 garlic clove, crushed
Salt
Freshly ground black pepper
6-8 eggs

Imperial
1 oz butter
2 oz onion, peeled and finely chopped
4 oz green pepper, cored, seeded and finely chopped
1 lb ripe tomatoes, skinned and chopped
1 garlic clove, crushed
Salt
Freshly ground black pepper
6-8 eggs

Melt the butter in a saucepan and add the onion and green pepper. Cook gently until soft. Stir in the tomatoes and garlic, cover and simmer for 10 minutes. Adjust the seasoning.

Meanwhile, hard-boil the eggs. Cool slightly, then shell and halve lengthways. Arrange in a warmed shallow serving dish. Pour the hot sauce over the eggs and serve at once.

Cheese and chive hotties.

Eggs with tomato-pepper sauce.

Dark chocolate swirl cake.

DARK CHOCOLATE SWIRL CAKE

Metric	Imperial
175 g butter or block margarine	6 oz butter or block margarine
175 g caster sugar	6 oz caster sugar
2 eggs, beaten	2 eggs, beaten
5 x 15 ml spoons cocoa powder	5 tablespoons cocoa powder
175 ml milk	6 fl oz milk
1 x 5 ml spoon vanilla essence	1 teaspoon vanilla essence
225 g plain flour	8 oz plain flour
1.5 x 5 ml spoons bicarbonate of soda	1½ teaspoons bicarbonate of soda
Pinch of salt	Pinch of salt
1 square bakers' unsweetened chocolate, melted	1 square bakers' unsweetened chocolate, melted
125 g icing sugar	4 oz icing sugar
50 g plain chocolate-flavoured cake covering, melted	2 oz plain chocolate-flavoured cake covering, melted

Grease and bottom-line two straight-sided 19 cm (7½ inch) sandwich tins. Cream 125 g (4 oz) of the fat until soft. Gradually work in the caster sugar and continue creaming until light and fluffy. Beat in the eggs, little by little. Mix the cocoa and 6 x 15 ml spoons (6 tablespoons) of the milk to a smooth paste. Stir in the remaining milk with the essence.

Sift the flour with the bicarbonate of soda and salt and beat into the creamed ingredients, alternating with the cocoa liquid. Spoon into the prepared sandwich tins. Swirl the unsweetened chocolate around the top of one cake. Bake in a preheated moderate oven (180°C/350°F, Gas Mark 4) for about 30 minutes. Leave to cool in the tins before turning out.

Beat the remaining fat until soft. Sift in the icing sugar and continue to cream well. Work in the cake covering. Use to sandwich the cakes together. Makes a 19 cm (7½ inch) sandwich cake

SUNDAY NIGHT SNACK SUPPER FOR SIX

Cheese and tomato fries, Celery sticks, radishes and chicory/Fresh fruit or Melon and pear compôte

BEFOREHAND

Cheese and tomato fries
Can be made early in the day and fried when needed.
Celery sticks, radishes and chicory
Prepare and keep refrigerated in polythene bags or covered containers until needed.
Melon and pear compôte
Can be made on Friday or Saturday; keep refrigerated.

CHEESE AND TOMATO FRIES

Metric
12 slices of white bread
Butter or soft margarine
Dijon mustard
350 g Edam cheese, thinly sliced
225 g tomatoes, skinned and thinly sliced
Salt
Freshly ground black pepper
Oil and butter for frying
Watercress to garnish

Imperial
12 slices of white bread
Butter or soft margarine
Dijon mustard
12 oz Edam cheese, thinly sliced
8 oz tomatoes, skinned and thinly sliced
Salt
Freshly ground black pepper
Oil and butter for frying
Watercress to garnish

Spread the slices of bread with butter or margarine and mustard. Make six cheese and tomato sandwiches, placing the tomatoes in the centre with plenty of seasoning. Press well together. Cut off the crusts and cut each sandwich into triangles. Shallow fry quickly in mixed hot oil and butter until golden brown on both sides and the cheese starts to ooze. Serve as soon as possible, garnished with watercress.
Note: If preferred, the sandwiches can be grilled rather than fried. In this case, prepare by brushing or spreading the outside of the sandwich triangles with melted or softened fat.

MELON AND PEAR COMPÔTE

Metric
100 g sugar
300 ml water
4 x 15 ml spoons Kirsch
3 x 15 ml spoons lemon juice
4 large ripe pears, peeled, cored and sliced
1 medium ripe honeydew melon
Blanched finely shredded lemon rind to decorate

Imperial
4 oz sugar
$\frac{1}{2}$ pint water
4 tablespoons Kirsch
3 tablespoons lemon juice
4 large ripe pears, peeled, cored and sliced
1 medium ripe honeydew melon
Blanched finely shredded lemon rind to decorate

Dissolve the sugar in the water in a shallow pan. Bring to the boil and stir in the Kirsch and strained lemon juice. Add the pear slices, cover and poach gently until tender – about 20 minutes.

Meanwhile, divide the melon into eighths and discard the seeds. Remove the flesh from the skin in one piece and cut across into thin slices. Place in a large bowl. While still hot, pour the pears with their syrup over the melon and mix well together. Cool, cover and chill well before serving, decorated with lemon rind.

Above: Cheese and tomato fries. Right: Melon and pear compôte.

PARTIES OUT OF DOORS

Whether for a picnic, a barbecue, or a buffet supper on the balcony, catering for any outdoor meal demands food to suit the occasion. For a picnic, take food which can be prepared in bake-and-take containers, such as quiches, flans and pâtés. Accompany them with salad greens, in polythene containers, with the dressing taken separately, and lots of fresh fruit.

Don't buy expensive and elaborate equipment unless you are regular outdoor-eaters. Polythene wraps and foil are usually adequate and disposable equipment is cheap enough for the odd occasion. If you take your picnicking seriously, you'll need a good suppy of rigid polythene containers of all sizes.

Take soups, ice cubes and fruit salads in wide necked vacuum flasks.

For barbecue parties at home, you'll need lots of foil, throwaway plates and extra-large absorbent paper napkins, tongs and a pair of thick gloves for whoever operates the barbecue. To drink, serve vin ordinaire, beer, a hot punch – or a chilled fruit cup on a warm summer's evening. Finish the meal with plenty of hot coffee.

SIMPLE PATIO PARTY FOR SIX TO EIGHT

Pan pizza, Blue cheese rarebits, Ratatouille aux champignons, Lemon-dressed avocado salad, Tossed green salad/Apricot cheesecake

BEFOREHAND

Pan pizza
Cook one in advance, as far as topping it with sardines and olives (see recipe note).

Blue cheese rarebits
Make the egg mixture early in the day; spread over the toast and grill when required.

Ratatouille aux champignons
Prepare the day before and refrigerate. Heat through, if required, in a preheated moderate oven (180°C/350°F, Gas Mark 4) for 45 minutes, or until hot.

Avocado salad
Prepare the cucumber and celery in the afternoon. Make the dressing. Prepare the avocados and complete the salad just before serving.

Tossed green salad
Prepare the vegetables and keep in polythene bags in the refrigerator.

Apricot cheesecake
Make the day before, but leave in mould in the refrigerator. Turn out and dredge with icing sugar when required.

PAN PIZZA

Metric	Imperial
325 g self-raising flour	12 oz self-raising flour
Pinch of salt	Pinch of salt
50 g butter or margarine	2 oz butter or margarine
About 175 ml water	About 6 fl oz water
4 x 15 ml spoons oil	4 tablespoons oil
4 x 15 ml spoons tomato paste	4 tablespoons tomato paste
1 x 397 g can tomatoes, drained and roughly chopped	1 x 14 oz can tomatoes, drained and roughly chopped
1 x 5 ml spoon dried oregano or marjoram	1 teaspoon dried oregano or marjoram
Freshly ground black pepper	Freshly ground black pepper
175 g Cheddar cheese, grated	6 oz Cheddar cheese, grated
1 x 250 g can sardines, drained	1 x 9 oz can sardines, drained
Black olives	Black olives

Sift together the flour and salt and rub in the fat. Add enough water to mix to a soft dough. Knead the dough gently. Divide in two and roll or press out half to fit a 25 cm (10 inch) diameter frying pan.

Heat half the oil in the frying pan and fry the dough until golden – about 5 minutes. Turn the dough over and spread half the tomato paste over the cooked side. Top with half of the tomatoes, herbs and pepper. Sprinkle half the cheese over. Top with half the sardines and olives. When the second side is brown – 5 to 7 minutes – place the pizza under a hot grill and cook until the cheese melts and bubbles. Serve in wedges from the pan. Make the second pizza the same way. Makes 2 pizzas, each to serve 3 to 4

Note: Cook one pizza in advance, as far as topping with sardines and olives. Remove carefully, sliding onto a heatproof plate, when the second side is brown. Keep warm and cook under the grill while the second pizza is cooking in the pan.

BLUE CHEESE RAREBITS

Metric	Imperial
225 g Danish blue cheese, grated	8 oz Danish blue cheese, grated
6 x 15 ml spoons dry white wine	6 tablespoons dry white wine
8 egg yolks	8 egg yolks
6 x 15 ml spoons milk	6 tablespoons milk
Freshly ground black pepper	Freshly ground black pepper
Salt	Salt
16 slices of rye bread, toasted	16 slices of rye bread, toasted

Blue cheese rarebits; Pan pizza; Ratatouille aux champignons; Lemon-dressed avocado salad.

Put the cheese and wine into a heavy-based saucepan and stir over a low heat until the cheese has melted. Beat the egg yolks with the milk and pepper. Off the heat, stir into the cheese mixture. Return to the heat, and cook gently, stirring constantly, until the mixture thickens. Adjust the seasoning, adding salt if necessary, and spoon onto the slices of toast. Pop them under a hot grill to glaze golden brown. Serve as soon as possible. Makes 16

RATATOUILLE AUX CHAMPIGNONS

Metric	Imperial
1 medium aubergine, thickly sliced	1 medium aubergine, thickly sliced
Salt	Salt
2 x 15 ml spoons oil	2 tablespoons oil
25 g butter	1 oz butter
500 g small button mushrooms	1 lb small button mushrooms
4 medium tomatoes, skinned, quartered and seeded	4 medium tomatoes, skinned, quartered and seeded
1 small green pepper, cored, seeded and sliced	1 small green pepper, cored, seeded and sliced
225 g courgettes, thickly sliced	8 oz courgettes, thickly sliced
1 garlic clove, crushed	1 garlic clove, crushed
2 x 15 ml spoons tomato paste	2 tablespoons tomato paste
Large pinch of ground coriander	Large pinch of ground coriander
Freshly ground black pepper	Freshly ground black pepper
Chopped parsley to garnish	Chopped parsley to garnish

Good hot or cold, coriander gives this dish a subtle flavour.

Sprinkle the aubergine slices with salt and leave for 40 minutes, then rinse under the cold tap to remove the excess salt. Drain well.

Heat the oil and butter in a large flameproof casserole. Reserve half the mushrooms and add the remainder with all the other vegetables, together with the garlic, tomato paste, coriander and seasoning. Stir well to mix thoroughly. Cover and cook in a preheated moderate oven (180°C/350°F, Gas Mark 4) for 50 to 60 minutes, stirring once or twice.

Ten minutes before the cooking is completed, stir in the reserved mushrooms. Adjust the seasoning and serve garnished with parsley.

LEMON-DRESSED AVOCADO SALAD

Metric	Imperial
½ small cucumber, peeled and diced	½ small cucumber, peeled and diced
Salt	Salt
150 ml vegetable oil	¼ pint vegetable oil
4 x 15 ml spoons lemon juice	4 tablespoons lemon juice
2 x 5 ml spoons thin honey	2 teaspoons thin honey
Freshly ground black pepper	Freshly ground black pepper
2 ripe avocados, peeled, stoned and sliced	2 ripe avocados, peeled, stoned and sliced
4 celery stalks, trimmed and thinly sliced	4 celery stalks, trimmed and thinly sliced
50 g salted peanuts	2 oz salted peanuts
Paprika or chopped parsley to garnish	Paprika or chopped parsley to garnish

Sprinkle the cucumber with salt and leave for 20 minutes to draw out the juices. Dry on absorbent kitchen paper.

Put the oil, lemon juice, honey, 1 x 2.5 ml spoon (½ teaspoon) salt and pepper to taste in a screwtop jar and shake well. Dice one avocado and toss both with the cucumber, celery, avocados and nuts. Pile into a serving dish. Serve immediately, dusted with paprika or parsley.

Apricot cheesecake.

APRICOT CHEESECAKE

Metric	Imperial
75 g granulated sugar	3 oz granulated sugar
200 ml water	⅓ pint water
500 g fresh apricots, halved and stoned	1 lb fresh apricots, halved and stoned
225 g semi-sweet biscuits, crushed	8 oz semi-sweet biscuits, crushed
175 g butter or block margarine, melted	6 oz butter or block margarine, melted
1 x 5 ml spoon mixed spice	1 teaspoon mixed spice
50 g caster sugar	2 oz caster sugar
4 x 5 ml spoons powdered gelatine	4 teaspoons powdered gelatine
Thinly pared rind and juice of 2 large thin-skinned lemons	Thinly pared rind and juice of 2 large thin-skinned lemons
225 g cream cheese	8 oz cream cheese
225 g cottage cheese	8 oz cottage cheese
1 large can condensed milk	1 large can condensed milk
Icing sugar	Icing sugar

Dissolve the granulated sugar in the water in a saucepan. Add the apricot halves and poach gently until tender. Then chop roughly.

Mix the biscuit crumbs with the melted butter or margarine, spice and caster sugar. Use three-quarters of the crumb mixture to line the bottom and sides of 21.5 cm (8½ inch) spring-release mould (bottom-lined with non-stick paper). Refrigerate until set.

Sprinkle the gelatine over the lemon juice in a heatproof cup to soften it. Place in a pan of hot water and stir to dissolve the gelatine. Put the lemon rind, cheeses, condensed milk and gelatine in a blender and blend until smooth. Fold in the chopped apricots. Pour the mixture into the crumb case. Scatter the remaining crumbs over and refrigerate until set.

Turn out, upside-down, dredge heavily with icing sugar and mark with a lattice design, using a knife.

Patio Party for Twelve to Sixteen

Tunafish creams, Dressed leeks/Battalian beef bake, Red cabbage and sweetcorn salad, Tossed green salad/Peach and apple soufflé, Shortcake gâteau

Beforehand

Tunafish creams
Make these the evening before; cover with cling film and refrigerate. Remove them from the refrigerator 2 hours before serving; garnish and cover again with film.

Dressed leeks
Prepare the leeks to the cooking stage the day before; store them in a polythene bag in a cool place. Make up the dressing. Finish preparing in the morning.

Battalian beef bake
Prepare up to the addition of the Parmesan; store, covered, in the refrigerator.

Red cabbage and sweetcorn salad
Prepare and finely shred the cabbage the day before; store in a polythene bag in a cool place.

Tossed green salad
Prepare the vegetables and keep in polythene bags in the refrigerator.

Peach and apple soufflé
Make the soufflé the day before and refrigerate; remove from the refrigerator 1 hour before serving. Discard the collar.

Shortcake gâteau
Make the walnut shortcake base the day before; wrap it in kitchen foil.

Tunafish Creams

Metric	Imperial
450 ml soured cream	¾ pint soured cream
4 x 15 ml spoons mayonnaise	4 tablespoons mayonnaise
Salt	Salt
Freshly ground black pepper	Freshly ground black pepper
Large dash of Worcestershire sauce	Large dash of Worcestershire sauce
2 x 15 ml spoons snipped fresh chives	2 tablespoons snipped fresh chives
4 x 5 ml spoons capers, chopped	4 teaspoons capers, chopped
1 x 15 ml spoon peeled and finely grated onion	1 tablespoon peeled and finely grated onion
1 x 12.5 g packet powdered gelatine	1 x ½ oz packet powdered gelatine
4 x 15 ml spoons water	4 tablespoons water
2 x 198 g cans tuna, drained and flaked	2 x 7 oz cans tuna, drained and flaked
4 eggs, hard-boiled and chopped	4 eggs, hard-boiled and chopped
To garnish:	**To garnish:**
3 firm tomatoes, sliced	3 firm tomatoes, sliced
Parsley sprigs	Parsley sprigs

Mix together the soured cream, mayonnaise, seasoning, Worcestershire sauce, chives, capers and onion. Dissolve the gelatine in the water in a small heatproof bowl over a pan of hot water. Cool slightly, then stir into the soured cream mixture, followed by the tuna and eggs. Mix thoroughly and spoon into individual soufflé or cocotte dishes. Chill until set. Garnish with tomato slices and parsley.

Below: Tunafish creams.

Battalian beef bake.

BATTALIAN BEEF BAKE

Metric
3 x 15 ml spoons corn oil
350 g onions, peeled and sliced
1 garlic clove, crushed
750 g prime collar or slipper of
  bacon joint, rind removed,
  cut into 1 cm cubes
1.25 kg lean minced beef
Thinly pared rind and juice of
  1 large orange
1 x 397 g can peeled tomatoes
2 bay leaves
Freshly ground black pepper
1 x 2.5 ml spoon Worcestershire
  sauce
Salt
2 kg potatoes, peeled
50 g butter or margarine
50 g plain flour
750 ml milk
1 x 5 ml spoon made mustard
100 g mature Cheddar cheese,
  grated
2 x 15 ml spoons freshly grated
  Parmesan cheese

Imperial
3 tablespoons corn oil
12 oz onions, peeled and sliced
1 garlic clove, crushed
1½ lb prime collar or slipper of
  bacon joint, rind removed,
  cut into ½ inch cubes
2½ lb lean minced beef
Thinly pared rind and juice of
  1 large orange
1 x 14 oz can peeled tomatoes
2 bay leaves
Freshly ground black pepper
½ teaspoon Worcestershire sauce
Salt
4 lb potatoes, peeled
2 oz butter or margarine
2 oz plain flour
1¼ pints milk
1 teaspoon made mustard
4 oz mature Cheddar cheese,
  grated
2 tablespoons freshly grated
  Parmesan cheese

Heat the oil in a large pan and fry the onions and garlic until soft but not coloured. Add the bacon and cook gently for 10 minutes, then stir in the mince. Cook for a further 10 minutes, stirring frequently.

Cut the orange rind into fine julienne strips and blanch in boiling water for 5 minutes. Drain. Add the orange strips, orange juice, tomatoes, with the can liquid, bay leaves, pepper and Worcestershire sauce to the meat mixture and bring to the boil. Cover the pan and simmer gently for 45 minutes. Check the seasoning and adjust if necessary.

Cook the potatoes in boiling salted water until almost tender. Drain, cool and slice. Turn the meat mixture into a shallow 3.4 litre (6 pint) casserole (or two 2.3 litre (4 pint) casseroles) and arrange the potato slices in an overlapping pattern over the meat.

Melt the butter or margarine in a saucepan. Stir in the flour and cook for 1 minute. Gradually stir in the milk and bring to the boil. Add seasoning and the mustard. Simmer for 3 minutes, then remove from the heat and stir in the Cheddar cheese until melted. Spoon the sauce over the potato slices and sprinkle with the Parmesan cheese.

Cook in a preheated hot oven (220°C/425°F, Gas Mark 7) for about 20 minutes.

Reduce the oven temperature to moderate (180°C/350°F, Gas Mark 4) and cook for a further 25 minutes or until really hot and the cheese is brown. Serve immediately.

DRESSED LEEKS

Metric
1.5 kg leeks
9 x 15 ml spoons oil
3 x 15 ml spoons cider vinegar
1 x 5 ml spoon French mustard
25 g peeled and finely chopped
  onion
2 x 5 ml spoons caster sugar
1 x 2.5 ml spoon salt
Freshly ground black pepper

Imperial
3 lb leeks
9 tablespoons oil
3 tablespoons cider vinegar
1 teaspoon French mustard
1 oz peeled and finely chopped
  onion
2 teaspoons caster sugar
½ teaspoon salt
Freshly ground black pepper

Trim about half the green part from the leeks. Cut the remainder of the leeks into 3mm (⅛ inch) slices and wash thoroughly. Drain, then blanch in boiling salted water for 3 to 4 minutes. Drain and cool quickly in cold water. Drain well.

In a screwtop jar, shake together the remaining ingredients. Pour over the leeks and toss together. Leave to marinate for at least 2 hours.

Dressed leeks.

RED CABBAGE AND SWEETCORN SALAD

Metric	Imperial
1.5 kg red cabbage, cored and finely shredded	3 lb red cabbage, cored and finely shredded
150 ml French dressing (see page 91)	¼ pint French dressing (see page 91)
1 cucumber, diced	1 cucumber, diced
Salt	Salt
Freshly ground black pepper	Freshly ground black pepper
2 x 312 g cans sweetcorn kernels, drained	2 x 11 oz cans sweetcorn kernels, drained
1 x 2.5 ml spoon finely grated lemon rind	½ teaspoon finely grated lemon rind
1 x 5 ml spoon clear honey	1 teaspoon clear honey

Put the cabbage in a large bowl with the dressing. Toss and leave for 2 hours. Put the diced cucumber and seasoning in a bowl and leave for 2 hours.

Drain off any excess moisture from the cucumber and add with the corn, lemon rind and honey to the cabbage. Toss thoroughly.

SHORTCAKE GÂTEAU

Metric	Imperial
250 g plain flour, sifted	10 oz plain flour, sifted
50 g ground rice	2 oz ground rice
200 g butter	8 oz butter
100 g caster sugar	4 oz caster sugar
Finely grated rind of 1 lemon	Finely grated rind of 1 lemon
50 g walnuts, finely chopped	2 oz walnuts, finely chopped
1 egg yolk	1 egg yolk
300 ml whipping cream	½ pint whipping cream
2 x 435 g cans loganberries or raspberries, or 225 g thawed frozen berries, well drained	2 x 15½ oz cans loganberries or raspberries, or 8 oz thawed frozen berries, well drained
Icing sugar	Icing sugar

Put the flour, ground rice, butter, sugar and lemon rind in a bowl and rub together until the mixture resembles breadcrumbs. Add the walnuts and egg yolk and knead together to give a soft dough. Chill, wrapped in a polythene bag, for 30 minutes.

Roll out two-thirds of the dough into a rectangle 30 by 15 cm (12 by 6 inches) and place carefully on a baking sheet. Roll out the remaining dough and cut into six 7.5 cm (3 inch) rounds with a fluted pastry cutter. Cut each in half to form semi-circles. Place on another baking sheet.

Bake in a preheated moderate oven (180°C/350°F, Gas Mark 4), allowing about 30 minutes for the rectangle and about 20 minutes for the semi-circles, or until light brown and firm to the touch. While on the baking sheet, cut the rectangle in half lengthways with a sharp knife. Cool on the baking sheet, then remove to a wire rack. Wrap in foil to store.

About 1 hour before required, whip the cream until stiff. With a forcing bag fitted with a large rose vegetable nozzle, pipe two-thirds in a thick line down the centre of one shortbread rectangle half. Spoon almost all the loganberries or raspberries over the piped cream. Place the second rectangle half over the berries and press down lightly. Pipe the remaining cream in whirls down the centre. Arrange the shortbread semi-circles along the cream and mount a whole berry between each. Dust with icing sugar.

Above: Red cabbage and sweetcorn salad. Right: Shortcake gâteau; Peach and apple soufflé.

PEACH AND APPLE SOUFFLÉ

Metric	Imperial
500 g cooking apples, peeled, cored and sliced	1¼ lb cooking apples, peeled, cored and sliced
1 x 435 g can peach slices	1 x 15½ oz can peach slices
6 eggs, separated	6 eggs, separated
275 g caster sugar	10 oz caster sugar
2 x 15 ml spoons lemon juice	2 tablespoons lemon juice
5 x 5 ml spoons powdered gelatine	5 teaspoons powdered gelatine
3 x 15 ml spoons water	3 tablespoons water
2 x 15 ml spoons orange-flavoured liqueur	2 tablespoons orange-flavoured liqueur
150 ml single cream	¼ pint single cream
300 ml double cream	½ pint double cream
Few black grapes (some frosted) and candied angelica to decorate	Few black grapes (some frosted) and candied angelica to decorate

Stew the apples in 6 x 15 ml spoons (6 tablespoons) of the peach can syrup until soft. Cool. Sieve or liquidize with the drained peaches. Put the egg yolks, sugar and lemon juice in a heatproof bowl over a pan of hot water and whisk until very thick and creamy and the whisk leaves a trail when lifted. Remove from the heat and whisk until cool.

Dissolve the gelatine in the water in a heatproof bowl over a pan of hot water, then cool slightly. Whisk the fruit purée into the egg mixture, followed by the gelatine and liqueur. Whip the creams together until thick but not stiff and fold into the mixture. Finally, whisk the egg whites until stiff and fold in. Turn into a 1.5 litre (2½ pint) soufflé dish fitted with a paper collar and chill in the refrigerator until set.

Use a round-bladed knife to remove the collar from the soufflé, and decorate the top with grapes and angelica cut into diamonds.
Note: To frost grapes, first dip them into egg white, then coat thoroughly in caster sugar. Leave to dry.

PICNIC FOR EIGHT ON BEACH OR BOAT, USING A CAMPING STOVE

Picnic stick/Sausage and apple burgers, Selection of cold meats, French bread, butter, Radishes/Ice cream, Butterscotch sauce

PICNIC STICK

Make two

Metric	Imperial
65 g butter	2½ oz butter
2 x 15 ml spoons milk	2 tablespoons milk
4 eggs, lightly beaten	4 eggs, lightly beaten
Salt	Salt
Freshly ground black pepper	Freshly ground black pepper
1 x 30 cm French loaf	1 x 12 inch French loaf
100 g salami, thinly sliced and skinned	4 oz salami, thinly sliced and skinned
2 firm tomatoes, sliced	2 firm tomatoes, sliced
Thinly sliced cucumber	Thinly sliced cucumber
Black olives	Black olives

Above: Picnic stick. Right: Sausage and apple burgers; Selection of cold meats; Butterscotch sauce.

Melt 15 g (½ oz) of the butter in a saucepan. Add the milk, then stir in the eggs and seasoning. Cook gently, stirring constantly, until the eggs thicken and become creamy. Don't let them become dry. Remove from the heat while still a little runny. Turn out of the pan and cool.

Split the French loaf lengthways, without cutting all the way through, and butter the cut surfaces using the remaining butter. Place a little of the scrambled egg in the centre of each salami slice. Fold or roll them up and wedge upright in the French loaf. Fill the gaps with any remaining scrambled egg and put slices of tomato and cucumber along the sides. Finish with black olives. Eat fresh. Serves 4

SAUSAGE AND APPLE BURGERS

Metric	Imperial
1 x 40 g packet dried onion slices	1 x 1.4 oz packet dried onion slices
2 x 42 g packets quick-dried apple flakes	2 x 1½ oz packets quick-dried apple flakes
750 g pork sausage meat	1½ lb pork sausage meat
50 g fresh white breadcrumbs	2 oz fresh white breadcrumbs
2 x 5 ml spoons dried mixed herbs	2 teaspoons dried mixed herbs
Salt	Salt
Freshly ground black pepper	Freshly ground black pepper
1 egg, beaten	1 egg, beaten
25 g seasoned flour	1 oz seasoned flour
1 x 15 ml spoon oil	1 tablespoon oil

Reconstitute the onion slices and apple flakes separately as directed on the packets. Press out excess moisture and put them in a large bowl. With a wooden spoon, work in the sausage meat, breadcrumbs, mixed herbs and seasoning. Bind together with the beaten egg. Shape the sausage mixture into eight round cakes about 2 cm (¾ inch) thick. Turn in seasoned flour to coat.

Fry the burgers in the oil in a large pan for about 20 minutes, until well browned, turning once. Serve in soft buns with apple chutney, onion rings, tomato slices, etc.

A selection of cold meats to serve as an addition to this menu could include honey glazed ham, tongue, Danish salami, ham sausage, German garlic sausage and thinly sliced cold pork. Wrap each kind of meat separately in waxed or greaseproof paper and pack in a lidded plastic box. Take homemade chutney or French mustard to serve with the cold meats.

BUTTERSCOTCH SAUCE

Metric	Imperial
90 g dark soft brown sugar	3½ oz dark soft brown sugar
175 g golden syrup	6 oz golden syrup
50 g butter	2 oz butter
150 ml single cream	¼ pint single cream
2 x 15 ml spoons lemon juice	2 tablespoons lemon juice

Heat the sugar, syrup and butter in a pan for 5 minutes, stirring to dissolve the sugar. Off the heat, stir in the cream and lemon juice. (Keeps well in a screwtop jar for several days.)
Note: Remove the ice cream from the freezer at the last possible moment and take in an insulated container or wide-mouthed vacuum jar. (Or buy it near the picnic site!)

Picnic Ideas

Harvest Pasties

Metric	Imperial
2 x 15 ml spoons oil	2 tablespoons oil
100 g peeled and diced carrot	4 oz peeled and diced carrot
100 g trimmed and diced celery	4 oz trimmed and diced celery
100 g diced leek	4 oz diced leek
1 x 5 ml spoon yeast extract	1 teaspoon yeast extract
1 x 5 ml spoon Worcestershire sauce	1 teaspoon Worcestershire sauce
1 x 220 g can baked beans	1 x 7¾ oz can baked beans
Salt	Salt
Freshly ground black pepper	Freshly ground black pepper
225 g shortcrust pastry, made with 225 g plain flour and 100 g fat	8 oz shortcrust pastry, made with 8 oz plain flour and 4 oz fat
1 egg, beaten	1 egg, beaten

Heat the oil in a pan and fry the vegetables gently until soft – about 10 minutes. Stir in the yeast extract, Worcestershire sauce, baked beans and seasoning to taste. Cool.

Roll out the dough on a floured surface and cut out four rounds, each 16 cm (6½ inches) in diameter. Divide the vegetable mixture between the four rounds. Brush the edges with egg and bring the sides to the centre. Press together with the fingertips to seal. Place on a baking sheet. Using scissors, snip the pastry edge in diagonal cuts, about 1 cm (½ inch) inwards. Glaze with beaten egg and bake in a preheated moderately hot oven (190°C/375°F, Gas Mark 5) for 20 minutes. Glaze again with egg and return to the oven for a further 10 to 15 minutes baking. Wrap each pastry in foil for carrying to the picnic. Makes 4

Mini Heroes

Metric	Imperial
1 x 454 g packet brown bread mix	1 x 1 lb packet brown bread mix
Beaten egg	Beaten egg
175 g butter or soft margarine	6 oz butter or soft margarine
3 x 15 ml spoons horseradish relish	3 tablespoons horseradish relish
3 x 113 g packets sliced Danish salami	3 x 4 oz packets sliced Danish salami
1 x 298 g can green cut asparagus spears, drained	1 x 10½ oz can green cut asparagus spears, drained

Prepare and knead the dough according to the packet instructions. Wrap about one-sixth in greaseproof paper and keep in the refrigerator. Divide the remaining dough into 16 even pieces. Shape into finger rolls and place on lightly greased backing sheets. Loosely cover with oiled cling wrap and leave to rise in a warm place until double in size.

Shape the refrigerated dough into 16 plaits the same length as the rolls. Make an indentation along each proved roll and place a plait in each. Glaze with beaten egg. Bake in a preheated hot oven (220°C/425°F, Gas Mark 7) for 15 to 20 minutes. Cool.

Split the rolls (which should be eaten fresh) and spread each half with the butter or margarine and horseradish, creamed together. Fill with slices of salami rolled around asparagus pieces. Cover with cling wrap until required. (Wrap individually in cling wrap or foil for taking to the picnic.) Serves 8

Below: Harvest pasties; Mini heroes. Right: Picnic sandwich box; Tuna quiche.

PICNIC SANDWICH BOX

Metric	Imperial
1 small uncut crusty bloomer loaf	1 small uncut crusty bloomer loaf
75 g butter, melted	3 oz butter, melted
225 g pork sausage meat	8 oz pork sausage meat
100 g cooked ham, diced	4 oz cooked ham, diced
100 g cooked tongue, diced	4 oz cooked tongue, diced
50 g onion, peeled and chopped	2 oz onion, peeled and chopped
2 eggs	2 eggs
150 ml milk	$\frac{1}{4}$ pint milk
Salt	Salt
Freshly ground black pepper	Freshly ground black pepper
2 eggs, hard-boiled and halved	2 eggs, hard-boiled and halved

Cut horizontally across the loaf, two-thirds of the way up, and remove this 'lid'. Gently ease away the bread from around the edge of the crust. Make 100 g (4 oz) breadcrumbs from the bread. Brush the cavity of the loaf and the lid with some of the melted butter.

Combine the sausage meat, chopped meats, breadcrumbs and onion. Beat the two eggs and milk together. Season well. Combine with the meat mixture. Place one third of the filling in the bread case and arrange the halved hard-boiled eggs lengthways on top. Pack around with the remaining filling, then top with the bread lid.

Secure the loaf in a parcel-like fashion with string. Use the remaining melted butter to brush all over the loaf. Place on a baking sheet. Bake in a preheated moderately hot oven (200°C/400°F, Gas Mark 6) for 15 minutes. Cover with foil and continue baking for 45 minutes. When cool, remove the string. Wrap in foil for carrying to the picnic. Cut in thick slices to serve. Serves 8

TUNA QUICHE

Metric	Imperial
225 g dry shortcrust pastry mix	8 oz dry shortcrust pastry mix
1 x 15 ml spoon oil	1 tablespoon oil
175 g plump spring onions, trimmed and cut into 6 mm slices	6 oz plump spring onions, trimmed and cut into $\frac{1}{4}$ inch slices
1 x 198 g can tuna, drained and flaked	1 x 7 oz can tuna, drained and flaked
2 eggs	2 eggs
300 ml milk	$\frac{1}{2}$ pint milk
Salt	Salt
Freshly ground black pepper	Freshly ground black pepper
Grated Parmesan cheese	Grated Parmesan cheese

Make up the pastry dough as instructed on the packet. Roll out and use to line a 23 cm (9 inch) flan dish. Bake blind in a preheated moderately hot oven (200°C/400°F, Gas Mark 6) for 15 minutes or until the pastry shows signs of browning.

Heat the oil in a frying pan and fry the spring onions for about 3 minutes. Drain well. Arrange the onions and tuna in the pastry case. Whisk together the eggs and milk and season well. Pour over the filling in the pastry case. Sprinkle the centre with Parmesan cheese. Bake in a preheated moderate oven (180°C/350°F, Gas Mark 4) for 30 to 35 minutes until the filling sets and lightly browns. Take to the picnic in the flan dish, foil wrapped. Serves 6

CURRIED BACON FLAN

Metric
175 g shortcrust pastry, made
  with 175 g plain flour 75 g fat
15 g margarine
100 g celery heart, sliced
100 g streaky bacon rashers,
  rinds removed, chopped
1 x 5 ml spoon mild curry powder
3 eggs, beaten
150 ml unsweetened natural
  yogurt
Salt
Freshly ground black pepper
225 g tomatoes, skinned and
  thinly sliced
Chopped parsley to garnish

Imperial
6 oz shortcrust pastry, made with
  6 oz plain flour and 3 oz fat
½ oz margarine
4 oz celery heart, sliced
4 oz streaky bacon rashers, rinds
  removed, chopped
1 teaspoon mild curry powder
3 eggs, beaten
¼ pint unsweetened natural
  yogurt
Salt
Freshly ground black pepper
8 oz tomatoes, skinned and
  thinly sliced
Chopped parsley to garnish

Roll out the dough and use to line a 21.5 cm (8¼ inch) loose-bottomed French fluted flan tin. Bake blind in a moderately hot oven (200°C/400°F, Gas Mark 6) until the pastry is quite dry and just beginning to colour. Cool.

Melt the margarine in a small frying pan and fry the celery and bacon until the celery is golden brown. Stir in the curry powder and cook for 2 minutes to draw out the flavour.

Mix the eggs with the yogurt. Add the pan ingredients and seasoning, and turn into the flan case. Top with the tomato slices. Bake in a preheated moderately hot oven (190°C/375°F, Gas Mark 5) for about 25 minutes. Cool, then sprinkle with parsley. Carry in the tin. Serves 6

Left: Curried bacon flan. Above: Farmhouse cake.

FARMHOUSE CAKE

Metric
225 g wholemeal flour
225 g plain flour
1 x 5 ml spoon mixed spice
1 x 5 ml spoon bicarbonate of
  soda
175 g block margarine
225 g sugar
100 g sultanas, cleaned
100 g seedless raisins, cleaned
3 x 15 ml spoons chopped mixed
  peel
1 egg, beaten
300 ml milk

Imperial
8 oz wholemeal flour
8 oz plain flour
1 teaspoon mixed spice
1 teaspoon bicarbonate of soda
6 oz block margarine
8 oz sugar
4 oz sultanas, cleaned
4 oz seedless raisins, cleaned
3 tablespoons chopped mixed
  peel
1 egg, beaten
½ pint milk

Grease and flour a 20 cm (8 inch) cake tin. Sift the flours, spice and bicarbonate of soda into a bowl. Rub the fat into the dry ingredients until the mixture resembles fine breadcrumbs. Stir in the sugar, fruit and peel. Make a well in the centre and pour in the egg and some of the milk. Gradually work into the dry ingredients, adding more milk if necessary to give a dropping consistency. Put the mixture into the tin and level the top. Bake in a preheated moderate oven (160°C/325°F, Gas Mark 3) for about 2 hours, until firm to the touch. Turn out and cool on a wire rack. Wrap in foil and put in a firm container for carrying to the picnic.
Makes a 20 cm (8 inch) round cake

BARBECUES

Barbecue food needs to be spicy and satisfying. Choose your favourites from the following selection.

BARBECUE BASTING SAUCE

Combine a 225 g (8 oz) jar of tomato chutney, 1 x 5 ml spoon (1 teaspoon) each of dry mustard, soft brown sugar and salt, 1 x 15 ml spoon (1 tablespoon) Worcestershire sauce, 1 x 15 ml spoon (1 tablespoon) lemon juice, 120 ml (4 fl oz) each dry red wine and corn oil, a crushed garlic clove and a dash of Tabasco. This can be used for any meat or poultry.

With any barbecue grill, have a big salad bowl on hand, made with finely shredded cabbage, sliced radishes and sweet peppers, broken walnut pieces and snipped chives, moistened with French dressing or topped with mayonnaise.

Delicious extras for a barbecue are wedges of eating apple or halves of fresh juicy apricots, bacon-wrapped on skewers.

BARBECUE SAUCE

Metric	Imperial
50 g butter	2 oz butter
100 g onion, peeled and finely chopped	4 oz onion, peeled and finely chopped
1 x 226 g can tomatoes	1 x 8 oz can tomatoes
2 x 5 ml spoons tomato paste	2 teaspoons tomato paste
2 x 15 ml spoons vinegar	2 tablespoons vinegar
2 x 15 ml spoons demerara sugar	2 tablespoons demerara sugar
2 x 5 ml spoons dry mustard	2 teaspoons dry mustard
2 x 15 ml spoons Worcestershire sauce	2 tablespoons Worcestershire sauce

Melt the butter in a saucepan and fry the onion until soft but not browned. Stir in the remaining sauce ingredients and simmer, partially covered, for 25 minutes. Serve with barbecued chicken pieces, chops or sausages.

BARBECUE-STYLE MUSTARD CHICKEN

Several hours before, spread the mustard butter over the chicken pieces and keep them in the refrigerator until required for grilling.

Metric	Imperial
1 x 1.75 kg chicken	1 x 3½ lb chicken
50 g butter, softened	2 oz butter, softened
3 x 15 ml spoons coarse-grain mustard	3 tablespoons coarse-grain mustard
Grated rind of 1 lemon	Grated rind of 1 lemon
1 x 15 ml spoon lemon juice	1 tablespoon lemon juice
1 x 5 ml spoon chopped fresh tarragon or rosemary	1 teaspoon chopped fresh tarragon or rosemary
Salt	Salt
Freshly ground black pepper	Freshly ground black pepper

Joint the chicken into eight pieces and trim off any excess fat, leaving the skin on. In a bowl, cream the butter and work in the mustard a little at a time, using a wooden spoon. Add the lemon rind, then gradually beat in the lemon juice and the herbs. Season well. Spread the mustard butter over the chicken pieces, coating evenly.

Heat the grill and cook the chicken on the rack for 10 to 15 minutes on each side until the skin is crisp and golden and the chicken is tender. Some of the mustard mixture may slide off, in which case spoon it from the grill pan over the chicken when serving.

When cooking is done on a barbecue, keep back some of the mustard butter and spread it on the chicken pieces as they cook.
Serves 4 to 6

Barbecue-style mustard chicken, which can be cooked in batches.

HERRING PARCELS WITH MUSTARD BUTTER

The fish boats can be prepared several hours ahead and kept cool, covered, until needed for cooking.

Metric	Imperial
75 g butter, softened	3 oz butter, softened
2 x 15 ml spoons Dijon mustard	2 tablespoons Dijon mustard
2 x 15 ml spoons chopped parsley	2 tablespoons chopped parsley
Salt	Salt
Freshly ground black pepper	Freshly ground black pepper
2 herrings or mackerel, cleaned and heads removed	2 herrings or mackerel, cleaned and heads removed
½ lemon, cut into wedges	½ lemon, cut into wedges

Combine the softened butter with the mustard, parsley and seasoning. Shape two pieces of foil, each 23 by 23 cm (9 by 9 inches) into two boat-shapes suitable to hold the fish. Spread a little of the savoury butter on the bottom of the foil. Fill the cavity of each fish with more of the savoury butter, reserving 2 x 5 ml spoons (2 teaspoons). Make three slits at a slant on each side of each fish.

Place each fish in a foil 'boat' and top with the reserved butter. Cook over the barbecue for about 10 to 15 minutes, turning once during cooking. Serve in the boat to keep the juices and garnish with the lemon wedges. Serves 2

Note: For lemon tarragon butter, beat 125 g (4 oz) butter with 3 x 15 ml spoons (3 tablespoons) lemon juice, 1 x 15 ml spoon (1 tablespoon) chopped fresh tarragon and seasoning. Score the fish and spread with the butter. Place in foil boats and cook as above.

Below: Herring parcels with mustard butter. Right: Apricot cheese sponge cake; Strawberry mallows; Minced meat shashlik.

MINCED MEAT SHASHLIK

The meatballs can be made and threaded onto the skewers, with the onions and bay leaves, several hours ahead. Keep covered and cool. Brush with oil just before cooking.

Metric	Imperial
500 g lean minced beef (minced twice)	1 lb lean minced beef (minced twice)
1 x 5 ml spoon salt	1 teaspoon salt
1 x 1.25 ml spoon freshly ground black pepper	¼ teaspoon freshly ground black pepper
1 x 15 ml spoon peeled and grated onion	1 tablespoon peeled and grated onion
1 x 15 ml spoon Worcestershire sauce	1 tablespoon Worcestershire sauce
4 large onions	4 large onions
Bay leaves	Bay leaves
Oil	Oil
2 small tomatoes, halved	2 small tomatoes, halved
Fine strips of canned pimiento (optional)	Fine strips of canned pimiento (optional)

Combine the beef, salt, pepper, grated onion and Worcestershire sauce well together. Shape into small balls about the size of a large walnut. Put the onions in a bowl. Pour boiling water over and leave for 2 to 3 minutes. Drain and peel, then quarter. Thread onto four skewers with the meatballs and bay leaves. Brush with oil. Cook on the barbecue, turning until almost cooked.

Place the seasoned tomato halves on the skewers and cook for a further 5 minutes. Serves 4

Note: The shashlik can be cooked under a preheated grill for 10 minutes, turning once. The sliced pimiento can be added to the juices in the grill pan and spooned over the shashlik before serving.

APRICOT CHEESE SPONGE CAKE

Metric	Imperial
2 x 15 ml spoons apricot jam	2 tablespoons apricot jam
1 x 18 cm bought sponge flan case	1 x 7 inch bought sponge flan case
225 g cream cheese	8 oz cream cheese
1 sachet Dream topping	1 sachet Dream topping
150 ml milk	¼ pint milk
4 x 15 ml spoons lemon juice	4 tablespoons lemon juice
Grated rind of 1 lemon	Grated rind of 1 lemon
25 g sultanas, cleaned	1 oz sultanas, cleaned
Jam for topping	Jam for topping

Spread the apricot jam on the bottom of the flan case. Beat the cheese until soft. Make up the Dream topping with the milk and beat into the cheese. Beat in the lemon juice and rind and the sultanas. Pile into the flan case and drizzle on a little more jam. Serves 4 to 6

STRAWBERRY MALLOWS

Metric	Imperial
4 chocolate caramel bars	4 chocolate caramel bars
4 x 15 ml spoons single cream	4 tablespoons single cream
20 strawberries	20 strawberries
20 marshmallows	20 marshmallows

Round off the party in a spectacular – but simple – way. Melt the caramel bars gently (over a low heat or in a double saucepan), then stir in the cream. Keep warm.

Spear a berry and a marshmallow on a skewer and grill until the mallow starts to brown – but no longer. Dip into the chocolate caramel sauce and serve immediately. Serves 6

POSH PICNIC FOR SIX FOR TRANSPORTING IN THE BACK OF THE CAR

Cold avocado soup/Seafood quiches/Melton Mowbray pie, Chicory and black olive salad/Fresh lime mousse, Strawberries and cream

BEFOREHAND

Cold avocado soup
Make a day or two beforehand. When cool, refrigerate in a lidded polythene bowl or vacuum flask which can be put straight into the picnic basket on the day. Chop parsley or chives and keep in the refrigerator in a polythene bag. Stir soup before serving and sprinkle each cupful with the garnish.

Seafood quiches
Make the day before or on the morning of the picnic allowing time for the quiches to cool.

Melton Mowbray pie
Make a day or two beforehand and wrap lightly; keep refrigerated.

Chicory and black olive salad
Mix the dressing a day or two beforehand and keep in a screwtop jar (not in the refrigerator). Prepare chicory the day before; refrigerate in a polythene bag.

Fresh lime mousse
Make the day before and keep in refrigerator, lightly covered.

Cold avocado soup; Seafood quiches.

COLD AVOCADO SOUP

Metric	Imperial
25 g butter	1 oz butter
25 g plain flour	1 oz plain flour
150 ml milk	$\frac{1}{4}$ pint milk
900 ml chicken stock	$1\frac{1}{2}$ pints chicken stock
1 x 1.25 ml spoon salt	$\frac{1}{4}$ teaspoon salt
Freshly ground black pepper	Freshly ground black pepper
1 small green pepper, cored, seeded and chopped	1 small green pepper, cored, seeded and chopped
1 ripe avocado	1 ripe avocado
Chopped parsley or snipped fresh chives to garnish	Chopped parsley or snipped fresh chives to garnish

Melt the butter in a saucepan. Stir in the flour and cook gently over a low heat for about 3 minutes, without browning. Remove from the heat and gradually stir in the milk, then the stock. Add the salt, pepper and green pepper and bring to the boil. Simmer, covered, for 15 minutes.

Meanwhile, halve and stone the avocado. Scrape out the flesh and mash to a smooth cream. Mix some of the thickened stock with the avocado and stir it back into the pan. Cook the soup for a few minutes but do not boil it. Strain to remove the green pepper. Allow to cool. Serve garnished with parsley or chives. Take to the picnic in a vacuum flask.

SEAFOOD QUICHES

Metric	Imperial
200 g shortcrust pastry, made with 200 g plain flour and 115 g fat	7 oz shortcrust pastry, made with 7 oz plain flour and $3\frac{1}{2}$ oz fat
100 g shelled prawns, chopped	4 oz shelled prawns, chopped
75 g smoked salmon, cut into strips	3 oz smoked salmon, cut into strips
300 ml single cream	$\frac{1}{2}$ pint single cream
4 egg yolks	4 egg yolks
Salt	Salt
Freshly ground black pepper	Freshly ground black pepper
2 x 15 ml spoons chopped parsley	2 tablespoons chopped parsley

Roll out the dough and use to line six 10 cm (4 inch) shallow patty pans or individual tartlet tins. Knock up the edges.

Divide the prawns and salmon equally between the uncooked pastry cases. Beat the cream and egg yolks together. Season to taste, remembering that the salmon tends to be salty. Add half the chopped parsley. Spoon into the pastry cases placed on a baking sheet. Bake in a preheated moderately hot oven (200°C/400°F, Gas Mark 6) for 10 minutes. Reduce the heat to moderate (180°C/350°F, Gas Mark 4) and cook for a further 20 to 25 minutes until the pastry is beginning to colour and the filling is lightly set.

Take in the patty pans, foil-wrapped and placed in a square container to hold firm, for transportation. Garnish with the remaining parsley just before serving. Makes 6

Melton Mowbray pie; Chicory and black olive salad.

MELTON MOWBRAY PIE

Metric	Imperial
For the pastry:	**For the pastry:**
225 g plain flour	8 oz plain flour
1 x 5 ml spoon salt	1 teaspoon salt
100 g lard	4 oz lard
5 x 15 ml spoons milk and water mixed	5 tablespoons milk and water mixed
Beaten egg to glaze	Beaten egg to glaze
For the filling:	**For the filling:**
500 g lean pork, finely diced	1 lb lean pork, finely diced
Salt	Salt
Freshly ground black pepper	Freshly ground black pepper
1 sage leaf, finely chopped, or 1 x 1.25 ml spoon dried sage	1 sage leaf, finely chopped, or ¼ teaspoon dried sage
2 x 15 ml spoons water	2 tablespoons water
Melted jellied stock	Melted jellied stock

Sift the flour and salt together and rub in 50 g (2 oz) of the lard. Melt the remaining lard in the milk and water and stir into the flour. Knead until smooth. Reserve one-quarter of the dough and keep covered. Roll out the remainder on a floured surface to a 25 cm (10 inch) circle. Use to line a 15 cm (6 inch) greased and bottom-lined round cake tin.

Mix the pork with seasoning, the sage and water. Fill the pastry case. Brush the top edge of the dough with beaten egg. Roll out the reserved dough into a circle and use to cover the pie. Crimp the edges to seal, cut a small hole in the centre and glaze with beaten egg. Bake in a preheated hot oven (220°C/425°F, Gas Mark 7) for 30 minutes, then reduce the heat to moderate (160°C/325°F, Gas Mark 3) and continue baking for 1½ hours.

Cool and remove from the tin. Top up the pie with melted jellied stock through the hole. Make sure the pie has cooled and the stock firmly jellied before wrapping it for the picnic.

CHICORY AND BLACK OLIVE SALAD

Metric	Imperial
2 x 15 ml spoons vinegar	2 tablespoons vinegar
2 x 5 ml spoons honey	2 teaspoons honey
2 onions, peeled and finely chopped	2 onions, peeled and finely chopped
4 x 15 ml spoons salad oil	4 tablespoons salad oil
2 x 15 ml spoons lemon juice	2 tablespoons lemon juice
Pinch of sugar	Pinch of sugar
Pinch of salt	Pinch of salt
4 heads of chicory, trimmed and thinly sliced	4 heads of chicory, trimmed and thinly sliced
12 black olives, stoned	12 black olives, stoned

Put the vinegar, honey, onions, oil, lemon juice, sugar and salt in a screwtop jar and shake well together. Put the chicory and olives in a large lidded plastic bowl and pour over the dressing. Toss. Place the lid firmly on top for transportation. Toss well again before serving.

FRESH LIME MOUSSE

Metric	Imperial
3 eggs, separated	3 eggs, separated
100 g caster sugar	4 oz caster sugar
Finely grated rind and juice of 2 limes	Finely grated rind and juice of 2 limes
1 x 15 ml spoon powdered gelatine	1 tablespoon powdered gelatine
150 ml double cream	¼ pint double cream
Sliced strawberries to decorate	Sliced strawberries to decorate

Put the egg yolks in a deep heatproof bowl over warm water with the sugar and lime rind and whisk until thick and mousse-like. (If using an electric mixer no heat is needed.) Meanwhile, soak the gelatine in the strained lime juice in a small heatproof bowl. Dissolve by standing the bowl in a pan of gently simmering water. Whip the cream to the floppy stage, then fold it through the mousse with the dissolved gelatine. Whisk the egg whites until stiff and fold in.

Turn into six individual unbreakable dishes or one large unbreakable plastic bowl. Refrigerate until firm. Decorate with sliced strawberries. Cover firmly with cling-wrap (or lids) before transportation. Keep as cool as possible.

Note: Instead of the rind and juice of the 2 fresh limes, 6 x 15 ml spoons (6 tablespoons) of "Lazy Lime Juice" can be used.

Fresh lime mousse.

BUFFET PARTIES

A help-yourself party is the best way of entertaining more than a handful of people, and careful planning can ensure that preparations go smoothly and that the party itself is a success. Choose a menu to suit your mood, your purse and your kitchen – and your culinary skill. Even if you haven't a freezer, you can do a lot of cooking beforehand, such as making meringues, gâteaux bases, pastry cases and fillings.

List the utensils and dishes you'll need for cooking as well as for serving, and borrow from friends if necessary. For the actual party, arrange the cold savouries, with cutlery, plates and napkins, on a table sited so that guests can move around freely and help themselves from all sides, and make sure there are enough serving spoons. Bring in hot dishes at the last possible minute. The desserts should be on another table or on a trolley in the kitchen, ready to be wheeled in; another table or sideboard will be needed for the drinks.

WINTER PARTY FOR TWELVE

Beef and wine potato pie, Courgette and orange salad, Platter salad (see page 128) /Caramel mousse

BEFOREHAND

Beef and wine potato pie
Prepare up to and including covering with mousseline potatoes. Cover and refrigerate.

Courgette and orange salad
Prepare the courgettes the day before, but don't combine with the dressing until the afternoon of the party.

Platter salad
Prepare, bag up and chill the salad items. If using chicory, wash it but leave slicing until assembly time. Fennel, if used, should be used sparingly; slice it thinly and brush at once with lemon juice or marinate in dressing. Prepare a large amount of mustardy French dressing (see page 91).

Caramel mousse
Make this the day before; keep it chilled, undecorated.

BEEF AND WINE POTATO PIE

Make two

Metric	Imperial
1.5 kg chuck steak	3 lb chuck steak
225 g lean streaky bacon, rinds removed	8 oz lean streaky bacon, rinds removed
50 g lard	2 oz lard
3 x 15 ml spoons plain flour	3 tablespoons plain flour
300 ml red wine	$\frac{1}{2}$ pint red wine
150 ml stock	$\frac{1}{4}$ pint stock
1 x 2.5 ml spoon mixed herbs	$\frac{1}{2}$ teaspoon mixed herbs
1 bay leaf	1 bay leaf
1 garlic clove, crushed	1 garlic clove, crushed
225 g onions, peeled and sliced	8 oz onions, peeled and sliced
175 g small button mushrooms	6 oz small button mushrooms
For the mousseline potatoes:	**For the mousseline potatoes:**
1.5 kg old potatoes, peeled and boiled	3 lb old potatoes, peeled and boiled
150 ml hot milk	$\frac{1}{4}$ pint hot milk
3 eggs, separated	3 eggs, separated
75 g Cheddar cheese, grated	3 oz Cheddar cheese, grated
50 g butter	2 oz butter
2 x 15 ml spoons chopped parsley	2 tablespoons chopped parsley
Salt	Salt
Freshly ground black pepper	Freshly ground black pepper

Mince the chuck steak and bacon, or ask your butcher to do it for you. Melt half the lard and quickly fry the mince until it starts to brown. Stir in the flour and cook for a few minutes. Add the wine and stock slowly, stirring all the time. Add the herbs, bay leaf and garlic. Turn the mixture into a large entrée-type ovenproof dish or a 30.5

cm (12 inch) diameter shallow casserole. Cover and bake in a preheated moderate oven (180°C/350°F, Gas Mark 4) for 30 minutes.

For the mousseline potatoes, sieve the potatoes. Beat the hot milk, egg yolks, grated cheese, butter and chopped parsley into the potatoes. Season to taste. Whisk the egg whites until stiff and fold in.

Melt the rest of the lard and fry the onions until golden. Add the mushrooms and cook for 5 minutes. Drain well and stir into the mince. Cover with the mousseline potatoes and return to a moderately hot oven (200°C/400°F, Gas Mark 6) to bake for about 30 minutes or until golden brown. Serves 6

Note: If preparing ahead of time, cover the mince with the mousseline potatoes, then allow to cool. Cover the dish or casserole and refrigerate. When needed, reheat in a moderately hot oven (200°C/400°F, Gas Mark 6) for 50 minutes, covering with foil after 30 minutes if the top is too brown.

COURGETTE AND ORANGE SALAD

Metric	Imperial
1.5 kg courgettes, cut into 1 cm slices	3 lb courgettes, cut into $\frac{1}{2}$ inch slices
Salt	Salt
6 oranges	6 oranges
175 ml mayonnaise	6 fl oz mayonnaise
120 ml single cream	4 fl oz single cream
Chopped parsley to garnish	Chopped parsley to garnish

Blanch the courgettes in boiling salted water for 3 minutes. Drain and rinse in cold water. Pat dry on absorbent kitchen paper.

Grate the rind from the oranges and add to the mayonnaise with the cream. Peel the oranges and separate into segments. Put with any juice in a bowl with the courgettes. Toss in the mayonnaise mixture. Cover and chill for several hours.

Turn into a serving dish and garnish with parsley.

CARAMEL MOUSSE

Metric	Imperial
4 eggs, separated	4 eggs, separated
4 egg yolks	4 egg yolks
100 g caster sugar	4 oz caster sugar
1.2 litres lukewarm milk	2 pints lukewarm milk
500 g granulated sugar	1 lb 2 oz granulated sugar
400 ml warm water	14 fl oz warm water
9 x 5 ml spoons powdered gelatine	9 teaspoons powdered gelatine
6 x 15 ml spoons lemon juice	6 tablespoons lemon juice
600 ml whipping cream	1 pint whipping cream
Broken walnuts to decorate	Broken walnuts to decorate

Whisk all the egg yolks and caster sugar in a saucepan until thick. Add the milk and cook over a low heat without boiling, stirring all the time, until the custard thickens slightly. Cool.

Dissolve the granulated sugar in half the water. Boil to a rich dark caramel, then immediately pour in the remaining water. (Cover your hand while you do this as the caramel splutters.) Stir over a low heat to amalgamate, then pour into the custard.

Soak the gelatine in the lemon juice in a small heatproof bowl and dissolve by standing the bowl in a pan of simmering water. Add to the cool custard mixture. Chill until the mixture begins to set.

Lightly whip the cream. Whisk the egg whites until stiff. Fold half the cream and all the egg whites into the setting custard mixture. Turn into two 1.8 litre (3 pint) ring moulds or glass dishes and refrigerate until set. Decorate with whirls of the remaining whipped cream and walnuts. Makes 2 mousses, each to serve 6

Above: Caramel mousse. Below: Beef and wine potato pie; Courgette and orange salad.

Buffet Supper for Ten to Twelve Using Convenience Foods

Smoked mackerel salad, Tivoli salad, Walnut cheesies, Poppy seed knots/Lemon chiffon pie, or Apricot orange flan (see page 14)

Beforehand

Smoked mackerel salad
Early in the day, prepare the potato, mackerel and celery up to the addition of the dressing. Keep in covered containers in the refrigerator.

Tivoli salad
Prepare the vegetables, meat and cheese on the morning of the party. Fold the mayonnaise through just before serving.

Walnut cheesies
Better made on the afternoon of the party, but can be made the day before; in this case, keep them whole and refresh when needed.

Poppy seed knots
Better if made fresh, but can be made before. Refresh when needed.

Lemon chiffon pie
Make the day before, apart from decoration.

Apricot orange flan
Make the flan cases a day or two before; keep in airtight containers, or foil-wrapped. Fill during the afternoon.

Left: Smoked mackerel salad.

Smoked Mackerel Salad

Metric	Imperial
1 kg small new potatoes (or use canned ones)	2 lb small new potatoes (or use canned ones)
750 g smoked mackerel fillets, skinned	1½ lb smoked mackerel fillets, skinned
300 ml soured cream	½ pint soured cream
120 ml mayonnaise	4 fl oz mayonnaise
6 x 15 ml spoons horseradish sauce	6 tablespoons horseradish sauce
Salt	Salt
Freshly ground black pepper	Freshly ground black pepper
500 g celery, trimmed and sliced	1 lb celery, trimmed and sliced
Paprika	Paprika
Lemon wedges	Lemon wedges

Boil the potatoes in their skins until tender, then peel, halve and cool. Divide the mackerel into fork-size pieces.

In a large bowl, mix the soured cream with the mayonnaise, horseradish and seasoning. Stir in the fish and vegetables. Cover and chill well. Serve the salad sprinkled with paprika and accompanied by lemon wedges.

Tivoli Salad

Metric	Imperial
3 x 340 g cans pork and ham, thickly sliced, or equivalent in thickly sliced cooked ham, cut into small cubes.	3 x 12 oz cans pork and ham, thickly sliced, or equivalent in thickly sliced cooked ham, cut into small cubes
350 g Samsoe cheese, cut into small cubes	12 oz Samsoe cheese, cut into small cubes
1 x 450 g (approx) can sweetcorn kernels, drained	1 x 16 oz (approx) can sweetcorn kernels, drained
1.5 x 15 ml spoons peeled and finely chopped onion	1½ tablespoons peeled and finely chopped onion
1 large crisp lettuce, separated into leaves	1 large crisp lettuce, separated into leaves
Snipped fresh chives to garnish	Snipped fresh chives to garnish
For the dressing:	**For the dressing:**
6 x 15 ml spoons mayonnaise	6 tablespoons mayonnaise
3 x 15 ml spoons cream	3 tablespoons cream
2-3 x 15 ml spoons lemon juice	2-3 tablespoons lemon juice
Freshly ground black pepper	Freshly ground black pepper

Mix together the meat, cheese, sweetcorn and onion. Combine the mayonnaise and cream with lemon juice to sharpen. Season with pepper. Fold the mayonnaise dressing through the meat and cheese.

Arrange a bed of lettuce on a dish and pile the meat and cheese mixture on top. Garnish with chives. Serves 10

Walnut cheesies; Poppy seed knots; Tivoli salad.

WALNUT CHEESIES

Metric
1 x 283 g packet brown bread mix
100 g cream cheese
1-2 x 15 ml spoons single cream
25 g walnuts, finely chopped
Salt
Freshly ground black pepper

Imperial
1 x 10 oz packet brown bread mix
4 oz cream cheese
1-2 tablespoons single cream
1 oz walnuts, finely chopped
Salt
Freshly ground black pepper

Make up and knead the dough according to the packet instructions. Roll out on a floured surface to a 30 cm (12 inch) square. Beat the cheese with the cream, walnuts and seasoning and spread over the dough. Roll up like a Swiss roll and cut into nine even-sized slices. Place, cut sides down, in a greased and bottom-lined 16 cm (6½ inch) square cake tin. Cover loosely with oiled cling wrap and leave to rise until double in size, about 40 minutes.

Bake in a preheated very hot oven (230°C/450°F, Gas Mark 8) for about 20 minutes. Cool on a wire rack. Serve slightly warm, pulled apart like Chelsea buns. Makes 9

POPPY SEED KNOTS

Metric
1 x 283 g packet white bread mix
200 ml lukewarm milk
Beaten egg to glaze
Salt
Poppy seeds

Imperial
1 x 10 oz packet white bread mix
7 fl oz lukewarm milk
Beaten egg to glaze
Salt
Poppy seeds

Make up the dough according to the packet instructions, using the milk instead of water. Divide the kneaded dough into eight and roll each piece into a long sausage shape. Tie into a single knot. Place well apart on a greased baking sheet, cover loosely with oiled cling wrap and leave to rise in a warm place for about 40 minutes, or until double in size.

Brush evenly with beaten egg to which a pinch of salt has been added. Sprinkle with poppy seeds and bake in a preheated very hot oven (230°C/450°F, Gas Mark 8) for about 12 minutes. Cool. Break open and spread with butter to serve. These are at their best on the day they are made. Makes 8
Note: To vary, use celery seeds instead of poppy seeds, and grate 50 g (2 oz) mature cheese into the dry bread mix before making up.

Lemon chiffon pie; Apricot orange flan (see recipe page 14).

LEMON CHIFFON PIE

Make two

Metric	Imperial
125 g digestive biscuits, crushed	4 oz digestive biscuits, crushed
50 g butter, melted	2 oz butter, melted
1 x 2.5 ml spoon ground ginger	½ teaspoon ground ginger
2 medium lemons	2 medium lemons
1 small can condensed milk, or ½ large can	1 small can condensed milk, or ½ large can
1 x 5 ml spoon powdered gelatine	1 teaspoon powdered gelatine
1 egg white	1 egg white
150 ml whipping cream, lightly whipped	½ pint whipping cream, lightly whipped

Mix the biscuits with the melted butter and ground ginger. Press into an 18 cm (7 inch) loose-bottomed flan tin, lining the bottom and sides. Place in the refrigerator to firm up.

Pare a few strips of lemon rind free of all white pith. Cut into fine shreds and blanch in boiling water for a few seconds. Drain well. Grate the remaining lemon rind and squeeze the juice from the lemons. Whisk the condensed milk with 5 x 15 ml spoons (5 tablespoons) strained lemon juice and the grated lemon rind until the mixture thickens. Soak the gelatine in a further 1 x 15 ml spoon (1 tablespoon) lemon juice in a small heatproof bowl, then dissolve by standing the bowl in a pan of simmering water. Add to the condensed milk mixture.

Whisk the egg white until stiff and fold into the lemon mixture, then pour into the flan case. Refrigerate until set. Decorate with whirls of lightly whipped cream and the shreds of lemon rind.
Serves 3 to 4

SUMMER BUFFET FOR TWENTY

Curried cucumber soup (cold) /Liver pâté, Blue cheese quiche, Pink mushrooms, French bread, Garlic bread, Cold glazed bacon (see page 93), Rice salad, Greek-style, Platter salad with Celery seed dressing/Grape and banana vacherin, Compôte of peaches, Lemon sugar cookies

BEFOREHAND

Curried cucumber soup
Make the day before and keep refrigerated, covered. Remove from the refrigerator about 30 minutes before serving, and garnish when serving.

Liver pâté
Make several days ahead; keep, covered, in the refrigerator.

Blue cheese quiche
Prepare and cook the pastry the day before. Complete the quiches during the afternoon of the party.

Pink mushrooms
Make the day before and keep, covered, in the refrigerator.

Garlic bread
Prepare in the morning of the party and wrap ready for heating through later.

Cold glazed bacon
Prepare two or three days ahead; keep, covered, in the refrigerator.

Rice salad
Make the day before and keep in a cool place or the refrigerator. Unmould about 2 hours before serving; leave in a cool place (not the refrigerator).

Platter salad
Prepare during the afternoon of the party. Prepare the dressing the day before.

Grape and banana vacherin
Make the meringue rounds several days ahead; foil-wrap. Assemble with cream and fruit just before the party.

Compôte of peaches
Prepare the day before, but don't add the almonds until just before serving.

Lemon sugar cookies
Make several days ahead. Keep in airtight container.

Liver pâté; Curried cucumber soup.

CURRIED CUCUMBER SOUP

Metric	Imperial
150 g butter	5 oz butter
750 g onions, peeled and very finely chopped	1½ lb onions, peeled and very finely chopped
5 cucumbers	5 cucumbers
1 x 15 ml spoon mild curry powder	1 tablespoon mild curry powder
5 x 15 ml spoons plain flour	5 tablespoons plain flour
10 chicken stock cubes	10 chicken stock cubes
4 litres boiling water	7 pints boiling water
2 litres milk	3½ pints milk
Salt	Salt
Freshly ground black pepper	Freshly ground black pepper
Cucumber slices to garnish	Cucumber slices to garnish

Melt the butter in a large pan and fry the onions, without colouring, for 10 minutes. Add the cucumbers, grating them coarsely straight into the pan. Fry for a further 5 minutes. Stir in the curry powder and flour and cook for a few minutes.

Dissolve the stock cubes in the water and add to the pan, stirring. Bring to the boil. Cover, reduce the heat and simmer for 30 minutes.

Add the milk and reheat without boiling. Adjust the seasoning. Chill and serve cold with a garnish of wafer-thin slices of cucumber.

LIVER PÂTÉ

Metric	Imperial
225 g pigs' liver	8 oz pigs' liver
225 g calves' liver	8 oz calves' liver
500 g fat pork	1 lb fat pork
75 g onion, peeled and chopped	3 oz onion, peeled and chopped
1 garlic clove, crushed	1 garlic clove, crushed
Salt	Salt
Freshly ground black pepper	Freshly ground black pepper
150 ml dry white wine	¼ pint dry white wine
5 x 15 ml spoons brandy	5 tablespoons brandy
5 x 15 ml spoons olive oil	5 tablespoons olive oil
1 x 2.5 ml spoon dried thyme	½ teaspoon dried thyme
225 g streaky bacon rashers, rinds removed	8 oz streaky bacon rashers, rinds removed
2 eggs, beaten	2 eggs, beaten
100-125 g chicken livers, quartered	4 oz chicken livers, quartered
Juniper berries	Juniper berries
3 bay leaves	3 bay leaves
150 ml liquid aspic jelly	¼ pint liquid aspic jelly

Divide the liver and pork into small strips, discarding any skin and ducts. Place these in a bowl with the onion, garlic, seasoning, wine, brandy, oil and thyme. Cover and marinate overnight.

Stretch the rashers of bacon, using a blunt-edged knife, and use to line a 1.5 litre (2½ pint) capacity terrine dish, leaving the rashers hanging over the edge of the terrine. Drain the marinade from the other ingredients and reserve the liquid. Mince the liver mixture and return to the marinade with the eggs and chicken livers. Mix well. Turn into the lined dish. Draw the rashers over the top, cover and bake in a water bath in a preheated moderate oven (160°C/325°F, Gas Mark 3) for 1 hour. Lower the heat to cool (150°C/300°F, Gas Mark 2) and cook for a further 1¼ to 1½ hours or until firm.

Place a weight on the pâté and leave to cool overnight. Decorate with juniper berries, bay leaves and aspic for serving.

Blue Cheese Quiche

Make two

Metric	Imperial
For the pastry:	**For the pastry:**
225 g plain flour	8 oz plain flour
150 g butter or margarine	5 oz butter or margarine
1 egg yolk	1 egg yolk
2 x 15 ml spoons water	2 tablespoons water
For the filling:	**For the filling:**
175 g onions, peeled and chopped	6 oz onions, peeled and chopped
175 g streaky bacon rashers, rinds removed, chopped	6 oz streaky bacon rashers, rinds removed, chopped
225 g Stilton cheese, crumbled	8 oz Stilton cheese, crumbled
2 eggs	2 eggs
1 egg yolk	1 egg yolk
150 ml double cream	¼ pint double cream
150 ml milk	¼ pint milk
Salt	Salt
Freshly ground black pepper	Freshly ground black pepper

Sift the flour into a bowl. Rub in the butter or margarine until the mixture resembles breadcrumbs, then bind with the egg yolk and water. Roll out and use to line a 24 cm (9½ inch) flan dish. Bake blind in a preheated moderately hot oven (200°C/400°F, Gas Mark 6) for about 25 minutes, or until the pastry is beginning to colour and the bottom is quite dry. Cool.

Meanwhile, fry the onions and bacon together until the fat runs and the onion is tender. Cool, then scatter into the pastry case. Sprinkle the cheese on top of the onion and bacon. Whisk the eggs and egg yolk with the cream, milk and seasoning. Pour into the flan case.

Bake in a preheated moderately hot oven (190°C/375°F, Gas Mark 5) for about 45 minutes or until golden brown and set, covering if necessary with foil or greaseproof paper to prevent over-browning.

Pink Mushrooms

Metric	Imperial
1 kg button mushrooms	2 lb button mushrooms
300 ml dry red wine	½ pint dry red wine
300 ml vegetable oil	½ pint vegetable oil
4 x 15 ml spoons red wine vinegar	4 tablespoons red wine vinegar
2 x 5 ml spoons sugar	2 teaspoons sugar
1 x 5 ml spoon dry mustard	1 teaspoon dry mustard
Few grains of cayenne	Few grains of cayenne
12 cocktail onions, finely chopped	12 cocktail onions, finely chopped
8 small pickled gherkins, finely chopped	8 small pickled gherkins, finely chopped
3 x 15 ml spoons chopped parsley	3 tablespoons chopped parsley
Salt	Salt
Freshly ground black pepper	Freshly ground black pepper
Chopped parsley to garnish	Chopped parsley to garnish

Trim the mushroom stems level with the caps. Simmer the whole mushrooms in the wine in a saucepan for about 15 minutes or until the wine evaporates and the mushrooms turn pink. Tip into a bowl. Shake together the remaining ingredients in a screwtop jar. Spoon over the warm mushrooms. Leave them to cool and chill well before serving, garnished with parsley.

Right: Blue cheese quiche; Garlic bread.

Rice Salad, Greek-Style

Metric	Imperial
900 g brown rice	2 lb brown rice
150 ml French dressing (see page 91)	¼ pint French dressing (see page 91)
225 g onions, peeled and finely chopped	8 oz onions, peeled and finely chopped
1 green pepper, cored, seeded and chopped	1 green pepper, cored, seeded and chopped
1 red pepper, cored, seeded and chopped	1 red pepper, cored, seeded and chopped
4 celery stalks, trimmed and chopped	4 celery stalks, trimmed and chopped
1 x 397 g can pimientos, drained	1 x 14 oz can pimientos, drained
Black olives, stoned	Black olives, stoned

Cook the rice as directed on the packet. Drain the rice and, while still hot, pour over the dressing. Mix well. Add the onions, green and red peppers and celery. Chop all but two of the pimientos and stir into the rice mixture.

Brush two 1.5 litre (2½ pint) plain ring moulds with oil. Make a pattern on the bottom using the remainder of the pimientos, sliced and the black olives. Carefully spoon the rice mixture into the ring moulds. Cool to set, then turn out onto flat plates.

Makes 2 salads, each to serve 10

Platter Salad

Prepare a salad of diced red and green eating apples, chopped walnuts and celery and dress with lemon juice. Arrange in the centre of a round dish. Surround with diced cucumber, sliced radishes and thinly sliced chicory. Serve with a dressing made with 150 ml (¼ pint) French dressing (see page 91) to which 1 x 5 ml spoon (1 teaspoon) each of celery seeds and creamed horseradish have been added.

Rice salad Greek-style; Pink mushrooms; Platter salad.

GRAPE AND BANANA VACHERIN

Make two

Metric	Imperial
6 egg whites	6 egg whites
350 g caster sugar	12 oz caster sugar
300 ml whipping cream, whipped	½ pint whipping cream, whipped
3 large bananas, sliced	3 large bananas, sliced
225 g black grapes, halved and pipped	8 oz black grapes, halved and pipped
Lemon juice	Lemon juice
Chocolate curls to decorate	Chocolate curls to decorate

Whisk four of the egg whites until stiff, then beat in 4 x 5 ml spoons (4 teaspoons) of the sugar and continue whisking until the mixture will stand up in stiff peaks. Fold in a further 200 g (7 oz) sugar. Pipe the mixture in two 25 cm (10 inch) rounds on non-stick paper-lined baking sheets, using a 1 cm (½ inch) plain nozzle. Dry in a preheated very cool oven (120°C/250°F, Gas Mark ½) for 1 hour.

Make up the remaining egg whites and sugar into a meringue mixture as above. Pipe a border of small meringues round the edge of one of the baked meringue rounds. Return this to the oven and dry both rounds for a further hour. Remove the paper and cool.

Sandwich the meringue rounds together with the whipped cream, bananas and grapes. Lightly brush any exposed pieces of banana with lemon juice to prevent discoloration. Serve as soon as possible, decorated with chocolate curls.

COMPÔTE OF PEACHES

Metric	Imperial
550 g sugar	1¼ lb sugar
1.5 litres water	2½ pints water
Piece of vanilla pod	Piece of vanilla pod
20 yellow flesh peaches, peeled, stoned and sliced	20 yellow flesh peaches, peeled, stoned and sliced
5 x 15 ml spoons lemon juice	5 tablespoons lemon juice
Flaked almonds	Flaked almonds

Dissolve the sugar in the water with the vanilla pod. Bring to the boil and boil for 3 minutes. Discard the vanilla pod and add the peach slices. Cook gently for 5 minutes. Remove the pan from the heat. Add the lemon juice and leave the fruit until cold.

Brown a few flaked almonds under the grill and sprinkle over the peaches in a serving dish. Serve with thin crisp biscuits or soft sponge fingers. (See Lemon sugar cookies, below.)

Note: To peel the peaches, place them in boiling water, count to 10, then plunge them into cold water. Carefully remove the skins.

LEMON SUGAR COOKIES

Metric	Imperial
225 g plain flour	8 oz plain flour
1 x 5 ml spoon baking powder	1 teaspoon baking powder
Pinch of salt	Pinch of salt
Pinch of grated nutmeg	Pinch of grated nutmeg
100 ml vegetable oil	4 fl oz vegetable oil
100 g caster sugar	4 oz caster sugar
1 egg	1 egg
Grated rind of 1 small lemon	Grated rind of 1 small lemon
Granulated sugar	Granulated sugar

Sift together the flour, baking powder, salt and nutmeg. Combine the oil and caster sugar in a bowl, then beat in the egg and lemon rind. Add the dry ingredients to the oil mixture. Mix well. Shape into balls about 2 cm (¾ inch) in diameter. Dip the tops of the balls into granulated sugar and place, sugar side up, on greased baking sheets, about 5 cm (2 inches) apart. Press the tops of the biscuits with the prongs of a fork to make a criss-cross pattern. Bake in a preheated moderately hot oven (190°C/375°F, Gas Mark 5) for 10 to 12 minutes. Cool on a wire rack. Makes 30

Lemon sugar cookies; Compôte of peaches; Grape and banana vacherin.

Slimmers' Special for Eight

Apple tuna salad/Swiss veal, Tossed green salad/Grape delight

Beforehand

Apple tuna salad
Make up the salad about 1½ hours before serving time. The apple shouldn't discolour if you use sufficient lemon juice.

Swiss veal
This can be partly prepared, up to but not including the addition of the egg yolks and yogurt, the day before. To reheat when required, put the mixture in a casserole and cook in a preheated moderate oven (180°C/350°F, Gas Mark 4) for about 1 hour. Then add the egg yolks and yogurt and complete the preparation according to the recipe.

Tossed green salad
Prepare the vegetables and store in polythene bags in the refrigerator.

Grape delight
Halve and pip the grapes the day before; store in the refrigerator. Make up the sweet 1 hour before serving time.

Apple Tuna Salad

Metric	Imperial
2 x 198 g cans tuna, drained and flaked	2 x 7 oz cans tuna, drained and flaked
2 small green peppers, cored, seeded and chopped	2 small green peppers, cored, seeded and chopped
8 medium red-skinned apples	8 medium red-skinned apples
For the cheese dressing:	**For the cheese dressing:**
225 g cottage cheese	8 oz cottage cheese
Juice of 1 lemon	Juice of 1 lemon
Salt	Salt
Freshly ground black pepper	Freshly ground black pepper

Mix the tuna with the green peppers. Core the apples and scoop out the inside of each, leaving a 6 mm (¼ inch) wall. Chop the scooped-out apple and add to the tuna mixture.

Combine the cottage cheese, lemon juice and seasoning and sieve or blend until smooth and creamy. Add 1 to 2 x 15 ml spoons (1 to 2 tablespoons) to the tuna mixture and mix thoroughly. Pile into the apple shells and chill. Serve the rest of the dressing separately.

Swiss Veal

Metric	Imperial
2 kg pie veal, cubed	4 lb pie veal, cubed
Seasoned flour	Seasoned flour
2 x 15 ml spoons cooking oil	2 tablespoons cooking oil
225 g carrots, peeled and diced	8 oz carrots, peeled and diced
225 g shallots, peeled and chopped	8 oz shallots, peeled and chopped
1 x 15 ml spoon lemon juice	1 tablespoon lemon juice
300 ml stock	½ pint stock
150 ml dry white wine	¼ pint dry white wine
1 bouquet garni	1 bouquet garni
4 egg yolks, beaten	4 egg yolks, beaten
300 ml unsweetened natural yogurt	½ pint unsweetened natural yogurt
Salt	Salt
Freshly ground black pepper	Freshly ground black pepper
Chopped parsley to garnish	Chopped parsley to garnish

Dust the veal lightly with the seasoned flour. Heat the oil and fry the veal until pale golden. Add the carrots, shallots, lemon juice, stock, wine and bouquet garni and simmer gently until the meat is tender – about 1½ hours. Alternatively, turn the mixture into a casserole and cook in a preheated moderate oven (180°C/350°F, Gas Mark 4) for about 1½ hours.

Mix the egg yolks with the yogurt. Add a little of the hot stock, then stir into the meat mixture and adjust the seasoning. Reheat gently without boiling and serve sprinkled with chopped parsley.

Grape Delight

Metric	Imperial
3 egg whites	3 egg whites
450 ml apricot yogurt	¾ pint apricot yogurt
225 g black grapes, halved and seeded	8 oz black grapes, halved and seeded
225 g white grapes, halved and seeded	8 oz white grapes, halved and seeded

Whisk the egg whites until stiff and fold in the yogurt. Layer the yogurt and grapes into eight glasses. Top with grapes.

Above: Grape delight. Right: Apple tuna salad; Swiss veal.

COFFEE PARTIES

There are lots of good reasons for giving a coffee party; to welcome a new neighbour, or to say goodbye to an old one; to raise money for a favourite cause; or simply to be sociable and entertain friends. If it's to be a money-raising venture, it's a good idea to start planning ahead.
Biscuits, buns and cakes can all be made in advance and stored in airtight containers until they're needed. The home-made preserves and pickles in this chapter keep well – chutneys actually mature with keeping. Lemon curd, fudge and truffles all keep for 2 or 3 weeks. Label jars clearly – and put sweets and biscuits in transparent bags or in small boxes. Wrap them with cling film and stick a descriptive label on top.
The cakes, teabreads and other goodies in this chapter can be made for eating at the coffee morning – or for selling. If larger quantities than those indicated in the basic recipe are needed, make two or three batches, instead of doubling or trebling the ingredients.

COFFEE PARTY FOR TWELVE

Parkerhouse rolls with unsalted butter, honey, apricot jam, Salted twisters and Cheese crescents (see page 66; double the quantity), Malt bread with unsalted butter/Date streusel, Coffee battenberg, Cherry Madeira ring, Spiced carrot cake

COFFEE

The coffee should be piping hot when you serve it, accompanied by hot – but not boiled – milk. It must be fresh; if you can't get it freshly roasted and freshly ground, buy the coffee in flavour-sealed containers (cans or bags). Make it in the way you find most successful, whether it's in a jug, percolator, or cafetière, or whether you use the espresso or filter method.

For every 24 to 26 servings (allow 200 ml ($\frac{1}{3}$ pint) per serving) you'll need 275 to 350 g (10 to 12 oz) of fresh or instant coffee, 3.5 litres (6 pints) of water, and 1.75 litres (3 pints) of milk. Allow 500 g (1 lb) of sugar for these quantities. If you are using instant coffee and want to make it in bulk, allow 100 g (4 oz) to 3.5 litres (6 pints) of water.

If you make the coffee in advance – and this will almost certainly be necessary if you are to be prepared for most of your guests to arrive simultaneously – strain it after infusion and then reheat it, without boiling, when required. If you have, or can borrow, some large vacuum flasks or jugs, it's a good idea to fill them with freshly made coffee beforehand and to keep them topped up as the party progresses. Milk can be kept hot in this way, or in a double saucepan.

Malt bread; Parkerhouse rolls.

PARKERHOUSE ROLLS

Make two batches

Metric	Imperial
1 x 283 g packet white bread mix	1 x 10 oz packet white bread mix
2 x 15 ml spoons finely chopped fresh thyme	2 tablespoons finely chopped fresh thyme
200 ml water, hand hot	$\frac{1}{3}$ pint water, hand hot
Melted butter to glaze	Melted butter to glaze

Mix together the dry bread mix and chopped thyme and stir in the water. Mix the dough together in the bowl, then turn onto a lightly floured surface and knead for about 5 minutes. Roll out the dough to 1 cm ($\frac{1}{2}$ inch) thick. Cut out eight rounds with a 6.5 cm ($2\frac{1}{2}$ inch) plain cutter, re-rolling the dough as necessary. With the dull edge of the knife, make a crease just off-centre of each round. Brush with melted butter and fold over so that the larger part overlaps, pressing well together. Place on baking sheets, cover with oiled cling film and leave to rise in a warm place until doubled in size.

Brush again with melted butter and bake in a preheated very hot oven (230°C/450°F, Gas Mark 8) for 10 to 12 minutes. Transfer from baking sheets to a wire rack to cool. Eat fresh. (Any leftovers are delicious split and toasted.) Makes 8

MALT BREAD

Metric	Imperial
25 g fresh yeast	1 oz fresh yeast
About 350 ml tepid water	About 13 fl oz tepid water
450 g plain flour	1 lb plain flour
1 x 5 ml spoon salt	1 teaspoon salt
3 x 15 ml spoons malt extract	3 tablespoons malt extract
2 x 15 ml spoons black treacle	2 tablespoons black treacle
25 g butter or margarine	1 oz butter or margarine
225 g sultanas, cleaned	8 oz sultanas, cleaned
For the glaze (optional):	**For the glaze (optional):**
1 x 15 ml spoon sugar	1 tablespoon sugar
1 x 15 ml spoon water	1 tablespoon water

Cream the yeast and water together. Sift the flour and salt into a mixing bowl. Warm the malt extract, treacle and butter or margarine until just melted, then stir into the flour with the yeast liquid. Combine well. Add the sultanas and beat for 5 minutes.

Divide the mixture between two greased 20.5 x 10 cm (8 x 4 inch) top measurement loaf tins. Cover and leave to rise in a warm place for 45 minutes, or until the dough almost fills the tins.

Bake in a preheated moderately hot oven (200°C/400°F, Gas Mark 6) for 40 to 45 minutes. When cooked the loaves may be brushed with the sugar and water glaze. Makes 2 loaves

DATE STREUSEL

Make two

Metric	**Imperial**
125 g shortcrust pastry, made with 125 g plain flour and 60 g fat	4 oz shortcrust pastry, made with 4 oz plain flour and 2 oz fat
350 g stoned dates, chopped	12 oz stoned dates, chopped
3 x 15 ml spoons lemon juice	3 tablespoons lemon juice
4 x 15 ml spoons soft dark brown sugar	4 tablespoons soft dark brown sugar
1 x 2.5 ml spoon bicarbonate of soda	½ teaspoon bicarbonate of soda
6 x 15 ml spoons water	6 tablespoons water
75 g plain flour	3 oz plain flour
1 x 2.5 ml spoon mixed spice	½ teaspoon mixed spice
40 g butter or block margarine	1½ oz butter or block margarine
25 g granulated sugar	1 oz granulated sugar
Grated rind of 1 lemon	Grated rind of 1 lemon

Bottom-line a 21.5 cm (8½ inch) straight-sided sandwich tin with greaseproof paper. Roll out the dough and use to line the tin. Prick with a fork and bake blind in a preheated moderately hot oven (200°C/400°F, Gas Mark 6) for 15 minutes.

Place the dates in a small saucepan with the lemon juice, brown sugar, bicarbonate of soda and water. Heat gently to dissolve the sugar and soften the dates. Cool.

Sift the flour with the spice. Rub in the fat, then stir in the granulated sugar and lemon rind. Spread the date mixture in the pastry case and sprinkle the crumble mixture on top. Bake in a preheated moderately hot oven (190°C/375°F, Gas Mark 5) for about 25 minutes, or until golden brown. Cool in the tin.

Coffee battenberg; Date streusel.

COFFEE BATTENBERG

Metric	**Imperial**
175 g butter or margarine	6 oz butter or margarine
175 g caster sugar	6 oz caster sugar
3 eggs, beaten	3 eggs, beaten
175 g self-raising flour, sifted	6 oz self-raising flour, sifted
4 x 5 ml spoons coffee essence (Camp)	4 teaspoons coffee essence (Camp)
1 x 15 ml spoon milk	1 tablespoon milk
10 x 15 ml spoons ginger marmalade or apricot jam	10 tablespoons ginger marmalade or apricot jam
2 x 226 g packets marzipan	2 x 8 oz packets marzipan
Crystallised ginger, chopped, to decorate (optional)	Crystallised ginger, chopped, to decorate (optional)

Grease a 20 cm (8 inch) square cake tin or two 24 by 11 cm (9½ by 4½ inch) loaf tins – top measurement. Divide the square tin in half by bottom-lining with foil, making a pleat down the centre. Support by cardboard inside the pleat.

Cream the fat and sugar well together and gradually beat in the eggs, keeping the mixture fairly stiff. Lightly beat in the flour. Divide the mixture in half. Fold the coffee essence into one portion and the milk into the other.

Spoon one flavour into each side of the tin (or separate loaf tins). Bake in a preheated moderately hot oven (190°C/375°F, Gas Mark 5) for about 30 minutes. Turn out onto a wire rack and cool.

Trim each piece of cake and divide in half lengthways. Sandwich alternately together with half of the marmalade or jam. Measure the Battenberg lengthways, and also add up the total of the four sides. Cut out a sheet of non-stick paper to these measurements and cut out the marzipan on top to fit it exactly. Spread the remaining marmalade or jam over the marzipan and wrap closely around the cake. Pinch the top edges and press in the crystallised ginger.

CHERRY MADEIRA RING

Make two

Metric	Imperial
125 g butter	4 oz butter
125 g caster sugar	4 oz caster sugar
Grated rind and juice of 1 large juicy lemon	Grated rind and juice of 1 large juicy lemon
2 large eggs, beaten	2 large eggs, beaten
175 g glacé cherries, halved	6 oz glacé cherries, halved
175 g plain flour	6 oz plain flour
1 x 5 ml spoon baking powder	1 teaspoon baking powder
125 g icing sugar	4 oz icing sugar

Cream the butter, caster sugar and lemon rind together until really light. Beat in the eggs, little by little, keeping the mixture stiff. Mix 125 g (4 oz) of the cherries with the flour and baking powder sifted together. Fold the flour and cherries lightly into the cream ingredients with 2 x 15 ml spoons (2 tablespoons) lemon juice. Turn into a greased 1.5 litre (2½ pint) plain ring mould. Bake in a preheated moderate oven (160°C/325°F, Gas Mark 3) for about 45 minutes, or until firm to the touch. Turn out onto a wire rack to cool.

Dissolve the sifted icing sugar in 1 to 2 x 15 ml spoons (1 to 2 tablespoons) lemon juice to give a coating consistency. Drizzle over the cake. Decorate with the remaining cherries before the icing sets.

Spiced carrot cake.

SPICED CARROT CAKE

Metric	Imperial
450 g wholemeal flour	1 lb wholemeal flour
Large pinch of salt	Large pinch of salt
1 x 2.5 ml spoon bicarbonate of soda	½ teaspoon bicarbonate of soda
1 x 15 ml spoon ground cinnamon	1 tablespoon ground cinnamon
1 x 2.5 ml spoon grated nutmeg	½ teaspoon grated nutmeg
1 x 1.25 ml spoon ground cloves	¼ teaspoon ground cloves
125 g butter	4 oz butter
500 g juicy carrots, peeled and grated	1 lb juicy carrots, peeled and grated
125 g dark brown sugar	4 oz dark brown sugar
75 g clear honey	3 oz clear honey
75 g treacle	3 oz treacle
About 2 x 15 ml spoons milk	About 2 tablespoons milk
2 x 15 ml spoons demerara sugar	2 tablespoons demerara sugar

Grease and bottom-line a 20 cm (8 inch) cake tin. Mix together the flour, salt, bicarbonate of soda and spices in a large bowl. Rub in the butter, then stir in the carrots. Warm the sugar, honey and treacle together over a low heat. Pour into a well in the centre of the dry ingredients. Mix to a stiff dropping consistency with the milk and turn into the prepared cake tin. Sprinkle with the demerara sugar and bake in a preheated moderately hot oven (190 °C/375°F, Gas Mark 5) for 1 to 1¼ hours until a skewer inserted in the centre comes out clean and dry. Turn out and cool on a wire rack.
Makes a 20 cm (8 inch) cake

Cherry Madeira ring, which may also be baked in a 1 kg (2 lb) loaf tin.

COFFEE PARTY FOR TWENTY

Date and apple teabread, Marmalade teabread, Chocolate butter crunch, Boston brownies, Cornish fairings, Ginger fridgies, Honey whirls

DATE AND APPLE TEABREAD

Make two

Metric	Imperial
225 g cooking apples, peeled, cored and sliced	8 oz cooking apples, peeled, cored and sliced
Grated rind of 1 lemon	Grated rind of 1 lemon
3 x 15 ml spoons lemon juice	3 tablespoons lemon juice
125 g stoned dates, chopped	4 oz stoned dates, chopped
125 g butter or block margarine	4 oz butter or block margarine
125 g soft dark brown sugar	4 oz soft dark brown sugar
2 eggs	2 eggs
225 g self-raising flour, sifted	8 oz self-raising flour, sifted

Put the apples into a heavy-based pan. Add the lemon rind and juice, cover tightly and stew until the apples are soft. Beat the apple purée until smooth (or use a potato masher) and, while still warm, stir in the dates. Cool.

Cream the butter or margarine and sugar together thoroughly. Beat in the eggs, flour and apple mixture until evenly mixed. Turn into a greased and bottom-lined 1.2 litre (2 pint) loaf tin. Bake in a preheated moderate oven (180°C/350°F, Gas Mark 4) for about 1 hour or until firm to the touch.

Turn out of the tin and cool on a wire rack. Wrap and keep for at least a day before serving, sliced and buttered.

Note: The teabread should have a cracked, rounded top.

MARMALADE TEABREAD

Make two

Metric	Imperial
225 g plain flour	8 oz plain flour
1.5 x 5 ml spoons baking powder	1½ teaspoons baking powder
1 x 2.5 ml spoon bicarbonate of soda	½ teaspoon bicarbonate of soda
1 x 5 ml spoon salt	1 teaspoon salt
50 g block margarine	2 oz block margarine
	4 oz demerara sugar

100 g demerara sugar	¼ pint milk
150 ml milk	1 egg, beaten
1 egg, beaten	4 tablespoons marmalade
4 x 15 ml spoons marmalade	5 oz seedless raisins, cleaned
150 g seedless raisins, cleaned	2 oz walnuts, chopped
50 g walnuts, chopped	

Grease and line a 23 by 11.5 cm (9 by 4½ inch) loaf tin (top measurements). Sift together the flour, baking powder, bicarbonate of soda and salt. Rub in the margarine and add the sugar. Combine the milk, beaten egg and marmalade and stir lightly into the batter, followed by the raisins and walnuts. Turn the batter into the prepared tin. Level the top and bake in a preheated moderate oven (180°C/350°F, Gas Mark 4) for about 1¼ hours. Cool for 10 minutes in the tin, then turn out and cool on a wire rack. Serve thickly sliced and buttered.

CHOCOLATE BUTTER CRUNCH

Metric	Imperial
125 g butter	4 oz butter
50 g caster sugar	2 oz caster sugar
125 g plain flour, sifted	4 oz plain flour, sifted
50 g ground rice	2 oz ground rice
Finely grated rind of 1 orange	Finely grated rind of 1 orange
50 g plain chocolate-flavoured cake covering, finely grated	2 oz plain chocolate-flavoured cake covering, finely grated

Grated chocolate and orange on a rich butter base make deliciously different shortbread. Cream the butter until soft, then gradually beat in the sugar until the mixture is light and creamy. Mix together the flour, ground rice and orange rind, then work into the creamed mixture with the chocolate. Knead lightly until the mixture forms a stiff dough. Pat into a 29 by 19 cm (11½ by 7½ inch) Swiss roll tin. Bake in a preheated moderate oven (160°C/325°F, Gas Mark 3) for 35 to 40 minutes until crisp and lightly browned. Cut into 16 fingers and leave in the tin to cool. Makes 16

Date and apple teabread; Marmalade teabread.

Chocolate butter crunch.

BOSTON BROWNIES

Metric	Imperial
4 x 15 ml spoons pure corn oil	4 tablespoons pure corn oil
50 g plain chocolate	2 oz plain chocolate
175 g caster sugar	6 oz caster sugar
75 g self-raising flour	2½ oz self-raising flour
1 x 1.25 ml spoon salt	¼ teaspoon salt
2 eggs, beaten	2 eggs, beaten
1 x 2.5 ml spoon vanilla essence	½ teaspoon vanilla essence
50 g walnuts, roughly chopped	2 oz walnuts, roughly chopped

Lightly oil and flour a 20 cm (8 inch) square tin. In a heatproof bowl over hot water, heat the oil and chocolate until melted. Sift together the dry ingredients and, off the heat, add to the chocolate mixture with the remaining ingredients. Beat well, then turn into the prepared tin. Bake in a preheated moderate oven (180°C/350°F, Gas Mark 4) for about 35 minutes. Leave in the tin to cool, then cut into squares or finger-shaped pieces. Makes about 24

CORNISH FAIRINGS

Make two batches

Metric	Imperial
100 g plain flour	4 oz plain flour
Pinch of salt	Pinch of salt
1 x 5 ml spoon baking powder	1 teaspoon baking powder
1 x 5 ml spoon bicarbonate of soda	1 teaspoon bicarbonate of soda
	1 teaspoon ground ginger
1 x 5 ml spoon ground ginger	½ teaspoon mixed spice
1 x 2.5 ml spoon mixed spice	2 oz block margarine
50 g block margarine	2 oz caster sugar
50 g caster sugar	3 tablespoons golden syrup
3 x 15 ml spoons golden syrup	

Sift the flour, salt, baking powder, bicarbonate of soda and the spices into a bowl. Rub in the margarine, then add the sugar. Warm the syrup and work into the flour to give a fairly stiff mixture. Roll into small balls and arrange, well spaced, on greased baking sheets. Bake fairly near the top of a preheated moderately hot oven (200°C/400°F, Gas Mark 6) for 5 to 8 minutes. Cool on a wire rack. Makes about 24

GINGER FRIDGIES

Make two batches

Metric	Imperial
225 g plain flour	8 oz plain flour
1 x 2.5 ml spoon bicarbonate of soda	½ teaspoon bicarbonate of soda
1 x 2.5 ml spoon salt	½ teaspoon salt
1 x 5 ml spoon ground ginger	1 teaspoon ground ginger
100 ml pure corn oil	4 fl oz pure corn oil
100 g soft brown sugar	4 oz soft brown sugar
100 g caster sugar	4 oz caster sugar
1 egg	1 egg
1 x 2.5 ml spoon vanilla essence	½ teaspoon vanilla essence
50 g flaked almonds	2 oz flaked almonds

Sift together the dry ingredients. Beat the oil, sugars, egg and essence together, then add to the dry ingredients with the nuts. Work together to give a manageable dough. Shape into a roll and wrap in greaseproof paper. Chill in the refrigerator for several hours, or overnight. Next day, or when required, cut the roll into 6 mm (¼ inch) slices and place them, widely spaced, on greased baking sheets. Bake in a preheated moderately hot oven (200°C/400°F, Gas Mark 6) for 10 to 12 minutes. Cool on a wire rack. Makes about 36

HONEY WHIRLS

Make two batches

Metric	Imperial
1 x 212 g packet frozen puff pastry, thawed	1 x 7½ oz packet frozen puff pastry, thawed
50 g margarine	2 oz margarine
4 x 15 ml spoons thick honey	4 tablespoons thick honey
Pinch of salt	Pinch of salt
50 g salted peanuts or walnut pieces, finely chopped	2 oz salted peanuts or walnut pieces, finely chopped

Roll out the dough thinly to an oblong 25 by 30 cm (10 by 12 inches). Mix together the remaining ingredients and spread evenly all over the surface. Roll up the dough from both the long edges so that the two rolls meet in the middle. Cut the roll into 14 even-sized pieces. Place, cut sides down, in an 18 cm (7½ inch) sandwich tin which has been greased and bottom-lined with non-stick paper. Bake in a preheated very hot oven (220°C/450°F, Gas Mark 8) for 20 minutes, or until brown and crisp. (The centre will be soft, but will harden on cooling.) Turn out immediately onto a plate, and pull apart into sections when cooler. Makes about 14

Left: Cornish fairings; Ginger fridgies; Boston brownies.
Below: Honey whirls.

BRING AND BUY IDEAS

CHERRY FUDGE

Metric	Imperial
900 g caster sugar	2 lb caster sugar
600 ml milk	1 pint milk
2 x 5 ml spoons powdered glucose	2 teaspoons powdered glucose
100 g butter	4 oz butter
100 g glacé cherries, chopped	4 oz glacé cherries, chopped
Vanilla essence	Vanilla essence

Butter a 23 cm (9 inch) square toffee tin. Dissolve the sugar in the milk in a large heavy-based saucepan. When completely dissolved, stir in the glucose and butter. Bring to the boil and boil gently until the temperature reaches 125°C/240°F. Add the cherries and a few drops of vanilla essence.

Stand the saucepan in cold water and beat the mixture until it turns thick and creamy. Pour at once into the buttered tin. Mark into squares when half set and leave until set. Makes 1 kg (2¼ lb)

Note: Make this a week ahead and leave wrapped. Cut into squares and put into polythene bags a day before the sale.

CHOCOLATE TRUFFLES

Metric	Imperial
225 g plain chocolate, grated	8 oz plain chocolate, grated
1 small can evaporated milk	1 small can evaporated milk
1 x 175 g packet trifle sponges, crumbled	1 x 6 oz packet trifle sponges, crumbled
65 g ground almonds	2½ oz ground almonds
350 g icing sugar, sifted	12 oz icing sugar, sifted
1-2 x 15 ml spoons rum	1-2 tablespoons rum
Chocolate vermicelli or desiccated coconut to decorate	Chocolate vermicelli or desiccated coconut to decorate

Put the chocolate and milk in a small saucepan and heat gently to melt the chocolate. Off the heat, stir in the remaining ingredients except the vermicelli or coconut. Allow the mixture to cool. Shape the mixture into bite-size balls and roll in vermicelli or coconut, or press into rigid foil sweet cases. Makes about 60

Note: Make up to a week ahead and store, covered, in the refrigerator.

MERINGUE SHELLS

Metric	Imperial
3 egg whites	3 egg whites
150 g caster sugar	6 oz caster sugar

Make these from the whites left over when you've used the yolks in biscuits and other goodies. Pack them by the half-dozen or dozen in polythene bags.

Line a baking sheet with non-stick paper. Whisk the egg whites until stiff, then whisk in half the sugar until the mixture becomes stiff again. Fold in the remaining sugar. Spoon into small heaps – or use a large star vegetable nozzle – keeping them well apart, on the baking sheet. Bake in a preheated very cool oven (130°C/250°F, Gas Mark ½) for 1½ to 2 hours or until dry. Leave to cool on a rack. Makes 18 to 24 (depending on size)

Right: Meringues. Far right: Lemon honey curd; Cherry fudge; Chocolate truffles; Lemon and apple chutney.

Note: Preserve fruits and vegetables in season for selling later. Always use scrupulously clean pots. Wash them in very hot water and dry them in a warm oven. Pots should be warm when filled.

LEMON AND APPLE CHUTNEY

Metric	Imperial
2 lemons	2 lemons
300 ml cider vinegar	½ pint cider vinegar
6 x 15 ml spoons thin honey	6 tablespoons thin honey
225 g granulated sugar	8 oz granulated sugar
1 x 2.5 ml spoon ground ginger	½ teaspoon ground ginger
225 g cooking apples, peeled, cored and sliced	8 oz cooking apples, peeled, cored and sliced
100 g onion, peeled and thinly sliced	4 oz onion, peeled and thinly sliced
25 g sultanas, cleaned	1 oz sultanas, cleaned

Halve the lemons lengthways, slice them thinly and discard the pips. Put the lemon slices in a pan, add water to cover and simmer, covered, for 45 minutes or until tender. Remove the slices from the liquid and reserve. Add the vinegar, honey, sugar and ginger to the liquid and heat gently until the sugar is dissolved.

Add the apples, onion, sultanas and cooked lemon slices and bring to the boil. Simmer uncovered for 20 to 25 minutes until the onion is soft and the liquid well reduced.

Pot and cover in the usual way with vinegar-proof covers. To allow the chutney to mature, store in a cool, dry place for 2 to 3 months before eating. Makes about 1 kg (2 lb)

LEMON HONEY CURD

Metric	Imperial
Finely grated rind and juice of 4 lemons	Finely grated rind and juice of 4 lemons
5 eggs, beaten	5 eggs, beaten
100 g butter	4 oz butter
225 g thick honey	8 oz thick honey
50 g caster sugar	2 oz caster sugar

Put all the ingredients into the top of a double boiler or into a deep heatproof bowl which fits over a saucepan. Place over a pan of simmering water and stir until the sugar has dissolved and the curd is thick enough to coat the back of a wooden spoon; this will take from 10 to 20 minutes. Do not allow the curd to boil or it will curdle. Stir continuously. Pour the curd into small pots and cover as for jam. Store in a cool place, preferably the refrigerator. Keeps about 1 month. Makes about 1 kg (2 lb)

Note: There should be 175 ml (6 fl oz) lemon juice, so squeeze another lemon, if necessary.

Lemon and
Apple

Lemon + Apple
Chutney

PINEAPPLE RELISH

Metric	Imperial
3 x 825 g cans pineapple	3 x 1 lb 13 oz cans pineapple
6 dried chillies, crushed	6 dried chillies, crushed
3 large garlic cloves, crushed	3 large garlic cloves, crushed
40 g mustard seeds	1½ oz mustard seeds
6 pieces of root ginger	6 pieces of root ginger
1.5 x 5 ml spoons ground mace	1½ teaspoons ground mace
1 x 5 ml spoon turmeric	1 teaspoon turmeric
450 ml white wine vinegar	¾ pint white wine vinegar
1 x 15 ml spoon salt	1 tablespoon salt

A slightly hot relish, this is good with ham, cold bacon or roast chicken.

Drain the pineapple, reserving 450 ml (¾ pint) of the syrup. Purée the fruit, with the measured syrup, in small amounts, to a medium-coarse texture. Put the chillies, garlic, mustard seeds and ginger in a muslin bag.

Put the puréed pineapple, muslin bag of spices, mace, turmeric, vinegar and salt in a pan and boil gently, stirring occasionally, until there is no free liquid. Discard the muslin bag. Pot into warm jars and seal with vinegar-proof covers. Makes six 225 g (8 oz) jars

BREAD AND BUTTER PICKLE

Metric	Imperial
6 large cucumbers, cut into chunks	6 large cucumbers, cut into chunks
750 g onions, peeled and thinly sliced	1½ lb onions, peeled and thinly sliced
6 x 15 ml spoons salt	6 tablespoons salt
1.2 litres distilled white vinegar	2 pints distilled white vinegar
350 g sugar	12 oz sugar
2 x 5 ml spoons celery seeds	2 teaspoons celery seeds
2 x 5 ml spoons mustard seeds	2 teaspoons mustard seeds

This pickle is especially good with English farmhouse Cheddar or Cheshire or cream cheese, wholemeal bread and country butter.

Put the cucumbers, onions and salt in a bowl. Toss and leave to stand for 1 hour. Pour off the brine, rinse well and drain.

Heat the vinegar, sugar and seeds and boil for 3 minutes. Pack the vegetables in jars. Add the hot vinegar mixture to cover and seal at once with vinegar-proof covers. Makes six 450 g (1 lb) jars

Bread and butter pickle.

Pineapple relish; Apple-mint jelly.

APPLE-MINT JELLY

Metric	Imperial
3 kg cooking apples, cut into pieces	6 lb cooking apples, cut into pieces
1.2 litres water	2 pints water
225 g fresh mint with stalks	8 oz fresh mint with stalks
750 g sugar	1½ lb sugar
175 ml lemon juice	6 fl oz lemon juice
900 ml distilled white vinegar	1½ pints distilled white vinegar
Green food colouring	Green food colouring

Traditional with lamb, this is a good way of using large windfall apples. Put the apples and water in a large pan and cook them to a pulp. Strain through a jelly bag. Boil the strained liquid for 15 minutes with half the mint, then remove the mint. Add the sugar, lemon juice and vinegar to the liquid and stir to dissolve the sugar. Bring to a fast rolling boil and boil for about 20 minutes or until setting point (110°C/222°F) is reached.

To test without a thermometer, spoon a little jelly onto a saucer, cool, then push it gently with your finger. It should wrinkle. If it does not, return to the heat and continue boiling and testing.

Stir in the rest of the mint leaves, chopped, and the green colouring. Cool the jelly until the mint is suspended. Pot and cover as for jam. Makes nine 225 g (8 oz) jars

SPICED PEPPER CHUTNEY

Metric	Imperial
500 g green peppers, cored, seeded and chopped	1 lb green peppers, cored, seeded and chopped
500 g onions, peeled and chopped	1 lb onions, peeled and chopped
1 kg tomatoes, quartered	2 lb tomatoes, quartered
1 kg cooking apples, peeled, cored and chopped	2 lb cooking apples, peeled, cored and chopped
225 g demerara sugar	8 oz demerara sugar
1 x 5 ml spoon ground allspice	1 teaspoon ground allspice
450 ml malt vinegar	¾ pint malt vinegar
1 x 5 ml spoon peppercorns	1 teaspoon peppercorns
1 x 2.5 ml spoon mustard seeds	½ teaspoon mustard seeds

Put the green peppers, onions, tomatoes, apples, sugar, allspice and vinegar in a large pan and stir well. Tie the peppercorns and mustard seeds in muslin and put in the pan. Bring to the boil and simmer, uncovered, for about 1½ hours or until well reduced. Discard the muslin bag. Pot and seal. Makes 2.3 kg (5 lb)

CORN RELISH

Metric
6 ripe corn cobs, trimmed
550 g white cabbage, cored
2 medium onions, peeled
2 red peppers, cored and seeded
2 x 5 ml spoons salt
2 x 5 ml spoons plain flour
1 x 2.5 ml spoon turmeric
175 g granulated sugar
2 x 5 ml spoons dry mustard
600 ml distilled white vinegar

Imperial
6 ripe corn cobs, trimmed
1¼ lb white cabbage, cored
2 medium onions, peeled
2 red peppers, cored and seeded
2 teaspoons salt
2 teaspoons plain flour
½ teaspoon turmeric
6 oz granulated sugar
2 teaspoons dry mustard
1 pint distilled white vinegar

Blanch the corn in boiling water for 3 minutes. Drain and cut the corn kernels away from the cobs. Coarsely mince the cabbage, onions and peppers. Mix the salt, flour, turmeric, sugar and mustard in a saucepan and gradually stir in the vinegar. Bring to the boil and add the minced vegetables and corn kernels. Simmer, stirring occasionally, for 30 minutes. Pour at once into hot jars. Cover with vinegar-proof paper. Makes seven 450 g (1 lb) jars

RASPBERRY CONSERVE

Metric
2 kg raspberries
2 kg sugar
A little butter

Imperial
4 lb raspberries
4 lb sugar
A little butter

Simmer the raspberries gently in a large pan in their own juice for about 15 minutes. Add the sugar, stir until dissolved, then bring to a fast rolling boil. Add a small knob of butter and boil until setting point (110°C/220°F) is reached – in about 10 minutes. To test for setting point, see Apple mint jelly above. Don't overboil. Pot as for jam. Makes about 3.2 kg (7 lb)

Below: Corn relish; Spiced pepper chutney; Raspberry conserve.

TEA PARTIES

Tea parties may be family affairs, get-togethers for friends or neighbours, a pleasant way of holding an informal committee meeting, or an enjoyable setting for a money-raising event.

If you are serving sandwiches, keep them small and dainty – we give you ideas for fillings later in the chapter. But more substantial savouries, some hot, based on bread rolls or scone mixes, will be welcome too. Provide Indian and China tea with lemon slices as well as milk and sugar.

If you are catering for a fairly large number of people, hand round the sandwiches and other goodies on trays lined with doilies or paper napkins; more varieties can be attractively presented that way. Label sandwiches with sandwich flags.

It's a good idea, if you are combining your tea party with a bring-and-buy sale, to make an extra supply of the cakes, biscuits and teabreads which you are serving, for your guests to buy and take home. Our choice of recipes will give you tempting ideas for tea parties of all kinds.

SANDWICHES AND SANDWICH FILLINGS

If you buy uncut sandwich loaves, you can control the thickness of the slices (and slicing is considerably simplified) if you use an electric carving knife! A large loaf, about 800 g (28 oz), gives 20 to 24 slices. A small loaf, about 400 g (14 oz), gives 10 to 12 slices. A long sandwich loaf, about 1.5 kg (3½ lb) gives 50 slices. About 100 g (4 oz) butter or margarine will be needed for spreading 10 to 12 sandwiches, and 225 g (8 oz) for bread rolls.

Ring the changes on different types of white bread – brown, white, wholemeal, granary, rye and so on, varying them with rolls on occasions.

Fillings should be well flavoured, so that they are not overwhelmed by the double layer of bread and butter. They must also be easy to spread or arrange. Don't use anything very moist, unless the sandwiches are to be eaten at once, or the filling will soak into the bread, making it soggy.

If you are using bread other than a sandwich loaf, pair the slices accurately to give a neat appearance. Stack up the made sandwiches and cut them in halves or quarters (after first removing the crusts). Use a really sharp knife. Wrap the sandwiches in polythene, aluminium foil or greasproof paper, or put them in a plastic box. Store in a cool place until they are needed.

Below: A variety of sandwich fillings and different types of bread.
Right: Cheese flakies; Cheese toast racks.

FILLINGS

Shelled cooked shrimp, chopped celery, shredded pineapple and mayonnaise. Cream cheese, chopped walnuts and seedless raisins. Minced cooked chicken, minced cooked ham and finely chopped pineapple. Chopped cooked ham, sliced hard-boiled egg and chopped pickled gherkin. Cream cheese, chopped celery and chopped green pepper. Chopped cooked tongue, mayonnaise, pinch of curry powder and chopped hard-boiled egg. Flaked canned crabmeat, chopped avocado and mayonnaise. Canned pâté and thinly sliced cucumber.

Cut the sandwiches into quarters or fancy shapes after removing the crusts – triangles, rounds and fingers. For an attractive effect, use brown and white bread together.

CHEESE TOAST RACKS

Metric	Imperial
1 x 283 g packet white bread mix	1 x 10 oz packet white bread mix
50 g mature Cheddar cheese, finely grated	2 oz mature Cheddar cheese, finely grated
2 x 15 ml spoons Parmesan cheese	2 tablespoons Parmesan cheese
200 ml warm water	$\frac{1}{3}$ pint warm water
40 g butter	$1\frac{1}{2}$ oz butter
1 x 2.5 ml spoon made mustard	$\frac{1}{2}$ teaspoon made mustard

Tip the bread mix into a bowl. Add the cheeses and mix with the warm water, according to the packet instructions. Knead for 5 minutes. Cut the dough in half, knead lightly and roll out each half to a 23 cm (9 inch) square.

Melt the butter with the mustard and brush half over the squares. Cut each square into 5 strips and stack these on top of each other. With a sharp knife, cut both stacks into four. Hold each quarter, cut side uppermost, and pinch the bases together. Press down well into greased deep bun tins. Prove, covered, in a warm place for about 45 minutes or until doubled in size.

Brush with the remaining butter mixture and bake in a preheated hot oven (220°C/425°F, Gas Mark 7) for about 25 minutes or until they sound hollow when tapped. Makes 8

CHEESE FLAKIES

Metric	Imperial
15 g fresh yeast	$\frac{1}{2}$ oz fresh yeast
5 x 15 ml spoons warm water	5 tablespoons warm water
25 g lard	1 oz lard
225 g plain flour, sifted	8 oz plain flour, sifted
1 x 2.5 ml spoon salt	$\frac{1}{2}$ teaspoon salt
1 egg, beaten	1 egg, beaten
125 g butter, softened	5 oz butter, softened
75 g Gruyère cheese	3 oz Gruyére cheese
Beaten egg to glaze	Beaten egg to glaze
Poppy seeds	Poppy seeds
1 x 112 g can sardines, drained	1 x $4\frac{3}{8}$ oz can sardines, drained
Grated Parmesan cheese	Grated Parmesan cheese
2 firm tomatoes, sliced	2 firm tomatoes, sliced

Mix the yeast with the water. Rub the lard into the flour and salt, then stir in the yeast mixture and egg. Mix and knead to a soft dough. Place in an oiled polythene bag and leave for 10 minutes in a cool place. Shape the butter into an oblong 23 by 7.5 cm (9 by 3 inches).

Roll out the dough to a 25 cm (10 inch) square. Place the butter in the centre. Fold the dough sides over and seal the top and bottom. Roll out to a 38 x 12.5 cm (15 x 5 inch) oblong. Fold the top third down and the bottom third up. Rest the dough for 10 minutes.

Repeat the process twice, then rest the dough for 30 minutes.

Divide the dough in half. Roll out one half to a 25 cm (10 inch) square. Cut into four squares, then halve each diagonally. Divide 50 g (2 oz) of the Gruyère cheese into eight cubes. Place a cube at the base of each dough triangle. Roll up into crescents. Egg-glaze and sprinkle with poppy seeds.

Roll out the remaining dough to a 30 x 20 cm (12 by 8 inch) oblong. Cut into six 10 cm (4 inch) squares. Place 3 sardines diagonally across each of three squares. Fold the corners over. Glaze and sprinkle with Parmesan. Use the tomatoes in the remaining three squares. Glaze and sprinkle with the remaining Gruyère cheese, grated. Leave, lightly covered, on baking sheets in a warm place for 20 minutes.

Bake in a preheated hot oven (220°C/425°F, Gas Mark 7) for 10 to 15 minutes. Cool on a rack. Makes 14

FROSTED HAZELNUT LAYER CAKE

Metric	Imperial
175 g plain flour	6 oz plain flour
2 x 5 ml spoons baking powder	2 teaspoons baking powder
225 g caster sugar	8 oz caster sugar
50 g demerara sugar	2 oz demerara sugar
50 g browned hazelnuts, chopped	2 oz browned hazelnuts, chopped
Finely grated rind of 1 lemon	Finely grated rind of 1 lemon
2 eggs, separated	2 eggs, separated
3 x 15 ml spoons vegetable oil	3 tablespoons vegetable oil
120 ml water	4 fl oz water
1 egg white	1 egg white
2 x 15 ml spoons lemon juice	2 tablespoons lemon juice
Pinch of cream of tartar	Pinch of cream of tartar
40 g butter, softened	1½ oz butter, softened

Grease and bottom-line two straight-sided 18 cm (7 inch) sandwich tins. Sift the flour and baking powder into a large mixing bowl. Stir in 50 g (2 oz) of the caster sugar, the demerara sugar, 40 g (1½ oz) of the nuts and the lemon rind. Whisk the egg yolks with the oil and water and stir into the dry ingredients. Beat well. Whisk the two egg whites until stiff and fold into the cake mixture. Turn into the prepared tins and bake in a preheated moderately hot oven (200°C/400°F, Gas Mark 6) for about 25 minutes. Turn out and cool on wire racks.

Split each cake into two layers. Whisk the remaining caster sugar, the egg white, lemon juice and cream of tartar in a deep heatproof bowl over a pan of simmering water until the mixture stands in stiff peaks. Whisk off the heat until cool, then beat into the softened butter. Sandwich the cake layers with the lemon icing, swirling the final layer of icing over the top. Decorate with the remaining nuts. Makes an 18 cm (7 inch) sandwich cake

COCONUT AND APRICOT SWISS ROLL

Metric	Imperial
2 large eggs	2 large eggs
65 g caster sugar	2½ oz caster sugar
50 g plain flour	2 oz plain flour
4 x 15 ml spoons desiccated coconut	4 tablespoons desiccated coconut
6 x 15 ml spoons apricot jam, warmed	6 tablespoons apricot jam, warmed

Grease a 28.5 by 18.5 by 2 cm (11¼ by 7¼ by ¾ inch) Swiss roll tin. Bottom-line with greaseproof paper, then grease again and dust with caster sugar and flour. Whisk the eggs and sugar in a deep heatproof bowl placed over a pan of hot water until thick. Remove from the heat and continue whisking until cold. Fold in the sifted flour with 3 x 15 ml spoons (3 tablespoons) of the coconut. Spread into the Swiss roll tin.

Bake in a preheated hot oven (220°C/425°F, Gas Mark 7) for about 8 minutes, or until the crust is golden brown and springs back when pressed lightly with a finger. Turn out at once onto a sheet of greaseproof paper dusted with the remaining coconut and a little caster sugar. Trim the edges. Spread straight away with the warm jam and roll up from the narrow edge using the paper to help roll it. Keep wrapped in the paper on a wire rack until cool. Serve on day of baking.

PEPPERKAKER

Metric	Imperial
100 g butter or block margarine	4 oz butter or block margarine
100 g demerara sugar	3½ oz demerara sugar
200 g molasses or golden syrup	7 oz molasses or golden syrup
1 x 5 ml spoon ground ginger	1 teaspoon ground ginger
1 x 5 ml spoon ground cinnamon	1 teaspoon ground cinnamon
1 x 2.5 ml spoon ground cloves	½ teaspoon ground cloves
2 x 5 ml spoons bicarbonate of soda	2 teaspoons bicarbonate of soda
1 egg	1 egg
500 g plain flour	1 lb 2 oz plain flour

Roughly cut up the butter or margarine and place in a large bowl. In a saucepan, bring the sugar, molasses or syrup and the spices to boiling point. Add the bicarbonate of soda and pour over the butter. Stir until the butter has melted. Beat in the egg and slowly mix in the sifted flour. Knead in the bowl to a smooth, manageable dough. Roll out and cut into a variety of shapes.

Place the biscuits on baking sheets and bake in a preheated moderate oven (160°C/325°F, Gas Mark 3) for 10 to 15 minutes. Cool on a wire rack. Makes about 48

MOCHA CUP CAKES

Metric	Imperial
2 x 15 ml spoons coffee essence (Camp)	2 tablespoons coffee essence (Camp)
200 ml water	⅓ pint water
75 g butter	3 oz butter
75 g caster sugar	3 oz caster sugar
1 x 15 ml spoon golden syrup	1 tablespoon golden syrup
225 g plain flour	8 oz plain flour
2 x 15 ml spoons cocoa powder	2 tablespoons cocoa powder
1 x 5 ml spoon bicarbonate of soda	1 teaspoon bicarbonate of soda
3 x 15 ml spoons milk	3 tablespoons milk
1 x 2.5 ml spoon vanilla essence	½ teaspoon vanilla essence
For the icing:	**For the icing:**
75 g plain eating chocolate	3 oz plain eating chocolate
40 g butter	1½ oz butter
4 x 15 ml spoons water	4 tablespoons water
300 g icing sugar	11 oz icing sugar

A rich fudgy frosting and syrup in the cake mixture keep these cakes deliciously moist. Bake each paper-caseful in a bun tin to keep its shape. In a large pan, gently heat together the coffee essence, water, butter, caster sugar and syrup, stirring until the sugar dissolves. Bring to the boil and simmer for 5 minutes. Cool. Sift the flour and cocoa together into the cool mixture. Dissolve the bicarbonate of soda in the milk and add to the pan with the vanilla essence. Beat until smooth.

Spoon the chocolate mixture into 20 paper cases (bottom measurement 5 cm/2 inches) and bake in a preheated moderate oven (180°C/350°F, Gas Mark 4) for 15 to 20 minutes. Cool on a wire rack.

To make the icing, melt the chocolate and butter in the water in a heatproof bowl over hot water. Sift in the icing sugar and beat until smooth. Keep the icing liquid over the hot water, adding a little extra water if necessary and beating it if it begins to set. Put a large spoonful of icing on each cake, tipping it to reach the edges. Makes about 20

Coconut and apricot Swiss roll; Frosted hazelnut layer cake; Pepperkaker; Mocha cup cakes.

WALNUT COFFEE ROCK CAKES

Metric	Imperial
100 g butter or block margarine	4 oz butter or block margarine
225 g self-raising flour, sifted	8 oz self-raising flour, sifted
50 g walnuts, chopped	2 oz walnuts, chopped
75 g demerara sugar	3 oz demerara sugar
1 egg	1 egg
2 x 15 ml spoons coffee essence	2 tablespoons coffee essence
About 3 x 15 ml spoons milk	About 3 tablespoons milk
75 g icing sugar	3 oz icing sugar

Rub half the fat into the flour. Mix in the chopped walnuts and demerara sugar. Beat the egg with 1 x 15 ml spoon (1 tablespoon) of the coffee essence and the milk. Add to the dry ingredients and mix to a firm dough, adding more milk only if really necessary. Spoon the mixture into 12 heaps on lightly greased baking sheets, allowing them room to spread. Bake in a preheated moderately hot oven (200°C/400°F, Gas Mark 6) for 15 to 20 minutes. Cool on wire racks.

Soften the remaining fat and beat in the sifted icing sugar and remaining coffee essence. Cut a small cap off each bun and sandwich back with the coffee buttercream. Dust with icing sugar for serving.
Makes about 12

Right: Walnut coffee rock cakes.
Below: Cheese scones (see recipe page 61); Toasted devilled fingers.

TOASTED DEVILLED FINGERS

Metric	Imperial
1 small crusty loaf	1 small crusty loaf
100 g butter or soft margarine	4 oz butter or soft margarine
Mild mustard chutney	Mild mustard chutney

Cut the loaf into average slices and butter liberally. Spread with a thick layer of chutney and sandwich in pairs. Just before they are required, toast the sandwiches on both sides under a hot grill. Cut into chunky fingers to serve. Serves 6 to 8

ST. CATHERINE'S CAKES

Metric	Imperial
125 g butter	4 oz butter
125 g caster sugar	4 oz caster sugar
1 large egg, beaten	1 large egg, beaten
225 g self-raising flour	8 oz self-raising flour
1 x 5 ml spoon mixed spice	1 teaspoon mixed spice
4 x 15 ml spoons ground almonds	4 tablespoons ground almonds
50 g currants, cleaned	2 oz currants, cleaned

St. Catherine is the patron saint of lace-making and in Honiton, East Devon, a place noted for its lace, these wheel-shaped biscuits are still eaten on her feast day, November 24. Traditionally they are eaten hot, with mulled ale and cider. Cream the butter and sugar together until light and fluffy. Gradually beat in the egg. Sift in the flour and spice and stir in the almonds and currants. Mix, handling lightly, until the dough begins to bind together, then knead again lightly. Roll out the dough on a floured surface to 6 mm (¼ inch) thick and 20 cm (8 inches) wide. (This is easier if only half the dough is handled at once.) Cut in 1 cm (½ inch) strips and wind round to form a Catherine wheel.

Arrange on greased baking sheets and bake in a preheated moderately hot oven (190°C/375°F, Gas Mark 5) for 10 to 15 minutes or until pale golden. Cool on a wire rack. Makes about 30

DANISH ALMOND FINGERS

Metric	Imperial
225 g plain flour	8 oz plain flour
Pinch of salt	Pinch of salt
25 g lard	1 oz lard
15 g fresh yeast	½ oz fresh yeast
5 x 15 ml spoons warm water	5 tablespoons warm water
1 egg, beaten	1 egg, beaten
1 x 15 ml spoon caster sugar	1 tablespoon caster sugar
150 g butter or margarine	5 oz butter or margarine
350 g almond paste (see page 77), cut into fingers	12 oz almond paste (see page 77), cut into fingers
Beaten egg to glaze	Beaten egg to glaze
Glacé icing (see page 57) to decorate	Glacé icing (see page 57) to decorate

Sift the flour and salt into a bowl and rub in the lard. Mix the yeast with the water. Make a well in the centre of the flour mixture and add the yeast mixture, egg and caster sugar. Mix to a soft dough. Knead until smooth. Cover and leave in a cool place for 10 minutes. Work the fat to a block 23 by 7.5 cm (9 by 3 inches).

Roll out the dough to a 25 cm (10 inch) square and place the butter in the centre. Fold the dough sides up over it. Roll out the dough to a 38 by 12.5 cm (15 by 5 inch) oblong. Fold the top third down and the bottom third up. Put it in a polythene bag and leave to rest for 10 minutes in a cool place. Repeat the process twice, resting finally for 30 minutes.

Roll out the dough to a 30 by 20 cm (12 by 8 inch) oblong. Cut into 12 strips 2.5 cm (1 inch) wide. Wrap loosely around the almond paste fingers. Place on a greased baking sheet. Cover and leave in a warm place for about 20 minutes, until spongy.

Brush with beaten egg and bake in a preheated hot oven (220°C/425°F, Gas Mark 7) for about 15 minutes. Brush with thin glacé icing while still warm. Makes 12

Danish almond fingers; St. Catherine's cakes.

SUSSEX PLUM HEAVIES

Metric	Imperial
225 g self-raising flour	8 oz self-raising flour
Pinch of salt	Pinch of salt
Pinch of ground cinnamon	Pinch of ground cinnamon
75 g lard	3 oz lard
75 g margarine	3 oz margarine
100 g currants, cleaned	4 oz currants, cleaned
50 g soft brown sugar	2 oz soft brown sugar
About 120 ml milk	About 4 fl oz milk
Beaten egg to glaze	Beaten egg to glaze

These are said to have been eaten in the open by shepherds and woodmen. Originally they were made with plain flour, which meant that they were indeed "heavy". By using self-raising flour, the result is a cross between a scone and flaky pastry. They are best eaten the day that they are made.

Sift the flour, salt and cinnamon into a bowl. Mix the fats together and rub one quarter into the flour. Add the currants and sugar and mix to a soft manageable consistency with the milk. Knead the dough lightly on a floured board and roll out to an oblong about 30 by 10 cm (12 by 4 inches).

Mark the dough into three and flake one-third of the remaining fat over the top two-thirds of the dough. Fold the bottom third up and the top third down and roll out to the original size. Repeat twice more until all the fat has been used. Leave to rest in the refrigerator for 1 hour.

Roll out the dough to 6 mm (¼ inch) thick and stamp out 5 cm (2 inch) rounds. Remove a 1 cm (½ inch) hole from the centre of each round. Place on lightly greased baking sheets and brush with beaten egg. Bake in a preheated very hot oven (230°C/450°F, Gas Mark 8) for about 7 minutes, then reduce the heat to moderately hot (190°C/375°F, Gas Mark 5) and bake for a further 5 minutes. Makes 24

Porter cake.

PORTER CAKE

Metric	Imperial
225 g butter	8 oz butter
Finely grated rind of 1 lemon	Finely grated rind of 1 lemon
225 g soft dark brown sugar	8 oz soft dark brown sugar
3 large eggs, beaten	3 large eggs, beaten
225 g seedless raisins, cleaned	8 oz seedless raisins, cleaned
225 g sultanas, cleaned	8 oz sultanas, cleaned
50 g chopped mixed peel	2 oz chopped mixed peel
50 g glacé cherries, quartered	2 oz glacé cherries, quartered
50 g almonds, chopped	2 oz almonds, chopped
275 g plain flour	10 oz plain flour
2 x 5 ml spoons mixed spice	2 teaspoons mixed spice
150 ml Guinness	¼ pint Guinness

In this traditional recipe, Guinness replaces the porter, a weak form of stout no longer produced. This moist, rich cake improves if aged for at least 24 hours, but preferably for a week. Wrap in foil and put in a tin. Cream the butter with the lemon rind and sugar until soft. Gradually add the eggs, beating well between each addition. Place the fruit and nuts in a large mixing bowl. Sift the flour and spice together and mix half into the fruit. Fold the remaining flour into the creamed ingredients, then the fruit, adding about 6 x 15 ml spoons (6 tablespoons) of the Guinness to give a dropping consistency.

Put the mixture in an 18 cm (7 inch) greased and lined round cake tin. Bake in a preheated moderate oven (160°C/325°F, Gas Mark 3) for 1 hour, then reduce the heat to cool (150°C/300°F, Gas Mark 2) and bake for a further 2 hours. Cool slightly in the tin, then while still warm, remove the cake from the tin. Prick the base well and spoon over the remaining Guinness. Makes an 18 cm (7 inch) cake

MIXED FRUIT SLAB CAKE

Metric	Imperial
450 g plain flour	1 lb plain flour
1 x 5 ml spoon baking powder	1 teaspoon baking powder
225 g clarified dripping	8 oz clarified dripping
250 g light soft brown sugar	9 oz light soft brown sugar
350 g mixed dried fruit, cleaned	12 oz mixed dried fruit, cleaned
125 g glacé cherries, halved	4 oz glacé cherries, halved
4 eggs, beaten	4 eggs, beaten
About 6 x 15 ml spoons milk	About 6 tablespoons milk

Make ahead – this improves with keeping. Sift together the flour and baking powder. Lightly rub in the dripping. Stir in the sugar, dried fruit and glacé cherries. Make a well in the centre and add the beaten eggs and milk. Mix to a stiff dropping consistency. Turn the mixture into a 20.5 cm (8 inch) square cake tin. Level the surface.

Bake in a preheated moderate oven (180°C/350°F, Gas Mark 4) for 30 minutes, then turn the heat down to cool (140°C/275°F, Gas Mark 1) and bake for 1½ to 2 hours longer or until golden and firm to the touch. Cool on a wire rack. Wrap in foil and keep in a tin.

Mixed fruit slab cake; Sussex plum heavies.

SIMNEL CAKE

Metric	Imperial
450 g (ready made weight) almond paste (bought or see page 77)	1 lb (ready made weight) almond paste (bought or see page 77)
225 g plain flour	8 oz plain flour
Pinch of salt	Pinch of salt
1 x 2.5 ml spoon grated nutmeg	$\frac{1}{2}$ teaspoon grated nutmeg
1 x 2.5 ml spoon ground cinnamon	$\frac{1}{2}$ teaspoon ground cinnamon
225 g currants, cleaned	8 oz currants, cleaned
100 g sultanas, cleaned	4 oz sultanas, cleaned
75 g chopped mixed peel	3 oz chopped mixed peel
100 g glacé cherries, quartered	4 oz glacé cherries, quartered
175 g butter	6 oz butter
175 g caster sugar	6 oz caster sugar
3 eggs	3 eggs
Milk to mix (if required)	Milk to mix (if required)
Egg white or apricot glaze	Egg white or apricot glaze

Grease and line an 18 cm (7 inch) round cake tin. Shape one-third of the almond paste into a round slightly smaller than the cake tin. Sift together the flour, salt and spices. Mix the currants, sultanas, peel and cherries.

Cream the butter and sugar together until pale and fluffy, then beat in the eggs, one at a time. Fold in the flour mixture, adding a little milk, if required, to give a dropping consistency. Fold in the fruit.

Put half the mixture into the prepared tin and place the round of almond paste on top. Cover with the rest of the mixture, spreading it evenly. Bake in a preheated cool oven (150°C/300°F, Gas Mark 2) for 2½ to 3 hours, until the cake is a rich brown and firm to the touch. Leave to cool on a wire rack.

From half the remaining almond paste, shape eleven small balls. Shape the rest into a round to fit the top of the cake. Brush the top surface of the cake with egg white or apricot glaze and place the almond paste round in position. Smooth it slightly with a rolling pin and pinch the edges into scallops with finger and thumb. Score the surface with a knife. Arrange the almond paste balls around the edge and, if liked for extra glaze, brush the whole with egg white. Grill until light golden brown, and finish with a ribbon and a bow when cold. Makes an 18 cm (7 inch) cake

CARAMEL SHORTBREAD

Metric	Imperial
175 g plain flour	6 oz plain flour
50 g caster sugar	2 oz caster sugar
175 g butter	6 oz butter
50 g soft brown sugar	2 oz soft brown sugar
1 large can condensed milk	1 large can condensed milk
100 g plain chocolate	4 oz plain chocolate

Sift the flour into a bowl. Add the caster sugar and rub in 125 g (4 oz) of the butter lightly with the fingertips until the mixture resembles fine crumbs. Press the mixture evenly into a Swiss roll tin measuring 29 by 19 cm (11½ by 7½ inches). Bake in a preheated moderate oven (170°C/325°F, Gas Mark 3) for about 30 minutes until just coloured. Allow to cool in the tin.

Heat the remaining butter and the soft brown sugar together in a saucepan. Stir in the condensed milk and heat gently until the sugar dissolves. Bring to the boil and cook, stirring continuously, until the caramel mixture is a creamy fudge colour. Pour over the shortbread and spread evenly. Leave to cool.

Melt the chocolate in a heatproof bowl over hot but not boiling water and pour over the caramel. Tap the tin on a hard surface to level the chocolate. Leave to set, then cut into fingers.
Makes about 32

MELTING MOMENTS

Metric	Imperial
100 g butter or block margarine	4 oz butter or block margarine
75 g sugar	3 oz sugar
1 egg yolk	1 egg yolk
Few drops of vanilla essence	Few drops of vanilla essence
150 g self-raising flour, sifted	5 oz self-raising flour, sifted
Crushed cornflakes	Crushed cornflakes

Cream the fat and sugar together and beat in the egg yolk. Flavour with vanilla essence, then stir in the flour to give a really stiff dough. Divide the dough into 20 to 24 portions. Form each into a ball and roll in crushed cornflakes.

Place the balls on greased baking sheets, well apart, and bake in a preheated moderately hot oven (190°C/375°F, Gas Mark 5) for 15 to 20 minutes. Cool on the baking sheets for a few moments before lifting onto a wire rack. Makes 20 to 24

Above: Simnel cake.

Caramel shortbread; Melting moments.

FOR A GRAND OCCASION

A wedding reception at home need not be a headache for the bride's mother providing she caters only for the numbers she can confidently manage. The celebration menu here would be just as suitable for an anniversary party as it is for a wedding reception. It is planned for 25 people, which in some cases means making double the quantity of the recipe. Unless you have very big pans and bowls, which in any case are heavy and awkward to cope with, it is more practical to make up recipes in two or more batches (we tell you when to do this). If you feel you can cater for more people, the quantities can be increased again but by making the recipes in three or more batches. The same basic advance preparation rules apply as for buffet parties.

Lay the buffet table so that people can help themselves from each end. Serve drinks from a separate table and brief some of the family to help.

BUFFET FOR TWENTY TO TWENTY-FIVE FOR A GRAND OCCASION

Crème vichyssoise or Cream of lemon soup, Walnut sablés/Cheese and asparagus quiche, Quiche lorraine/Rolled ham with chicken and almond mayonnaise, Jubilee eggs, Tossed green salad, Orange and chicory salad, Jellied beetroot and apple salad/Chocolate and rum cheesecake pie or Lemon cheesecake pie, Fruit salad or Strawberries or raspberries and cream/Cheese and biscuits/Coffee

BEFOREHAND

Several days ahead
Make the walnut sablés and keep in airtight tins. (When needed, refresh them in a preheated cool oven (150°C/300°F, Gas Mark 2) for a few minutes, then cool on a wire rack.)

The day before
Make the soup; refrigerate, covered. Make dry mix for the quiche pastry. Cook the chicken early in the day. Prepare the ham rolls, but don't glaze them; cover closely with cling film and keep in a cool place. Prepare the green salad ingredients; store in polythene bags in the refrigerator. Make up French dressing. Make the beetroot and apple salads. Make the cheesecakes without decorating them.

The morning of the party
Make up the fruit salad, without the bananas; keep cool. Make the quiches. Glaze the ham rolls.

The afternoon of the party
Decorate the cheesecakes. Make the orange and chicory salad.

At the last possible moment
Toss the salad. Add sliced bananas to the fruit salad. Reheat the quiches, if wished, in a preheated moderate oven (180°C/350°F, Gas Mark 4) for 30 minutes. Garnish dishes with parsley, etc. Make coffee when needed – the fresher the better.

CRÈME VICHYSSOISE

Make two batches

Metric	Imperial
6 leeks	6 leeks
50 g butter	2 oz butter
2 small onions, peeled and sliced	2 small onions, peeled and sliced
1 kg potatoes, peeled and diced	2 lb potatoes, peeled and diced
1.8 litres white stock	3 pints white stock
2 egg yolks	2 egg yolks
300 ml single cream	½ pint single cream
Salt	Salt
White pepper	White pepper
Snipped fresh chives to garnish	Snipped fresh chives to garnish

Trim the leeks, discarding most of the green tops, and slice thinly. Melt the butter in a 4.5 litre (8 pint) saucepan. Add the leeks and onions, and soften them without browning. Add the potatoes and stock and simmer for about 30 minutes. Sieve or purée in an electric blender. Return the purée to the saucepan. Add the egg yolks mixed with the cream and stir well. Reheat without boiling and adjust the seasoning. Chill and serve garnished with chives. Serves 12

CREAM OF LEMON SOUP

Make two batches

Metric	Imperial
75 g butter or margarine	3 oz butter or margarine
350 g onions, peeled and sliced	12 oz onions, peeled and sliced
350 g carrots, peeled and sliced	12 oz carrots, peeled and sliced
4 litres turkey or chicken stock	7 pints turkey or chicken stock
Thinly pared rind and juice of 3 large lemons	Thinly pared rind and juice of 3 large lemons
1 bouquet garni	1 bouquet garni
3 x 15 ml spoons arrowroot	3 tablespoons arrowroot
Salt	Salt
Freshly ground black pepper	Freshly ground black pepper
450 ml single cream	¾ pint single cream
Thin lemon slices to garnish	Thin lemon slices to garnish

Melt the butter or margarine in a large saucepan. Add the onions and carrots and cook gently until tender, stirring frequently. Stir in the stock and bring to the boil. Reduce the heat and cook for 5 minutes.

Meanwhile, pour boiling water over the lemon rind and leave for 1 minute. Drain. Add the rind, lemon juice and bouquet garni to the pan. Cover and cook for 1 hour or until the vegetables are really soft. Remove the bouquet garni.

Purée the soup, a little at a time, in an electric blender. In a clean pan, dissolve the arrowroot in a little of the soup, then add the remainder, stirring. Bring to the boil, stirring. Adjust the seasoning before adding the cream. Reheat but do not boil. Garnish with lemon slices. Serves 12

WALNUT SABLÉS

Metric	Imperial
100 g plain flour	4 oz plain flour
100 g butter	4 oz butter
100 g mature Cheddar cheese, grated	4 oz mature Cheddar cheese, grated
Pinch of salt	Pinch of salt
Pinch of dry mustard	Pinch of dry mustard
Beaten egg	Beaten egg
Few chopped walnuts	Few chopped walnuts

Sift the flour into a bowl. Rub the butter into the flour with the fingertips until the mixture resembles fine crumbs. Add the cheese, salt and mustard and work together to form a dough.

Roll out the dough to about 6 mm ($\frac{1}{4}$ inch) thick on a lightly floured board. Neaten the edges and cut into 5 cm (2 inch) squares. Cut each in half diagonally. Brush the sablés with beaten egg. Sprinkle with nuts and press them lightly into the dough. Place on a baking sheet and bake in a preheated moderately hot oven (200°C/400°F, Gas Mark 6) for about 10 minutes. Cool on a wire rack. Makes 30

Above: Walnut sablés. Below: Crème vichyssoise; Cream of lemon soup.

CHEESE AND ASPARAGUS QUICHE

Make two

Metric	Imperial
200 g shortcrust pastry, made with 200 g plain flour and 100 g fat	7 oz shortcrust pastry, made with 7 oz plain flour and 3½ oz fat
25 g butter or margarine	1 oz butter or margarine
3 x 15 ml spoons plain flour	3 tablespoons plain flour
300 ml milk	½ pint milk
100 g cheese, grated	4 oz cheese, grated
Salt	Salt
Freshly ground black pepper	Freshly ground black pepper
1 x 340 g can green asparagus spears, drained	1 x 12 oz can green asparagus spears, drained

Roll out the dough and use to line a 20 cm (8 inch) flan ring or deep pie plate. Bake blind in a preheated hot oven (220°C/425°F, Gas Mark 7) for 15 to 20 minutes or until the pastry is cooked but not browned.

Melt the fat in a saucepan. Stir in the flour and cook for 2 to 3 minutes. Remove the pan from the heat and gradually stir in the milk. Bring to the boil and continue to cook, stirring, until the sauce has thickened. Remove from the heat and stir in 75 g (3 oz) of the cheese and seasoning.

Place the asparagus in the pastry case, retaining a little for decoration. Pour the sauce over and decorate with the remaining asparagus. Sprinkle with the remaining cheese and brown under a preheated hot grill or in a preheated moderate oven (180°C/350°F, Gas Mark 4) for 30 minutes, before serving. Serves 8 to 10

Cheese and asparagus quiche.

Quiche lorraine.

QUICHE LORRAINE

Make two

Metric	Imperial
100 g shortcrust pastry, made with 100 g plain flour and 50 g fat	4 oz shortcrust pastry, made with 4 oz plain flour and 2 oz fat
2 eggs, beaten	2 eggs, beaten
1 x 5 ml spoon chopped fresh herbs (if available)	1 teaspoon chopped fresh herbs (if available)
150 ml double cream	¼ pint double cream
150 ml single cream	¼ pint single cream
Grated nutmeg	Grated nutmeg
Salt	Salt
Freshly ground black pepper	Freshly ground black pepper
100 g lean streaky bacon rashers, rinds removed	4 oz lean streaky bacon rashers, rinds removed
100-175 g Gruyère cheese, thinly sliced or diced	4-6 oz Gruyère cheese, thinly sliced or diced

Roll out the dough very thinly and use to line a 20 cm (8 inch) flan ring placed on a baking sheet. Bake blind in a preheated hot oven (200°C/425°F, Gas Mark 7) for 15 to 20 minutes.

Meanwhile, mix together the eggs, herbs, creams, nutmeg and seasoning. Fry the bacon rashers gently until just cooked. Drain on absorbent kitchen paper.

Arrange the cheese on the bottom of the pastry case. Place the bacon rashers on top and pour on the egg mixture. Continue to bake in a moderate oven (180°C/350°F, Gas Mark 4) for about 35 to 40 minutes or until just set. Serve warm, cut in wedges. Serves 6 to 7

ROLLED HAM WITH CHICKEN AND ALMOND MAYONNAISE

Metric	Imperial
1 x 1.6 kg oven-ready chicken	1 x 3½ lb oven-ready chicken
600 ml water	1 pint water
1 small onion, peeled and sliced	1 small onion, peeled and sliced
1 carrot, peeled and sliced	1 carrot, peeled and sliced
Slivers of lemon rind	Slivers of lemon rind
1 bay leaf	1 bay leaf
4 peppercorns	4 peppercorns
Salt	Salt
25 g butter	1 oz butter
25 g plain flour	1 oz plain flour
2-3 x 15 ml spoons mayonnaise	2-3 tablespoons mayonnaise
50 g flaked almonds, toasted	2 oz flaked almonds, toasted
20 slices of canned ham (about 750 g)	20 slices of canned ham (about 1¾ lb)
Aspic glaze (optional)	Aspic glaze (optional)
Stuffed olives to garnish	Stuffed olives to garnish

Put the chicken in a saucepan with the water, onion, carrot, lemon rind, bay leaf, peppercorns and salt. Bring to the boil, reduce the heat, cover and simmer until the chicken is tender – about 40 minutes. Drain the chicken, reserving the liquor and leave to cool.

Melt the butter in another saucepan. Add the flour and cook for 1 to 2 minutes. Gradually stir in the strained chicken cooking liquor. Bring to the boil and simmer for 3 to 4 minutes. Leave to cool, covered with buttered paper to prevent a skin forming.

Skin the chicken and remove the meat from the bones. Dice the meat and add to the sauce with mayonnaise to taste and the flaked almonds. Divide the chicken filling between the ham slices, placing it towards one end. Roll up. If liked, brush the rolls with aspic glaze. When set, press half a stuffed olive into the end of each roll, cut side outwards. Keep in a cool place until required. Makes 20

JUBILEE EGGS

Metric	Imperial
25 eggs, hard-boiled	25 eggs, hard-boiled
225 g liver pâté	8 oz liver pâté
120 ml thick mayonnaise	4 fl oz thick mayonnaise
Salt	Salt
Freshly ground black pepper	Freshly ground black pepper
Stoned green olives	Stoned green olives
Paprika	Paprika

Cut the eggs in half lengthways and carefully remove the yolks. Pass the yolks through a nylon sieve. Divide in half and add the pâté to one half. Beat very thoroughly until smooth. To the rest of the yolk add the mayonnaise and seasoning. Beat well.

Pipe the pâté mixture into half the egg whites, using a 1.25 cm (½ inch) plain nozzle. Pipe the mayonnaise mixture into the remaining egg whites with a star nozzle. Garnish the pâté eggs with sliced olives and the mayonnaise eggs with paprika. Makes 50

Rolled ham with chicken and almond mayonnaise; Jubilee eggs.

Orange and Chicory Salad

Metric	Imperial
3 x 15 ml spoons lemon juice	3 tablespoons lemon juice
1 x 5 ml spoon salt	1 teaspoon salt
Freshly ground black pepper	Freshly ground black pepper
1 x 5 ml spoon French mustard	1 teaspoon French mustard
1 x 15 ml spoon clear honey	1 tablespoon clear honey
9 x 15 ml spoons vegetable oil	9 tablespoons vegetable oil
9 oranges	9 oranges
12 heads of chicory, trimmed	12 heads of chicory, trimmed

Put the lemon juice, salt, pepper, mustard, honey and oil in a screwtop jar. Shake well until the dressing is smooth and creamy. Grate the rind from six of the oranges and add to the dressing. Remove the skin and pith from the all the oranges. Divide them into segments and place in a salad bowl together with any juice.

Reserving a few chicory leaves for garnish, thinly slice the remainder and add to the bowl. Pour over the dressing and toss gently. Leave for 1 to 2 hours. Garnish with the reserved chicory leaves.

Orange and chicory salad.

Jellied beetroot and apple salad.

Jellied Beetroot and Apple Salad

Make three

Metric	Imperial
1 x 142 g red jelly tablet	1 x 5 oz red jelly tablet
300 ml boiling water	½ pint boiling water
150 ml vinegar	¼ pint vinegar
2 x 15 ml spoons lemon juice	2 tablespoons lemon juice
50 g walnut halves	2 oz walnut halves
500 g cooked beetroot, skinned and sliced or diced	1 lb cooked beetroot, skinned and sliced or diced
2 eating apples, peeled, cored and sliced	2 eating apples, peeled, cored and sliced
Chicory to garnish	Chicory to garnish

Break up the jelly tablet. Put it in a bowl and dissolve it in the boiling water. Mix together the vinegar and lemon juice and make up to 300 ml (½ pint) with cold water. Add to the hot jelly liquid.

Put the walnut halves in the bottom of a 1.2 litre (2 pint) ring mould and add the beetroot and apples in layers. Pour on the liquid jelly and leave to set in the refrigerator. When required, unmould onto a flat plate and garnish with chicory. Serves 6

Note: Use shallow dishes if you don't have enough ring moulds to make three salads.

CHOCOLATE AND RUM CHEESECAKE PIE

Make three

Metric

For the biscuit base:
150 g digestive biscuits, crushed
75 g caster sugar
75 g butter, melted

For the filling:
100 g cottage cheese, sieved
100 g cream cheese
100 g caster sugar
100 g plain chocolate
15 g powdered gelatine
2 x 15 ml spoons water
2 x 15 ml spoons rum
150 ml double cream, whipped

Imperial

For the biscuit base:
6 oz digestive biscuits, crushed
3 oz caster sugar
3 oz butter, melted

For the filling:
4 oz cottage cheese, sieved
4 oz cream cheese
4 oz caster sugar
4 oz plain chocolate
½ oz powdered gelatine
2 tablespoons water
2 tablespoons rum
¼ pint double cream, whipped

For the decoration:
150 ml double cream
1 x 15 ml spoon milk
Curls of chocolate
Icing sugar

For the decoration:
¼ pint double cream
1 tablespoon milk
Curls of chocolate
Icing sugar

Mix the biscuits with the caster sugar and butter. Use to line the bottom and sides of a 20 cm (8 inch) fluted flan dish. Press into place with the back of a spoon. Chill until firm.

Cream the cheeses together and add the caster sugar. Melt the chocolate in a heatproof bowl over hot water. Add the chocolate to the cheese mixture and beat well. Dissolve the gelatine in the water in a heatproof bowl placed in a pan of hot water. Stir into the cheese mixture and chill until almost set.

Add the rum, then fold in the cream. Pour the filling into the crumb crust. Chill until firm.

To decorate, whip the cream with the milk and swirl this over the chocolate filling. Top with curls of chocolate dusted with icing sugar.
Serves 6 to 8

Chocolate and rum cheesecake pie.

LEMON CHEESECAKE PIE

Make three

Metric	Imperial
For the biscuit base:	**For the biscuit base:**
150 g digestive biscuits, crushed	6 oz digestive biscuits, crushed
75 g caster sugar	3 oz caster sugar
75 g butter, melted	3 oz butter, melted
For the filling:	**For the filling:**
1½ x 142 g lemon jelly tablets	1½ x 5 oz lemon jelly tablets
3 x 15 ml spoons water	3 tablespoons water
2 eggs, separated	2 eggs, separated
150 ml milk	¼ pint milk
Grated rind of 2 lemons	Grated rind of 2 lemons
4 x 15 ml spoons lemon juice	4 tablespoons lemon juice
350 g cottage cheese, sieved	12 oz cottage cheese, sieved
2 x 15 ml spoons caster sugar	2 tablespoons caster sugar
150 ml double cream, whipped	¼ pint double cream, whipped
To decorate:	**To decorate:**
150 ml double or whipping cream, whipped	¼ pint double or whipping cream, whipped
Angelica	Angelica

Mix the digestive biscuits with the caster sugar and butter. Use to line the bottom and sides of a 23 cm (9 inch) or 1.2 litre (2 pint) shallow open pie plate. Press in with the back of a spoon. Chill until firm.

Dissolve the jelly in the water in a pan over low heat. Do not boil. Beat together the egg yolks and milk and stir into the jelly. Heat for a few minutes without boiling. Remove from the heat and add the lemon rind and juice. Cool until beginning to set.

Stir in the sieved cottage cheese (or blend the jelly mixture and unsieved cheese in an electric blender). Whisk the egg whites until stiff. Add the caster sugar and whisk again until stiff. Fold quickly into the cheese mixture followed by the whipped cream. Spoon into the crumb crust, piling it up slightly. Chill until set, then decorate with the additional whipped cream and angelica, if liked.

Serves 6 to 8

FRUIT SALAD

Metric	Imperial
1 x 818 g can sliced peaches	1 x 1 lb 13 oz can sliced peaches
1 x 425 g can pineapple rings	1 x 15 oz can pineapple rings
2 dessert apples, cored and thinly sliced	2 dessert apples, cored and thinly sliced
4 oranges, peeled and segmented	4 oranges, peeled and segmented
225 g strawberries, hulled and sliced	8 oz strawberries, hulled and sliced
225 g white grapes, peeled and seeded	8 oz white grapes, peeled and seeded
4 x 15 ml spoons orange-flavoured liqueur	4 tablespoons orange-flavoured liqueur
Lemon juice	Lemon juice
4 bananas	4 bananas

Turn the contents from the cans into a large bowl. Cut the pineapple rings in half. Add the apples, oranges, strawberries, grapes, liqueur and lemon juice to taste. Stir well. Leave for at least 1 hour for the flavours to mix.

Just before serving, slice the bananas and add to the salad.

Serves 15

COFFEE FOR TWENTY

Allow 200 ml (⅓ pint) of coffee per person. You will need 275 g (10 oz) of ground coffee, 3.4 litres (6 pints) of water and 1.2 litres (2 pints) of milk, or 600 ml (1 pint) of single cream, for 20 people. Allow 500 g (1 lb) of sugar – demerara, white, or coffee crystals.

Below: Coffee for a crowd. Left: Lemon cheesecake pie; Fruit salad.

DROP IN FOR DRINKS

A drinks party calls for more than the crisps and other bits and pieces. Make a few of the goodies shown here – three or four cold ones, and at least one hot one, such as Talmouse, and a savoury dip – and your party will be a sure success. Serve dips in a bowl on a tray and surround the bowl with colourful bite-size pieces of raw carrot, cauliflower and celery or small crisp biscuits or potato crisps. Keep hot and cold savouries separate and serve some crisps and other bits and pieces – cocktail sausages, olives, gherkins, nuts.

If you're using any pastry cases or bases, they can be made a day or two in advance and kept in airtight tins. Refresh them shortly before filling by putting them into a warm oven for 10 to 15 minutes. Allow them to cool before adding the filling or topping. Do this as near as possible to serving time. The same applies to canapés based on savoury biscuits, whether homemade or bought.

TALMOUSE

Metric	Imperial
1 x 212 g packet smoked haddock fillets	1 x 7½ oz packet smoked haddock fillets
15 g butter	½ oz butter
15 g plain flour	½ oz plain flour
150 ml milk	¼ pint milk
Salt	Salt
Freshly ground black pepper	Freshly ground black pepper
1 x 368 g packet frozen puff pastry, thawed	1 x 13 oz packet frozen puff pastry, thawed
Beaten egg	Beaten egg

Cook the haddock fillets according to the directions on the packet. Allow to cool, then discard the skin and any bones and flake the flesh. Melt the butter in a saucepan. Add the flour and cook, stirring, for 1 minute. Remove from the heat and gradually stir in the milk. Return to the heat and bring to the boil, stirring constantly. Simmer until thickened. Remove the sauce from the heat. Season to taste with salt and pepper and fold in the flaked fish.

Roll out the pastry dough thinly and, with a 7.5 cm (3 inch) plain cutter, stamp out as many rounds as possible. Re-roll the dough as necessary. Brush the rim of each dough round with beaten egg. Put a little of the fish mixture in the centre of each round and shape up the round into a tricorn. Brush with more beaten egg and place on a baking sheet.

Bake in a preheated moderately hot oven (200°C/400°F, Gas Mark 6) for 20 minutes or until golden. Serve hot. Makes 24

DEVILS ON HORSEBACK

Metric	Imperial
1 x 450 g can prunes, drained	1 x 15½ oz can prunes, drained
34 whole browned almonds	34 whole browned almonds
350 g lean streaky bacon rashers, rinds removed	12 oz lean streaky bacon rashers, rinds removed

There should be 34 prunes in the can. Cut each almost in half and discard the stones. Replace with an almond.

Stretch the bacon rashers on a flat surface with the back of a knife, then cut each in half. Wrap a half rasher around each prune. Grill slowly until the bacon is brown and crisp. Serve on cocktail sticks. Makes 34

CHEESE OLIVES

Metric	Imperial
225 g full fat cream cheese	8 oz full fat cream cheese
15 stuffed olives	15 stuffed olives
Chopped walnuts	Chopped walnuts

Cream the cheese until it is soft. Take a heaped 5 ml spoonful (teaspoonful) and roll it around a stuffed olive to enclose it completely. Lightly coat in chopped walnuts. Cover the remaining olives in the same way. Chill the olives for about 1 hour. Before serving, cut each in half with a sharp knife. Makes 30

SARDINE PYRAMIDS

Metric	Imperial
20 to 24 cocktail grielle (rusk biscuits)	20 to 24 cocktail grielle (rusk biscuits)
Butter	Butter
2 x 106 g cans sardines, drained	2 x 4 oz cans sardines, drained
Lemon juice	Lemon juice
Salt	Salt
Freshly ground black pepper	Freshly ground black pepper
Paprika	Paprika
Chopped fresh parsley	Chopped fresh parsley

Lightly spread the cocktail grielle with butter. Mash the sardines with a seasoning to taste of lemon juice, salt and pepper. Mound some of the sardine mixture on each grielle and shape into a pyramid. Using a damp skewer, mark in a cross with paprika and chopped parsley. Makes 20 to 24

Left: Talmouse. Right: Sardine pyramids; Devils on horseback; Cheese olives.

PÂTÉ FLEURONS

Metric	Imperial
1 x 212 g packet frozen puff pastry, thawed	1 x 7 oz packet frozen puff pastry, thawed
Beaten egg	Beaten egg
1 x 107 g tube liver pâté	1 x 4¼ oz tube liver pâté
50 g butter	2 oz butter

Roll out the pastry dough thinly. Using a 3.7 cm (1½ inch) fluted round cutter, stamp out as many rounds as possible. Re-roll as necessary. Brush the rounds with beaten egg and fold over into semi-circles. Place on a baking sheet and leave in a cool place for at least 30 minutes.

Brush the semi-circles with beaten egg and bake in a preheated moderately hot oven (200°C/400°F, Gas Mark 6) for about 15 minutes. With a sharp knife, cut almost through the pastry to allow the steam to escape. Leave to cool on a wire rack.

Beat together the liver pâté and butter. Put into a piping bag fitted with a cake icing no. 8 nozzle. Pipe in a shell shape down the centre of each pastry fleuron. Makes about 52

PRAWN TITBITS

Metric	Imperial
100 g cheese pastry, made with 100 g plain flour (see page 56)	4 oz cheese pastry, made with 4 oz plain flour (see page 56)
Beaten egg	Beaten egg
1 x 100 g can prawns, drained	1 x 4 oz can prawns, drained
100 g butter, softened	4 oz butter, softened
1 x 2.5 ml spoon tomato paste	½ teaspoon tomato paste
Parsley sprigs to garnish	Parsley sprigs to garnish

Roll out the pastry dough to a rectangle 20 by 30 cm (8 by 12 inches). Trim the edges and cut into 2.5 cm (1 inch) wide strips, 5 cm (2 inches) long. Place on baking sheets and brush with beaten egg. Bake in a preheated moderately hot oven (200°C/400°F, Gas Mark 6) for about 15 minutes or until golden. Cool.

Sieve half the contents of the can of prawns. Beat in the butter and tomato paste. Put the shrimp butter into a piping bag fitted with a star vegetable nozzle and pipe lines on the cheese pastry bases. Garnish with the remaining whole canned prawns and parsley sprigs. Makes 48

CELERY SLICES

Metric	Imperial
100 g Danish blue cheese	4 oz Danish blue cheese
75 g full fat cream cheese	3 oz full fat cream cheese
8 celery stalks, trimmed	8 celery stalks, trimmed

Cream together the blue and cream cheeses. Put the cheese mixture into a piping bag fitted with a plain nozzle and pipe into the hollow of each celery stalk. Fit the celery stalks together in pairs, slightly interlocking them. Secure each end of each pair with an elastic band and leave in a cool place – not the refrigerator – for the stalks to firm up. Using a sharp knife, cut into approximately 1 cm (½ inch) slices. Makes about 30

SAVOURY BITES

Metric	Imperial
For egg and horseradish bites:	**For egg and horseradish bites:**
50 g butter	2 oz butter
2 x 5 ml spoons creamed horseradish	2 teaspoons creamed horseradish
24 salted crackers	24 salted crackers
3 eggs, hard-boiled and sliced	3 eggs, hard-boiled and sliced
24 pickled gherkin fans	24 pickled gherkin fans
For tomato bites:	**For tomato bites:**
225 g full fat cream cheese	8 oz full fat cream cheese
20 salted crackers	20 salted crackers
Tomato butterflies	Tomato butterflies
Black olives, stoned	Black olives, stoned

For the egg and horseradish bites, cream the butter and horseradish together well and spread onto the crackers. Top each with a slice of egg and a gherkin fan.

For the tomato bites, beat the cream cheese until soft. Put it into a piping bag fitted with a star vegetable nozzle and pipe a whirl of cheese onto each cracker. Garnish with tomato butterflies and a piece of black olive.

Prepare both these canapés as near as possible to serving time, as the crackers may soften. Makes 44

SALAMI CUSHIONS

Metric	Imperial
1 x 212 g packet frozen puff pastry, thawed	1 x 7 oz packet frozen puff pastry, thawed
100 g salami, finely chopped	4 oz salami, finely chopped
Beaten egg to glaze	Beaten egg to glaze

Roll out the dough to an oblong about 38 by 30 cm (15 by 12 inches). Cut in half. Dot the salami at 4 cm (1½ inch) intervals on one sheet. Brush the remaining sheet with water and lay it, wet side down, on the first sheet. Press the pastry well to form 'parcels' and cut into squares with a sharp knife or pastry wheel. Glaze with beaten egg and bake in a preheated hot oven (220°C/425°F, Gas Mark 7) for 8 to 10 minutes. Cool on a wire rack. Makes about 40
Note: These can be prepared the day before the party, but bake them just before they are needed. Wrap the uncooked 'cushions' in polythene and keep in the refrigerator overnight.

Left (clockwise from top): Celery slices; Prawn titbits; Egg and horseradish bites; Pâté fleurons; Tomato bites. Right: Salami cushions.

SPANISH DIP WITH MUSHROOMS

Metric	Imperial
25 g butter or margarine	1 oz butter or margarine
225 g tomatoes, skinned and chopped	8 oz tomatoes, skinned and chopped
1 large garlic clove, crushed	1 large garlic clove, crushed
1 x 2.5 ml spoon dried basil	½ teaspoon dried basil
2 x 15 ml spoons tomato paste	2 tablespoons tomato paste
Salt	Salt
Freshly ground black pepper	Freshly ground black pepper
150 ml thick mayonnaise	¼ pint thick mayonnaise
500 g small button mushrooms	1 lb small button mushrooms

Mushrooms make ideal dunkers, their special crispness contrasting deliciously with this rich velvety sauce.

Melt the butter or margarine in a small frying pan. Add the tomatoes, garlic, basil, tomato paste and seasoning and simmer gently for about 10 minutes, or until the tomato is well pulped. Cool slightly, then purée in a blender or sieve and leave to go cold.

Mix in the mayonnaise and adjust the seasoning. Serve as a dip with the mushrooms skewered on cocktail sticks. Serves 12 to 16

CHEESE AND WALNUT DIP

Metric	Imperial
500 g Wensleydale or mild soft cheese	1 lb Wensleydale or mild soft cheese
200 ml top of the milk	⅓ pint top of the milk
25 g onion, peeled and grated	1 oz onion, peeled and grated
Tomato paste	Tomato paste
Salt	Salt
Freshly ground black pepper	Freshly ground black pepper
40 g walnuts, finely chopped	1½ oz walnuts, finely chopped

With a fork, work the cheese until creamy, adding the milk a little at a time. Beat in the grated onion, tomato paste to taste and seasoning. Finally fold in the chopped walnuts. Serve with crisps, crackers and pretzels. Makes 600 ml (1 pint)

Spanish dip with mushrooms; Cheese and walnut dip.

PIQUANT COCKTAIL CROQUETTES

Metric	Imperial
25 g butter or margarine	1 oz butter or margarine
25 g plain flour	1 oz plain flour
150 ml milk	¼ pint milk
50 g pickled gherkins, very finely chopped	2 oz pickled gherkins, very finely chopped
1 x 15 ml spoon capers, very finely chopped	1 tablespoon capers, very finely chopped
25 g green olives, stoned and very finely chopped	1 oz green olives, stoned and very finely chopped
2 x 15 ml spoons chopped parsley	2 tablespoons chopped parsley
Salt	Salt
Freshly ground black pepper	Freshly ground black pepper
Beaten egg	Beaten egg
Fresh white breadcrumbs	Fresh white breadcrumbs
Oil for deep frying	Oil for deep frying

Melt the fat in a saucepan. Stir in the flour and cook for 1 minute. Gradually stir in the milk and bring to the boil. Simmer, stirring, for 1 minute. Add the gherkins, capers, olives, parsley and seasoning. Mix well, then turn the mixture onto a plate. Refrigerate until cold.

Shape the mixture into small barrels and coat with egg and breadcrumbs. Deep fry in oil heated to 190°C/375°F until crisp and golden. Drain on absorbent kitchen paper. Serve hot.
Makes about 20
Note: These can be made the day before and refreshed in a preheated moderately hot oven (200°C/400°F, Gas Mark 6) for 5 to 8 minutes. (Store them overnight in a polythene bag in the refrigerator.)

SCOTCH CHEESIES

Metric	Imperial
100-125 g Gorgonzola, Dolcelatte or Danish blue cheese, rind removed	4 oz Gorgonzola, Dolcelatte or Danish blue cheese, rind removed
500 g sausagemeat	1 lb sausagemeat
1 x 15 ml spoon French mustard	1 tablespoon French mustard
Salt	Salt
Freshly ground black pepper	Freshly ground black pepper
Plain flour	Plain flour
1 egg, beaten	1 egg, beaten
25 g dry white breadcrumbs	1 oz dry white breadcrumbs
Oil for deep frying	Oil for deep frying

Divide the cheese into 12 even-sized pieces. Pound the sausagemeat with the mustard and seasoning until well mixed. Divide into 12 portions. Roll each piece of cheese in sausagemeat, making sure the cheese is completely encased. Coat the balls lightly in flour, beaten egg and breadcrumbs, in that order, pressing the crumbs on well. Chill for 30 minutes to set the crumbs.

Deep-fry in oil heated to 190°C/375°F until golden brown. Drain well on absorbent kitchen paper. Leave to cool before serving. Makes 12

Left: Piquant cocktail croquettes; Scotch cheesies. Below: Herb chicken goujons with cucumber dip.

HERB CHICKEN GOUJONS WITH CUCUMBER DIP

Metric	Imperial
4 x 100 g chicken breasts, skinned and boned	4 x 4 oz chicken breasts, skinned and boned
Plain flour	Plain flour
Salt	Salt
Freshly ground black pepper	Freshly ground black pepper
1 egg, beaten	1 egg, beaten
1 x 85 g packet herby stuffing mix	1 x 3 oz packet herby stuffing mix
3 x 15 ml spoons oil	3 tablespoons oil
25 g butter	1 oz butter
For the dip:	**For the dip:**
75 g piece of cucumber, peeled and grated	3 oz piece of cucumber, peeled and grated
150 ml thick mayonnaise	¼ pint thick mayonnaise
Dash of Tabasco sauce	Dash of Tabasco sauce

With a sharp knife, slice each chicken breast into six long strips. Coat the strips evenly in lightly seasoned flour, then in egg and finally in dry stuffing mix. Heat the oil in a frying pan. Add the butter and when frothing, but not brown, fry the chicken goujons, half at a time, for 2 to 3 minutes on each side until golden brown. Drain well on absorbent kitchen paper. Leave to go cold.

To make the dip, mix the cucumber with the mayonnaise. Add a few drops of Tabasco and seasoning. Serve the goujons on cocktail sticks with the sauce separately. Serves 12

PARTY DRINKS

A drinks party can provide a very convivial way of entertaining without the need for a great deal of cooking but do provide some home-made savouries (see pages 166-71).
If you're not adept at making cocktails, stick to sherry (fino and amontillado), vermouth (sweet and extra dry) and white wine (dry and medium dry) or a non-vintage champagne or sparkling wine. Serve the vermouth straight, with ice and a sliver of lemon. For winter parties a hot mulled wine is popular and in summer a wine cup is very refreshing. Have a good supply of tonic water, ginger ale, tomato juice, orange juice and beer on hand. Order the drinks early, on a sale or return basis, paying only for bottles which are opened. Make lots of ice in advance if you have a freezer; or buy it in large bags from your off-licence.
Site the bar on a large table, covered with a cloth or sheet, at one end of the room. Remove most of the chairs and place ashtrays and coasters strategically to protect carpets and furniture.

COCKTAILS

HOW MANY DRINKS TO THE BOTTLE?

Sherry, port and vermouth, straight: 12 to 16 glasses.
Vermouths and spirits, in single nips for mixes: 30 drinks.
Spirits, served with tonic, soda or other minerals: 16 to 20 drinks.
A split bottle of tonic or soda: 2 to 3 drinks.
Table wines: 5 to 6 glasses.
A 600 ml (1 pint) can of tomato juice: 4 to 6 drinks.
A bottle of fruit cordial, diluted with 4 litres (7 pints) of water: 20 to 26 drinks.

SUGAR SYRUP FOR DRINKS

Metric	Imperial
450 g sugar	1 lb sugar
300 ml water	$\frac{1}{2}$ pint water

When making cups and punches, it is often more convenient to add the sugar in the form of a syrup, which dissolves more readily. Put the sugar in a saucepan with the water and dissolve it slowly. Bring it to the boil and boil to 105°C/220°F. Cool and bottle. Use as required.
Makes about 600 ml (1 pint)

Dry martini; Sweet martini.

CHAMPAGNE COCKTAIL

Metric	Imperial
4 dashes of Angostura bitters	4 dashes of Angostura bitters
1 small sugar lump	1 small sugar lump
Juice of $\frac{1}{4}$ lemon	Juice of $\frac{1}{4}$ lemon
1 x 15 ml spoon brandy (optional)	1 tablespoon brandy (optional)
Champagne, chilled in the bottle	Champagne, chilled in the bottle
Lemon slice to decorate	Lemon slice to decorate

Pour the bitters over the sugar lump in a champagne glass. Add the strained lemon juice and brandy, if used, and fill up with Champagne. Float a wafer-thin slice of lemon on top. Serves 1

BUCK'S FIZZ

Metric	Imperial
1 part fresh orange juice	1 part fresh orange juice
2 parts non-vintage Champagne	2 parts non-vintage Champagne

Chill the ingredients and stir together well just before serving. Serves 1

Buck's fizz; Bronx; Champagne cocktail.

174

Kir; Screwdriver.

BRONX

Metric	Imperial
Equal parts dry gin, Italian vermouth and French vermouth	Equal parts dry gin, Italian vermouth and French vermouth
Juice of ¼ orange	Juice of ¼ orange
Crushed ice	Crushed ice

Shake together the ingredients, then strain into a cocktail glass. Serves 1

DRY MARTINI COCKTAIL

Metric	Imperial
2 parts French vermouth	2 parts French vermouth
1 part dry gin	1 part dry gin
Cracked ice	Cracked ice
Stuffed olives or lemon rind curls	Stuffed olives or lemon rind curls

Shake the vermouth and gin together with some cracked ice in a shaker. Strain into a glass and add a stuffed olive or a curl of lemon rind. (The proportions of a martini are a matter of personal taste. Some people prefer two parts of gin to one of vermouth; others like equal parts of gin and vermouth.) Serves 1

SWEET MARTINI COCKTAIL

Metric	Imperial
2 parts Italian vermouth	2 parts Italian vermouth
1 part dry gin	1 part dry gin
Few drops of orange bitters (optional)	Few drops of orange bitters (optional)
Cracked ice	Cracked ice
1 Maraschino cherry	1 Maraschino cherry

Shake the vermouth, gin, bitters, if used, and ice together in a shaker. Strain into a glass. Serve with a cherry. Serves 1

SCREWDRIVER

Metric	Imperial
1 measure of vodka	1 measure of vodka
Orange juice	Orange juice

Put some ice cubes into a glass and pour in the vodka. Add orange juice to taste and stir lightly. Serves 1

KIR

Metric	Imperial
4 parts dry white wine (Chablis or similar)	4 parts dry white wine (Chablis or similar)
1 part crème de cassis	1 part crème de cassis

Chill the wine thoroughly before combining it with the cassis. Serve in a claret glass. Serves 1

JOHN COLLINS

Metric	Imperial
Juice of ½ lemon	Juice of ½ lemon
Dash of Angostura bitters	Dash of Angostura bitters
2 x 5 ml spoons caster sugar	2 teaspoons caster sugar
2 measures of gin	2 measures of gin
Ice	Ice
Soda water	Soda water
Lemon slice	Lemon slice

Shake the lemon juice, bitters, sugar and gin together and strain into a tall glass over ice. Fill with soda water and add a slice of lemon.

For a quick John Collins, mix two measures of gin and a dash of Angostura bitters, add ice and fill up the glass with fizzy lemonade. Serves 1

FRESH TOMATO COCKTAIL (NON-ALCOHOLIC)

Metric	Imperial
150 ml unsweetened natural yogurt	¼ pint unsweetened natural yogurt
4 ripe tomatoes, skinned and puréed and strained	4 ripe tomatoes, skinned and puréed and strained
2 drops of Worcestershire sauce	2 drops of Worcestershire sauce
1-2 drops of lemon juice	1-2 drops of lemon juice
Paprika	Paprika
Fresh mint sprigs	Fresh mint sprigs

Whisk together the yogurt, tomatoes, Worcestershire sauce and lemon juice with a dusting of paprika. Serve in tall glasses with a float of fresh mint. Serves 2 to 3

John Collins; Fresh tomato cocktail.

COLD CUPS AND PUNCHES

WHITE WINE CUP

Metric
Crushed ice
3 bottles of medium white wine
¾ bottle of dry sherry
4 x 15 ml spoons
    orange-flavoured liqueur
4 "splits" tonic water
3 cucumber slices, 1 slice of apple
    and 1 fresh borage sprig per jug

Imperial
Crushed ice
3 bottles of medium white wine
¾ bottle of dry sherry
4 tablespoons orange-flavoured
    liqueur
4 "splits" tonic water
3 cucumber slices, 1 slice of apple
    and 1 fresh borage sprig per jug

Mix all the ingredients in one or more jugs and chill before serving.
Serves 19 to 20

RED WINE CUP

Metric
2 bottles of red wine (preferably
    Rioja), well chilled
1 bottle (same capacity as the
    wine bottles) of soda water,
    well chilled
Sugar to taste, dissolved in
    water, or sugar syrup
    (see page 174)
Large pinch of ground
    cinnamon
Lemon and orange slices

Imperial
2 bottles of red wine (preferably
    Rioja), well chilled
1 bottle (same capacity as the
    wine bottles) of soda water,
    well chilled
Sugar to taste, dissolved in
    water, or sugar syrup
    (see page 174)
Large pinch of ground
    cinnamon
Lemon and orange slices

This is a simple version of Spanish sangria. Mix together the wine,
soda water, dissolved sugar or sugar syrup and cinnamon. Pour into a
punch bowl and stir in the fruit slices. (Ice cubes and a glass or two of
sherry or brandy could be added.) Serves about 12

Red wine cup; White wine cup.

Midsummer Night's Dream.

MIDSUMMER NIGHT'S DREAM

Metric
1 bottle of Riesling
1 bottle of Beaujolais
3 x 15 ml spoons
    orange-flavoured liqueur
1 dessert apple, cored and sliced
Pieces of melon
Orange slices, quartered
Few strawberries
Crushed ice
750 ml fizzy lemonade
Sugar syrup (see page 174) to
    taste

Imperial
1 bottle of Riesling
1 bottle of Beaujolais
3 tablespoons orange-flavoured
    liqueur
1 dessert apple, cored and sliced
Pieces of melon
Orange slices, quartered
Few strawberries
Crushed ice
1¼ pints fizzy lemonade
Sugar syrup (see page 174) to
    taste

Red wine and orange punch; Barbados rum punch.

Pour the wines and liqueur over the fruit and ice in a bowl. Chill, then add the lemonade and sugar syrup to taste. Serve ice-cold. Serves about 10

BARBADOS RUM PUNCH

Metric	Imperial
Rum	Rum
Orange juice	Orange juice
Grated nutmeg	Grated nutmeg

Mix rum with orange juice in the proportions you like and top up with ice-cold water. Serve in tumblers with just a sprinkling of nutmeg.

RED WINE AND ORANGE PUNCH

Metric	Imperial
1 orange	1 orange
12 cloves	12 cloves
2 bottles of red Burgundy	2 bottles of red Burgundy
1 x 540 ml can unsweetened orange juice	1 x 19 fl oz can unsweetened orange juice
24 sugar lumps	24 sugar lumps
6 x 15 ml spoons orange-flavoured liqueur	6 tablespoons orange-flavoured liqueur

Stud the orange with the cloves. Slice it and place it in a punch bowl. Pour the Burgundy and orange juice into a saucepan, add the sugar lumps and bring nearly to the boil. Add the liqueur and heat but don't boil. Pour over the orange slices. Serves 12

HOT PUNCHES AND CUPS

HUCKLE-MY-BUFF

Metric
1.2 litres draught beer
6 eggs, beaten
50 g sugar
Grated nutmeg
Brandy to taste

Imperial
2 pints draught beer
6 eggs, beaten
2 oz sugar
Grated nutmeg
Brandy to taste

A perfect drink to serve round the bonfire on Guy Fawkes night or after a Boxing Day walk in the country. Heat 600 ml (1 pint) of the beer with the eggs and sugar, but do not boil. Remove from the heat and add the remaining beer, a generous amount of nutmeg and brandy to taste. Serve in heatproof glasses.

You will need a large saucepan or flameproof casserole to make this punch. Serve it with a ladle. Serves 6

Huckle-my-buff.

Hot Honey Toddy

Metric
1 bottle of medium dry white
  wine
Thinly pared rind and juice of
  1 lemon
2 x 15 ml spoons thin honey
Few pieces of mace blade
1 x 5 cm cinnamon stick
4 x 15 ml spoons brandy

Imperial
1 bottle of medium dry white
  wine
Thinly pared rind and juice of
  1 lemon
2 tablespoons thin honey
Few pieces of mace blade
1 x 2 inch cinnamon stick
4 tablespoons brandy

Heat the wine, lemon rind and juice, honey and flavourings to just below boiling point. Remove from the heat, cover and leave to infuse for 1 hour.

Reheat the punch, but do not boil it. Strain it into a warmed jug. Add the brandy and serve immediately. (Run the punch into the glasses over the back of a spoon to prevent their cracking.)
Serves 6 to 8

Glühwein

Metric
600 ml red wine
75 g brown sugar
2 x 5 cm cinnamon sticks
1 lemon stuck with cloves
150 ml brandy

Imperial
1 pint red wine
3 oz brown sugar
2 x 2 inch cinnamon sticks
1 lemon stuck with cloves
¼ pint brandy

Put all the ingredients except the brandy in a pan, bring to simmering point and simmer gently, covered, for 2 to 4 minutes. Remove from the heat, add the brandy, strain and serve at once.
Serves about 4

Julglögg (Christmas Wine)

Metric
1 bottle of aquavit or gin
2 bottles of Burgundy
75 g seedless raisins, cleaned
100 g sugar
1 x 15 ml spoon cardamom seeds
  (optional)
6 cloves
1 x 5 cm cinnamon stick
Small piece of lemon rind

Imperial
1 bottle of aquavit or gin
2 bottles of Burgundy
3 oz seedless raisins, cleaned
4 oz sugar
1 tablespoon cardamom seeds
  (optional)
6 cloves
1 x 2 inch cinnamon stick
Small piece of lemon rind

Pour half the aquavit or gin into a saucepan with the wine. Add the raisins and sugar. Tie the spices and lemon rind in muslin and add to the pan. Cover and bring very slowly to the boil. Simmer for 30 minutes.

Add the remaining aquavit or gin and remove from the heat. Take out the muslin bag of spices and, just before serving, ignite the punch with a match. Serve in tumblers or punch glasses.
Serves 12 to 13

Glühwein; Julglögg; Hot honey toddy.

179

NON-ALCOHOLIC CUPS AND PUNCHES

VERANDAH PUNCH

Metric
Juice of 2 large juicy oranges
Juice of 3 thin-skinned lemons
150 ml sugar syrup (see page 174)
300 ml freshly made tea
3 x 175 ml bottles of ginger ale, well chilled
3 x 175 ml bottles of soda water, well chilled
Ice cubes
Orange slices to decorate

Imperial
Juice of 2 large juicy oranges
Juice of 3 thin-skinned lemons
¼ pint sugar syrup (see page 174)
½ pint freshly made tea
3 x 6 fl oz bottles of ginger ale, well chilled
3 x 6 fl oz bottles of soda water, well chilled
Ice cubes
Orange slices to decorate

Mix the fruit juices with the sugar syrup and tea. Cool, then strain into a bowl and chill. Just before serving, mix in the ginger ale and soda water. Add ice cubes and orange slices. Serves 9

SPICY FRUIT PUNCH

Metric
600 ml fresh or canned orange juice
300 ml canned pineapple juice
Pared rind and juice of 1 lemon
1 x 2.5 ml spoon grated nutmeg
6 cloves
1 x 2.5 ml spoon mixed spice
600 ml water
100-175 g sugar
6 'splits' of American ginger ale, chilled
Crushed ice
Pared orange or lemon rind to garnish

Imperial
1 pint fresh or canned orange juice
½ pint canned pineapple juice
Pared rind and juice of 1 lemon
½ teaspoon grated nutmeg
6 cloves
½ teaspoon mixed spice
1 pint water
4-6 oz sugar
6 'splits' of American ginger ale, chilled
Crushed ice
Pared orange or lemon rind to garnish

Mix the fruit juices, lemon rind and spices in a large jug. Put the water and sugar into a saucepan and heat gently to dissolve the sugar. Cool, then add the other ingredients from the jug. Chill. Strain the liquid and add the ginger ale and crushed ice just before serving. Garnish with pared orange or lemon rind. Serves 20

GRAPEFRUIT OR LIME SODA

Metric
1 ice cube, crushed
½ glass of soda water
2 x 15 ml spoons grapefruit juice or 1 x 15 ml spoon lime juice
1 x 15 ml spoon ice cream

Imperial
1 ice cube, crushed
½ glass of soda water
2 tablespoons grapefruit juice or 1 tablespoon lime juice
1 tablespoon ice cream

Whisk all the ingredients together with a rotary whisk until frothy, or blend at maximum speed for 1 minute in an electric blender. Pour into a large glass. Serves 1

GINGER SODA

Metric
¾ glass of ginger beer
¼ glass of lemonade
1 x 15 ml spoon ice cream

Imperial
¾ glass of ginger beer
¼ glass of lemonade
1 tablespoon ice cream

Make as for grapefruit or lime soda. Serves 1

PINEAPPLE CRUSH

Metric
1 x 539 ml can pineapple juice
Juice of 1 orange
Juice of 1 lemon
Sugar
1.2 litres ginger ale (chilled in the bottle)

Imperial
1 x 19 fl oz can pineapple juice
Juice of 1 orange
Juice of 1 lemon
Sugar
2 pints ginger ale (chilled in the bottle)

Combine the fruit juices, sweeten to taste and chill. Just before serving, add the ginger ale. Serves about 9

HOT SPICED PINEAPPLE CUP

Metric
2 x 400 ml cans pineapple juice
4 x 15 ml spoons sugar
2 x 15 ml spoons lemon juice
1 x 10 cm cinnamon stick

Imperial
2 x 15 fl oz cans pineapple juice
4 tablespoons sugar
2 tablespoons lemon juice
1 x 4 inch cinnamon stick

Simmer all the ingredients together for 10 minutes. Remove the cinnamon and pour the liquid into glasses. Serves 5

Hot spiced pineapple cup; Spicy fruit punch; Pineapple crush; Verandah punch.

LEMON CIDER CUP

Metric	Imperial
3 lemons	3 lemons
100 g caster sugar	4 oz caster sugar
1 cinnamon stick	1 cinnamon stick
600 ml boiling water	1 pint boiling water
1.2 litres cider, chilled	2 pints cider, chilled
1 'split' of soda water, chilled	1 'split' of soda water, chilled
Lemon slices	Lemon slices

Pare the rind from two of the lemons, free of any pith. Squeeze the juice from all the lemons. Put the rind, juice, sugar and cinnamon stick in a large jug. Pour on the boiling water and stir until the sugar has dissolved. Leave to cool, then strain into a bowl. Just before serving, add the cider, soda water and a lemon slice to float in each glass. Serves 12

APRICOT CIDER CUP

Metric	Imperial
1 x 820 g can apricots, drained	1 x 1 lb 13 oz can apricots, drained
1 x 5 cm cinnamon stick	1 x 2 inch cinnamon stick
15 g sweet almonds, blanched	½ oz sweet almonds, blanched
1.2 litres cider	2 pints cider
4 'splits' of tonic water	4 'splits' of tonic water

Rub the apricots through a sieve and put the purée into a large jug. Put the cinnamon, almonds and 300 ml (½ pint) of the cider in a pan. Bring to the boil, then remove from the heat and leave to stand for about 10 minutes. Cool, then add to the apricot purée. Just before serving, add remaining cider and tonic water and stir well. Serves 6

Below: Lemon cider cup; Ginger soda; Grapefruit or lime soda; Apricot cider cup.

QUANTITY GUIDE
APPROXIMATE QUANTITIES FOR BUFFET PARTIES

	1 portion	24-26 portions	Notes
Soups: cream or clear	200 ml (⅓ pint)	4.75 litres (1 gallon)	Serve garnished in mugs or cups.
Fish cocktail: shrimp, prawn, tuna or crab	25 g (1 oz)	750 g (1½ lb) fish 2-3 lettuces 900 ml (1½ pints) sauce	In stemmed glasses, garnished with a shrimp or prawn.
Meat with bone	150 g (5 oz)	3.25-3.50 kg (7-8 lb)	Cold roasts or barbecued chops.
boneless	75-100 g (3-4 oz)	2.25-3 kg (5-6½ lb)	Casseroles, meat balls, sausages, barbecued steaks.
Poultry: turkey	75-100 g (3-4 oz) boneless	7 kg (16 lb) (dressed)	
chicken	1 joint 150-225 g (5-8 oz)	6 x 1-1.5 kg (2½-3 lb) birds (dressed)	Serve hot or cold.
Delicatessen: ham or tongue	75-100 g (3-4 oz)	2.25-3 kg (5-6½ lb)	Halve the amounts if making stuffed cornets.
pâté for wine-and-pâté party	75-100 g (3-4 oz)	2.25-3 kg (5-6½ lb)	Halve the amount if pâté is starter course.
Salad vegetables lettuce	⅙	3-4	Dress at last minute.
cucumber	2.5 cm (1 inch)	2	
tomatoes	1-2	1.5 kg (3 lb)	
white cabbage	25 g (1 oz)	750 g (1½ lb)	For winter salads.
boiled potatoes	50 g (2 oz)	1.5 kg (3 lb)	For potato salads.
Rice or pasta	40 g (1½ oz) uncooked	1 kg (2 lb)	Can be cooked a day ahead; reheated for 5 min. in boiling water.
Cheese (for wine-and-cheese party)	75 g (3 oz)	1.75-2.25 kg (4½-5 lb) of at least 4 types	You'll need more if you serve a cheese dip, too.
Cheese (for biscuits)	25-40 g (1-1½ oz)	750 g-1 kg (1½-2 lb) cheese plus 500 g (1 lb) butter, 1 kg (2 lb) biscuits	Allow the larger amounts for an assorted cheese board.

APPROXIMATE TEA AND COFFEE QUANTITIES

	1 Serving	24-26 Servings		Notes
Coffee ground, hot	200 ml (⅓ pint)	225-250 g (8-9 oz) coffee 3.5 litres (6 pints) water	1.75 litres (3 pints) milk 500 g (1 lb) sugar	If you make the coffee in advance strain it after infusion. Reheat without boiling. Serve sugar separately.
ground, iced	200 ml (⅓ pint)	350 g (12 oz) coffee 3.5 litres (6 pints) water	1.75 litres (3 pints) milk sugar to taste	Make coffee (half sweetened, half not), strain and chill. Mix with chilled milk. Serve in glasses.
instant, hot	200 ml (⅓ pint)	50-75 g (2-3 oz) coffee 3.5 litres (6 pints) water	1.25 litres (2 pints) milk 500 g (1 lb) sugar	Make coffee in jugs as required. Serve sugar separately.

	1 Serving	24-26 Servings		Notes
instant, iced	200 ml (⅓ pint)	75 g (3 oz) coffee 1.25 litres (2 pints) water	3.5 litres (6 pints) milk sugar to taste	Make black coffee (half sweetened, half not) and chill. Mix with chilled creamy milk. Serve in glasses.
Tea Indian, hot	200 ml (⅓ pint)	50 g (2 oz) tea 4.75 litres (8 pints) water	900 ml (1½ pints) milk 500 g (1 lb) sugar	It is better to make tea in several pots rather than in one outsize one.
Indian, iced	200 ml (⅓ pint)	75 g (3 oz) tea 4.25 litres (7 pints) water	1.25 litres (2 pints) milk sugar to taste	Strain tea immediately it has infused. Sweeten half of it. Chill. Serve in glasses with chilled milk.
China	200 ml (⅓ pint)	50 g (2 oz) tea 5.5 litres (9 pints) water	2-3 lemons 500 g (1 lb) sugar	Infuse China tea for 2-3 minutes only. Put a thin lemon slice in each cup before pouring. Serve sugar separately.

SAVOURIES AND SWEETS

	Ingredients	Portions	Notes
Sausage rolls	675 g (1½ lb) shortcrust or flaky pastry or 2 x 312 g (2 x 12 oz) pkts frozen shortcrust or flaky pastry; 1 kg (2 lb) sausagemeat	25-30 medium or 50 small rolls	Pastry based on 675 g (1½ lb) flour, 350-450 g (¾-1 lb) fat.
Bouchées	450 g (1 lb) puff pastry or 2 x 227 g (2 x 8 oz) pkts frozen puff pastry; 600 ml (1 pint) thick white sauce; 275 g (10 oz) prepared filling	50 bouchées	Pastry based on 450 g (1 lb) flour, 350 g (12 oz) butter. Fillings: chopped cooked ham, chicken, egg, mushrooms, shrimps.
Cheese straws	225 g (8 oz) cheese pastry	100 cheese straws	225 g (8 oz) flour, 125 g (4 oz) fat, 125 g (4 oz) cheese.
Meringues	6 egg whites; 350 g (12 oz) caster sugar; 450 ml (¾ pint) whipped cream	50 (small) meringue halves	2 halves per head with cream; 1 half with fruit and cream, or ice cream.
Jelly	3 litres (2½ quarts)	25	
Trifle	2.5 litres (4 pints) custard; 25 sponge fingers; 1 large can fruit	25	Decorate with cream, glacé cherries, nuts, angelica.
Fruit salad	3 kg (6½ lb) fruit; 1.75-2.5 litres (3-4 pints) sugar syrup; 1 litre (1½ pints) cream	25	Can be prepared a day ahead and left submerged in syrup, but bananas should be added just before serving.

SALAD DRESSINGS

Mayonnaise	600 ml (1 pint) for 12 salad portions	900 ml-1 litre (1½-1¾ pints) for 24-26 salad portions	For 600 ml (1 pint), use 3 egg yolks, 400 ml (¾ pint) oil, 3 x 15 ml spoons (3 tablespoons) vinegar, 1.5 x 5 ml spoons (1½ teaspoons) each of dry mustard, salt and sugar, and 1 x 5 ml spoon (1 teaspoon) pepper.
French dressing	300 ml (½ pint) for 12 salad portions	450-600 ml (¾-1 pint) for 24-26 salad portions	Make in a lidded container and shake together just before serving.

HOW A FREEZER CAN HELP

Food and Storage time*	Preparation and Freezing	Thawing and Serving*
Meat and poultry, cooked dishes, casseroles, stews, curries, etc: 3 months If highly seasoned: 2 months	Prepare as desired; do not overcook. Have enough liquid to cover meat completely. Freeze when quite cold in rigid containers, foil dishes or foil-lined cookware.	Reheat in casserole from frozen. Allow at least 1 hour in oven at 200°C/400°F, Gas Mark 6. Reduce heat to 180°C/350°F, Gas Mark 4 and cook for 40 minutes, or until really hot.
Meat loaves, pâtés: 1 month	Follow recipe. When cold freeze in tin or dish, and when frozen remove from dish, wrap tightly in foil and overwrap in polythene.	Thaw overnight in refrigerator. For quicker thawing slice before freezing, place waxed paper between slices and wrap (see left).
Fish, cooked pies, fish cakes: 1-2 months	Follow recipe but omit any hard-boiled eggs from mixture. Freeze when cold in foil-lined containers. Remove when hard, then pack in sealed bags.	Thaw overnight in refrigerator or put straight in oven in ovenproof dish at 180°C/350°F, Gas Mark 4 until heated through.
Sauces, soups, stocks: 3 months If highly seasoned: 2 weeks	Prepare as usual. When cold, pour into rigid containers, seal well and freeze.	Thaw, covered, at room temperature, or heat in pan until boiling point is reached.
Pizza (yeast mixture) baked: up to 2 months	Bake as usual. When cold pack in foil or polythene, and freeze flat. When frozen pack in twos or threes in polythene bags.	Remove packaging and place frozen in oven at 200°C/400°F, Gas Mark 6, for about 20 mins. If thawed, reheat as above for 10-15 mins.
Pastry, cooked Pastry cases: 6 months Meat pies: 3-4 months Fruit pies: 6 months	Prepare and cook as usual. Brush pastry cases with egg white before filling. Cool. Wrap carefully (very fragile) in foil.	Thaw at room temperature for 2-4 hours. Then reheat if required hot. Allow flans to thaw for about 1 hour. Refresh in a warm oven.
Pancakes, unfilled: 3 months	Add 1 x 15 ml spoon (1 tablespoon) corn oil to basic 100 g (4 oz) flour recipe. Make pancakes; cool on a wire rack. Interleave with polythene film. Seal in polythene bags or foil. Freeze.	Thaw in packaging overnight in refrigerator or 2-3 hours at room temperature. To reheat place stack of pancakes, wrapped in foil, in oven at 190°C/375°F, Gas Mark 5 for 20-30 mins. Or separate pancakes and reheat in a lightly greased pan, 30 seconds on each side.
Desserts Mousses, creams, soufflés, etc: 2-3 months	Make as usual. Freeze unwrapped in foil-lined container until firm, then remove container and place dessert in polythene bag. Soufflés can be left in soufflé dish placed in polythene bag when firm.	Unwrap and thaw in refrigerator overnight (at least 6 hours).
Cream, fresh: 3 months	Use only pasteurised double or whipping cream. Half whip with a little sugar, 1 x 5 ml spoon (1 teaspoon) to 150 ml (¼ pint). Pack in waxed carton, leaving space for expansion.	Thaw in refrigerator for 24 hours or 12 hours at room temperature.
Cakes Sponges and layer cakes: 3 months (Frosted cakes lose quality after 2 months)	Bake in usual way. Leave until cold. Wrap in polythene film or foil. Freeze frosted cakes unwrapped. When firm, wrap, seal and pack in boxes for protection.	Unwrap frosted and cream cakes before thawing. Leave plain cakes in package. Allow 1-2 hours for small cakes, 4 hours for frosted and larger cakes at room temperature.
Scones and teabreads: 3 months	Bake in usual way. Freeze in polythene bag or foil.	Thaw in wrapping at room temperature for 2-3 hours.

Food and Storage time*	Preparation and Freezing	Thawing and Serving*
Frozen chicken: 12 months Turkey, duck: 9 months	Keep in the freezer in original wrapping.	Thaw in wrapping, preferably in refrigerator. Allow: 12 hours for birds up to 1.8 kg/4 lb; 24 hours for birds up to 5.5 kg/12 lb; 48-72 hours for birds over 5.5 kg/12 lb; joints 6 hours.

***Note:** The storage times given are the recommended maximum times food will keep in peak condition in a freezer. It will start to lose flavour and texture after that time. Although the change may be difficult to discern, the food remains safe to eat provided it is properly handled and cooked.

*Thawing times cannot be accurate as they depend on the temperature of the room, or the quantity of food already in the refrigerator and also the size of pack, but the times given in this table are a useful guideline.

PASTRY AND FILLING GUIDE

Tin sizes can only be approximate as manufacturers' ranges vary. Pastry amounts are generous to allow a certain flexibility for depths and metric proportions. Leftover trimmings can be used to make a pasty, turnover or a few tartlet cases.

Size of Tin	Pastry Required to Line
15 cm (6 inch)	100 g (4 oz) flour, etc.
18 cm (7 inch)	150 g (5 oz) flour, etc.
20.5 cm (8 inch)	200 g (7 oz) flour, etc.
23 cm (9 inch)	250 g (9 oz) flour, etc.
25.5 cm (10 inch)	300 g (11 oz) flour, etc.
28 cm (11 inch)	350 g (12 oz) flour, etc.

NB As a fluted flan *ring* is deeper than its equivalent size fluted flan tin, you'll need to use a size larger tin for a recipe that specifies a ring.

Fillings
15 cm (6 inch) flan needs half the amount of 20.5 cm (8 inch)
18 cm (7 inch) flan takes half the quantity of a 23 cm (9 inch)
25.5 cm (10 inch) flan needs twice the amount of a 20.5 cm (8 inch).

To bake blind:
Line the flan tin with rolled out pastry. Cover the pastry with greaseproof paper, or foil and dried beans, and bake at the usual temperature. Remove the beans and paper 5 to 10 minutes before the end of the cooking time. Small tartlet tins lined with pastry need only be pricked before baking.
To refresh savoury biscuits and pastries, flans or quiches, heat them in a warm oven (160°C/325°F, Gas Mark 3) for 5 to 10 minutes according to size and quantity.

INDEX

ACKNOWLEDGMENTS

The publishers would like to thank the following companies for their kindness in providing materials and equipment used in the photography for this book:

Liberty, Elizabeth David, Craftsmen Potters Association of Great Britain, David Mellor, Spode.

We should also like to thank the following who were concerned in the preparation of the book:

Carol Macartney, Consultant Editor; Margaret Coombes, Food Editor; Norma MacMillan, Editor; Brenda Holroyd, Associate Editor; Jill Eggleton, Caroline Young, Diana Wilkins and Alex Dufort, Home Economists.

Photography by: Barry Bullough: 2-8, 30, 31, 90-92, 106, 107, 110-119, 157 (bottom), 158-163; Paul Kemp: 12-23, 26, 27, 34-43, 54-59, 61, 126-129, 131, 146-148, 150-152, 153 (bottom right), 164-181; Philip Dowell: 10, 11, 24, 25, 32, 33, 44, 45, 52, 53, 60, 62, 63, 68, 69, 72, 73, 88, 89, 102, 103, 120, 121, 123-125, 130, 132, 133, 140-145, 153 (bottom left), 154, 155, 157 (top); Melvin Grey: 28, 29, 46-51, 64-67, 70, 71, 75-87, 93-101, 104, 105, 108, 109, 134-139; Robert Golden: jacket photograph p 185.

Notes

"LIZA GODDARD" – Lemon Syllabub.
½ Pt double cream
3 ~~tablespoons~~ Castor Sugar
2 Lemons — juice
Brandy
———

Apple & orange Desert —
Grated Apple
Oranges, Chopped.
Sugar to taste + Orange Juice?